GUIDE TO AFRICAN CINEMA

Reference Guides to the World's Cinema

Guide to the Cinema of Spain
Marvin D'Lugo

Guide to American Cinema, 1965–1995
Daniel Curran

GUIDE TO AFRICAN CINEMA

SHARON A. RUSSELL

Reference Guides to the World's Cinema
Pierre Horn, Series Editor

GREENWOOD PRESS
Westport, Connecticut • London

Library of Congress Cataloging-in-Publication Data

Russell, Sharon A., 1941–
    Guide to African cinema / Sharon A. Russell.
      p. cm.—(Reference guides to the world's cinema, ISSN
1090–8234)
    Includes bibliographical references and index.
    ISBN 0–313–29621–9 (alk. paper)
    1. Motion pictures—Africa—History. I. Title. II. Series.
PN1993.5.A35R87 1998
791.43'096—dc21   97–27560

British Library Cataloguing in Publication Data is available.

Library of Congress Catalog Card Number: 97–27560
ISBN: 0–313–29621–9
ISSN: 1090–8234

First published in 1998

Greenwood Press, 88 Post Road West, Westport, CT 06881
An imprint of Greenwood Publishing Group, Inc.

Printed in the United States of America

The paper used in this book complies with the
Permanent Paper Standard issued by the National
Information Standards Organization (Z39.48–1984).

10 9 8 7 6 5 4 3 2 1

To Karen, Mary Jean, and Sue
for the support of their friendship

CONTENTS

FOREWORD

For the first time, on December 28, 1895, at the Grand Café in Paris, France, the inventors of the *Cinématographe*, Auguste and Louis Lumière, showed a series of eleven two-minute silent shorts to a public of thirty-five people each paying the high entry fee of one gold Franc. From that moment, a new era had begun, for the Lumière brothers were not only successful in their commercial venture, but they also unknowingly created a new visual medium quickly to become, throughout the world, the half-popular entertainment, half-sophisticated art of the cinema. Eventually, the contribution of each member of the profession, especially that of the director and performers, took on enormous importance. A century later, the situation remains very much the same.

The purpose of Greenwood's *Reference Guides to the World's Cinema* is to give a representative idea of what each country or region has to offer to the evolution, development, and richness of film. At the same time, because each volume seeks to represent a balance between the interests of the general public and those of students and scholars of the medium, the choices are by necessity selective (although as comprehensive as possible) and often reflect the author's own idiosyncracies.

André Malraux, the French novelist and essayist, wrote about the cinema and filmmakers: "The desire to build up a world apart and self-contained, existing in its own right . . . represents humanization in the deepest, certainly the most enigmatic, sense of the word." On the other hand, then, every *Guide* explores this observation by offering discussions, written in a jargon-free style, of the motion-picture art and its practitioners, and on the other provides much-needed information, seldom available in English, including filmographies, awards and honors, and ad hoc bibliographies.

Pierre L. Horn
Wright State University

PREFACE

Any research project always poses difficult decisions about the material to be covered. While the author would like a work to be as inclusive as possible, many factors are involved in the process of selection. Time and space are the most obvious limitations on any project. The projected length of a text determines the number of topics that can be covered adequately. A guide is by its nature less inclusive than an encyclopedia. The time that can be devoted to a project is also a consideration. A work that takes years of research is different from one that is done in a shorter period of time. There is also the point that every author reaches when the research must stop and the writing begin or the job will never be finished. Film presents other challenges. Unlike books, many films are not available from libraries or even interlibrary loan. The task of locating a specific title can be challenging. All of these factors entered into the decisions I made in constructing this guide. I know my choices will not please everyone involved in work in this field. This is the case with any book. But I hope my explanation of how and why certain decisions were made will clarify those choices.

African film presents specific problems for the researcher. Finances and distribution have always been difficult for the filmmaker, and these same dilemmas confront those who pursue research in this area. Film distribution is subject to a complex maze of contracts that allow for the different kinds of screening in the United States from classroom use to the movie theater. A specific film may not be available because conflicts over its ownership can prevent distribution contracts. Many important films are not available to be screened in the United States. Others may be available in small private collections. Distributors who own the rights to films have different policies about allowing researchers access to their collections. While some are most accommodating, others charge prohibitive rental fees. Very few African films are available from even those video rental companies that feature foreign films. A check of the index of a video rental or sales catalogue will reveal very few tapes. One of the largest guides to video tapes, *Video Hound's Golden Movie Retriever* (1997), lists one Algerian film and eleven South African films, and the majority of those listed as South African use the country as the setting for action-adventure or horror. Such a situation makes viewing of the films, which are the primary texts for the researcher, a challenge.

While locating secondary sources is always part of the process of gathering information for a book, often the same problems that exist in locating films occur when tracing down information about these films. As the films are not popular, there are not many secondary sources to support them. Those books that do exist go out of print quickly and remain part of reference libraries' noncirculating collections. Many texts only exist in foreign publications. Much of the information I used in this book was purchased during trips to France. But every project presents its own unique dilemmas. Even though availability was not the primary criteria I used to select films and directors, I felt the guide would be most useful to others if it dealt with subjects that would be accessible to the general public. No analysis can ever be a substitute for an actual experience with the work. I hope this guide serves as an introduction to the subject and stimulates interest in African film. I also feel that if film after film is unavailable, interest can easily turn to frustration. Therefore, I did consider availability as one element of the selection process. With African film the challenges of viewing are connected to the topic itself and the attitude of the rest of the cinematic community to films from this region. The question of the effect of postcolonial attitudes on production and distribution is discussed further in the Introduction.

The relationship between the film or director and colonialism did play an important part in the selection process. Most people have a view of African film that is based on Hollywood-style productions, which often exhibit a fascination with the landscape and stereotyped perceptions of the inhabitants. These films are not monolithic in their presentation of the continent, but the vast majority fixate on the otherness of the people and the land. They are "Hollywood style" because not all come from the United States, but they share a visual style and a narrative technique that foreground a seamless presentation of the story and a dedication to commercialism at the expense of controversy or deep analysis. While a few do present negative images of colonialism, they accomplish this from the perspective of the European or American rather than the African.

There are a handful of recent films that examine colonial and postcolonial attitudes from a European perspective that manage to avoid the easy answers associated with the Hollywood style. These films posed the most difficult decisions in relation to the book. Claire Denis' *Chocolat* (1988) is a complex exploration of the colonial situation that contrasts past and present through the eyes of a young woman who remembers her childhood as she revisits modern Cameroon. I reluctantly eliminated it because of its European perspective. However, I did decide to include *A World of Strangers* (1962) primarily because its story is surrounded by documentary footage of South Africa. Until recently, most South African films represent some kind of compromise, and I included a few examples to suggest what is available in a country that is restructuring itself and its image. At the same time, I could not bring myself to include the controversial *The Gods Must Be Crazy* (1984). Some people defend its presentation of aspects of the South African culture. I have an African friend who loves watching it with his family and sees the Bushman hero as an example of the classic trickster. Some critics severely attack it for its denigration of the Bushman and a lack of recognition of the true situation in South Africa during the period covered by the film. As much as I understand the position of those who defend it, I still find the film perpetuates images of indigenous people as amusing savages. Another film I omitted because of concern about the operation of its images (aside from its length) is Trinh T. Minh-Ha's *Reassemblage* (1982). While I generally like her films and understand what she is attempting in this film, I have watched it with a class and observed that the nudity generates a different response from what she intended. These films are examples of the many choices I had to make about what could be excluded.

In some cases it was equally difficult whether to include a film. I have suggested some of the problems with South African films. In general North African films are extremely difficult to locate. I felt uneasy dealing in detail with a film I had not seen, so in cases where films were not available, I included some of the directors from the region to suggest the range of activity in this area. The two films that are readily accessible unfortunately are made by Europeans. But in both cases the films have an African perspective and were made with the collaboration of Africans. *The Battle of Algiers* (1966) and *Ramparts of Clay* (1970) document North African situations an attempt to be authentic in their representation of their subjects. I also had to make decisions about the length of films to be included. Many important documentaries are less than an hour in length. I decided features are generally more than an hour, and, with one exception, I have only included films that are more than sixty minutes. *Femmes aux yeux ouverts* (1994) is the only film under that time restriction added to the book because it provides a unique perspective on one of the most troubling aspects of modern African life, the role of women. In this film a woman director allows African women a voice that has been denied them.

While these specific considerations helped make certain choices possible, the larger structure of the book is dominated by an attempt to include films and directors who are trying to define a uniquely African perspective on the cinematic process and who accomplish this goal while balancing important thematic concerns with commercial considerations. Such distinctions are not always easy to determine when I have had no personal experience with the director or the work, and I have had to rely on the opinions of others. Since space limitations require a selection process, I have attempted to use such considerations as guidelines, but I also had to consider the quality of the work in each entry. In addition, I attempted to represent a variety of countries and different kinds of films from those that celebrate the past to those that present a humorous approach to the present or a fantastic view of the future. Each book is the product of an individual, and I am certain no one will be totally in accord with all of my decisions. I only hope the reader will understand and appreciate the difficulty inherent in making the selections.

There are other smaller choices that I made in developing this book. While some of the titles in this series deal with actors as well as directors and films, many of the sub-Sahara films use nonprofessional actors. A country like Egypt, for example, certainly has many famous actors, but since their work is not readily available, I decided not to include any actors in this book. In a guide, there is a need for consistency. All of the film titles list the original language title first even though the film may generally be known by another name. The entries are presented in alphabetical order. English and French language titles are ordered by excluding the initial article. When I refer to such a film in another entry, I use the most commonly known title. An entry in the index will refer the reader to the original language name. Many of the names and titles are in languages other than English. I have attempted to use the most common transcription of language into English. I have also used the same process for making decisions about the date of a film, which can vary from source to source. Where confusion might exist, I include both versions in the index. I have attempted to include as accurate a filmography as possible. Again I have had to rely on a variety of sources and have tried to determine the most accurate list possible. I have also included the commonly held versions of the titles in the various languages in which the film has a separate title, especially when a specific English one is available.

In the bibliography, I have included the texts I used. For further scholarship, any of the major texts listed will lead the researcher to other entries and information that cannot be included in a general overview of the topic. I have also added a list of the sources I located for the more readily accessible African films. My hope is that this book will introduce the topic to people around the country who do not have access to specialized libraries and collections and encourage a wider appreciation of the cinematic work being done on this continent.

An asterisk (*) after a name or title indicates that there is a main entry for this topic within this reference book.

Many people have helped me with this guide. I would especially like to thank F. Edward Reed for his assistance. Several of my colleagues provided insights into the material. I would also like to thank the Department of Communication of Indiana State University for continued support of my project.

GUIDE TO AFRICAN CINEMA

INTRODUCTION

If postcolonial Africa must continue to deal with the effects of its colonial past, African film bears a dual burden. It reflects the heritage of the continent at the same time that it must deal with the difficulties faced by any developing area in competing with established countries for a share of the film market. The directors who set out to make a film in an African country attempt to give voice to the unique problems of their homeland while trying to find the financing, production facilities, and distribution network that will bring the work to an audience and allow it to make enough money to permit the director to continue to work. To understand how African film communicates and what its goals and achievements are, one must examine its situation in world cinema and the forces that impact on it on the continent. Film both reflects and shapes the world it presents. I will begin by examining the effects of colonialism and then move to the specific attributes of African film.

COLONIALISM AND RACISM

While Africa shares economic and political problems with other developing nations, the effects of colonialism on this continent are manifested by complex social constructions that are both universal and unique. Many of the financial difficulties and the racism of the rest of the world are experienced by all African countries. Both North Africa and sub-Saharan Africa suffer from the racist attitudes displayed by the Western world. They also suffer from economic exploitation even if they have not been occupied by colonial powers. The legacy of colonialism has also resulted in political instability in many of the countries on the continent. But not

every country shared the same experiences with colonial powers. Liberation also came at different points, generally earlier in the fifties in the
north and later further south on the continent. The individual experiences
of each country both pre- and postliberation are all different, but certain
elements can be dealt with more broadly.

In *Unthinking Eurocentrism*, Ella Shohat and Robert Stam list and discuss types of racism: "Racism, then, is both individual and systemic, interwoven into the fabric both of the psyche and of the social system, at
once grindingly quotidian and maddeningly abstract" (23). They connect
racism with power and identify its expression in colonialism through five
mechanisms. First, it operates by "*the positing of lack*" that is expressed
by defining the colonized as lacking in the standards of European civili-
zation such as intellectual ability, social skills, or culture. Second, it is
manifested as "*the mania for hierarchy*" that results in the categorizing of
everything into superior or inferior levels such as one tribe over another,
one form of labor over another, one form of expression over another.
They combine three and four because of their relationship, "*the blaming
of the victim*" and "*the refusal of empathy*." The causes for poverty become
the fault of the poor, so there is no need to understand the sources of
their situations. The fifth is the culmination of all of the others, "*the sys-
tematic devalorization of life*," which can lead to genocide on a large scale
or the ability to ignore individual deaths because the people are of a different race. In *Le grand blanc de Lambaréné** (1995), the Cameroonian
filmmaker Bassek ba Kobhio demonstrates how Albert Schweitzer manifested all of these racist mechanisms under a cloak of humanitarianism. It
is important to keep this list in mind when examining African films that
expose the effects of Eurocentered racism. This Eurocentrist approach
then applies racist attitudes when judging the films and filmmakers.

THIRD WORLD AND THIRD CINEMA

Historically, racism allowed colonialism to operate by devaluing the indigenous populations and justifying their exploitation; in postcolonial situations, racism continues to operate under different labels. Many see the
term "Third World" as a continuation of Eurocentrist attitudes, but while
it does indicate power relationships between countries, this domination of
one group by another is not necessarily based on race. The term originated
as an extension of the French "third estate"—which identified the com-
moners—as opposed to the first estate, which were the nobility and the
second, the clergy. By analogy the United States, Europe, Australia, and
Japan are First World countries. The former socialist block of Eastern
European nations, the former Soviet Union, and possibly China formed
the Second World. The term "Third World" referred to those countries
outside of the power construct of First and Second. While many associate

the term with poor, nonwhite nations who are emerging from colonial domination, such a definition ignores resource rich areas of the world such as those possessing oil or mineral wealth like the Middle East, or countries whose dominant populations are European as in Latin America. The term has come to signify an inferiority to those designated by it. While "developing nations" may not be the perfect solution, many consider it a more positive way to refer to these countries. Of course, any term that attempts to cover such diversity with a single identity is never entirely satisfactory.

Filmmakers and film theorists have adapted the term "Third World" as "Third Cinema" while denying any of the pejorative implications of the phrase. In his essay "The Third Cinema Question: Notes and Reflections" in the collection *Questions of Third Cinema*, Paul Willemen explains the idea of Third Cinema as formulated by Fernando Solanas and Octavio Getino and later amplified by Julio Garcia Espinosa, Latin American filmmakers and theorists. They call Hollywood filmmaking First Cinema; Second Cinema is what is usually identified as experimental, art, or often European cinema. Third Cinema is based on connections between culture and social change and is opposed to the emotional manipulation of Hollywood or the experimentation of the art cinema. Just as it denies Hollywood's play with emotions, Third Cinema also calls for a clarity and ease of reading that may be absent from European cinema. Those who practice this type of filmmaking also call it imperfect cinema and refuse to dictate an aesthetics or to be controlled by dominant cinema's ideology. Keyan G. Tomaselli, Arnold Shepperson, and Maureen Eke define it: "As a cinema of emancipation it articulates the codes of an essentially First World technology into indigenous aesthetics and mythologies" (25).

Once the ideology of Third Cinema is articulated a mode of analysis that does not fall back into the traps and traditions of First Cinema must be developed and employed. While some list requirements for qualification as Third Cinema or stages of development to achieve an authentic filmmaking practice, other critics provide broad definitions. Such statements include a call for a clear style that links mind and emotion. As Willeman indicates, authors of the manifesto describing this cinema did not want to force a specific aesthetic approach (6).

Third Cinema most clearly refers to the more revolutionary manifestations of Latin American cinema, but recent writing on African film such as the work of Nwachukwu Frank Ukadike, Manthia Diawara, Lizbeth Malkmus, and Roy Armes make claims for an authentic African cinema that rejects the Hollywood model. These scholars attempt to identify the qualities of African Cinema that lead to accurate interpretation of its goals and also try to understand how such films are received by their primary audiences so they are not misinterpreted through the application of the codes reserved for Second Cinema. Many of those who wish to find authentic means of interpreting African film point to the role of oral tradition in people's lives. They also discuss the importance of the individual's connection to the community and the past. But before the unique qualities of African film can be examined it is important to identify the traits of First and Second Cinema, which it counters.

FIRST AND SECOND CINEMAS

For many, First Cinema's defining characteristic is its devotion to capitalism. Hollywood-style filmmaking is dependent on massive amounts of money to finance the stars and special effects that have recently set it apart from other forms of expression. In order for these films to make money, they must reproduce the bourgeois ideology of their intended audiences. Of course, First Cinema encompasses more than just the production of the United States. Many European films and even some Asian films can be identified with this Hollywood tradition. While Hollywood production is just a small share of the world market compared to the number of films made in India, for example, its forms and goals have often been considered the norm against which all other production is measured.

On the surface, the most obvious trait is a slick visual presentation that is the result of technical expertise and heavy investment in equipment that reflect capital investment. A film like *Lawrence of Arabia*, where generators were used to provide perfect lighting in the desert, is an example of this approach. In general more and more films in this style are shot on location, but lighting is still used to enhance the physical attractiveness of the stars and create a world where the composition of the image and its visual impact are improved through the application of lights. Lighting also erases imperfections in the natural world and can help cover temporary changes in shadows due to the movement of the sun or clouds. The amount of control of the lighting is often an indication of the expense of a film. Independently produced films and films from many European countries place less emphasis on such classic applications of light and attempt to reproduce a less studied photography. These films present images that are closer to those found outside of the Hollywood tradition.

While the amount of money available for a production may determine aspects of the image, First Cinema films share narrative and thematic concerns. In the cinema made in a capitalist mode, the story dominates the film, and its requirements cause the suppression of other stylistic elements such as editing. The narrative moves forward by focusing on the interactions of the characters. A scene traditionally begins with a long shot that introduces them and their spatial relationships. Two shots cover conversations that may also be presented with angle/reverse angle combinations. Close-ups show individual actions or reactions. To accommodate this organization, scenes are usually shot with a master take that covers all of the action and then is supplemented by the other shots. This type of filmmaking requires professional actors who can reproduce their lines for the different "takes" or versions of a shot. It is also only possible when the same lighting can be maintained over a period of time and when the cost of film and film processing is not a consideration.

The emphasis on story requires certain types of narrative structures as well. While time lines can be altered through flashbacks or framing stories, all must connect to the central account of the events. Temporal continuity is maintained within a shot and a sequence. In fact, a sequence is defined in relation to time and space: a series of shots taking place at the same time in the same place. Secondary plots mirror the primary one, sometimes providing a comic foil to the more serious plot. Stories follow patterns of cause and effect where the audience can perceive the operation of logic and reason in life. Events that are established early in the film relate to the ending and are instrumental in structuring the resolution. The audience expects some kind of correlation between the ending and the operation of good and evil in the world. Generally, evil should be punished and good rewarded.

The rules used to edit these films promote the narrative in such a way that the editing remains invisible. The action is matched between cuts and jump cuts in which the action is not matched are avoided. The logic of the narrative is also reflected in concerns about maintaining screen direction where the action is filmed from the same side in successive shots. These aspects of editing reflect concerns about spatial continuities. While the conventions that control the narrative can be ignored, they are generally observed in the classic Hollywood-style film.

Thematically, these films concentrate on the individual and the importance of the actions and decisions of the central characters. Such an approach emphasizes the role of the individual and the impact of a single person on the story. Characters often play heroic roles, and history is depicted as the result of personal intervention. The concentration on individuals supports a bourgeois notion of social organization and is connected to the cause/effect narrative pattern. The emphasis on the single character also reinforces a thematic belief that each person is in charge of her or his destiny, which absolves the larger societal structures of responsibility for the problems such a society must face.

Second Cinema challenges the traditional conventions of the Hollywood style. In its promotion of the director as the author of the work with a personal style that permeates the film, Second Cinema continues the concern with the role of the individual established by First Cinema. Many of these films express a concern with artistic expression and cinematic experimentation, which challenges the traditional patterns for the use of time and space and editing. These films may also voice anti-bourgeois sentiments that are connected to their stylistic explorations. But their revolutionary impact is blunted by their inaccessibility to the general audience.

Their efforts demonstrate the difficulty of attempting to alter the Hollywood mode without alienating the audience.

AFRICAN FILM AND THE HOLLYWOOD STYLE

While American films may not dominate world production, the Hollywood style controls the cinematic experience of people around the world. Films are just one aspect of the Western cultural domination of the media. Television and music along with the cinema and its stars have become a form of cultural colonization that often leaves little room for indigenous products. In some areas—like music—where a strong tradition predates the introduction of Western forms, the two cultures can exist side by side and even communicate and share influences. Western cinema and television enter a space where no history exists. Developing nations receive a sophisticated product that has been evolving and perfecting its message and the forms of its delivery for years without a chance to create their own styles. African filmmakers must face a public whose taste has been developed through exposure to foreign products at the same time they must overcome other problems that are the heritage of a colonial past such as a lack of production or training facilities or finances.

As the biographies in this book indicate, most African filmmakers must learn their craft abroad. They study film in the very countries whose cinematic products dominate their theaters. The styles they learn are those of alien cultures, and they must work in alien languages. Whichever country they select has developed its own traditions, which then become part of the educational experience. In addition many of the former colonial powers still control the production facilities that African filmmakers can use. The different former colonial powers established a variety of relationships with their colonies so the filmmaking situation varies in each country. But the general difficulty of creating indigenous centers for equipment and film processing has disturbed the creation of a stable industry on the continent with the exception of such longtime filmmaking centers as Egypt.

In addition to problems with the tools of the industry, finances have created impossible situations for Africans. Those filmmakers who wish to reflect their own languages may face a limited audience. Ousmane Sembene* began making films in French, but when he turned to films to reach a largely illiterate audience, he moved toward making films in indigenous languages like Wolof and Diola. He is fortunate in having an international reputation so his films can also be distributed with subtitles, but others must make more difficult choices about which audience they wish to reach. The film's language can also control distribution outside of the country of origin. A subtitled film generates less interest in the United States, for example, where most audiences reject foreign films for that reason. Subtitles also mark a film as exotic and hard to understand because foreign language films are associated with Second Cinema or European art films. But some foreign films seek such links and take part in a circuit of film festivals that build reputations both for the directors and their countries. Filmmakers who enter festivals run the risk of being seduced by this world into making so-called "festival films" that aim for an international market and lose contact with the very world they have set out to represent. The growth in prestige of FESPACO (Festival Panafricaine de Ouagadougou), which occurs every two years in Burkina Faso, helps to encourage genuine African cinematic expression at the same time that it provides a showplace to market these films. The process of developing indigenous film industries and getting their products to audiences is not one with easy solutions and will face African filmmakers for some time in the future.

DEVELOPING AFRICAN FILM STYLES

The theorists who present concepts of Third Cinema attempt to define the ways in which countries can move toward authentic filmmaking. Willemen, who forms his ideas into a series of options, suggests the first response is often to identify with dominant culture (18). In "Toward a Critical Theory of Third World Films," Teshome H. Gabriel calls this the phase of assimilation (31). He theorizes a series of stages for the development of Third World cinema. Both critics define this first period as one of an attempt to translate the qualities that make for successful Hollywood films into their own work. Filmmakers aim for entertainment and encourage audience's escapist fantasies that will be financially rewarding.

Willemen sees the next choice as one of confrontation. A national identity is established as a counter to colonialism. Filmmakers look for a past culture to set in opposition to modern distortions created by the colonizers. He suggests that filmmakers choosing this path may idealize the past rather than working toward more genuine cultural expressions (18–19). Gabriel identifies a second phase in a related manner as that of remembrance with the same traps of romanticizing a false past.

The two theorists differ most in their view of the ultimate goal or choice of the filmmaker. Gabriel defines the third phase as combative in the sense that the needs of the people govern the organization of the industry and the themes and styles of the films that are produced (33–34). He is concerned with the ideological impact of the cinema and a style that foregrounds this ideology over character. Willemen is less prescriptive. He looks for films that accurately present the complex social construction of a society both inside the culture and in the society's interactions with other cultures (19). Both can be seen as calling for a cinema that faces the complexities of the modern world at the same time that they integrate a real sense of the past of the society.

In both North African and sub-Saharan cinemas, there are films and filmmakers who represent all of the stages or choices suggested by Gabriel and Willemen. As North African films are not generally available in large numbers, one can only accept the views of Malkmus and Armes. From their descriptions in *Arab and African Film Making*, these works seem to concentrate on certain themes, especially those that deal with character and form. They deal with such genres as the epic, the comic, and the dramatic, which is often the melodramatic. They use specific films as examples of the operation of each of these forms, and their examples would seem to be films that are working toward a genuine expression of their cultures. However, the genres seem to lead the films toward styles that forego realism for more studied expressions. It is hard to judge the extent to which the varied cultures of the region may be reflected in the forms and subjects presented in these films, although the Islamic tradition that dominates this region does provide a worldview that may control approaches to the presentation of its society. In many of these countries, ongoing state control of film production and censorship of political, social, and religious content still limits the films that can be made and successfully distributed.

Diawara in *African Cinema: Politics & Culture* redefines the three types of Third Cinema in terms of existing African films. He ignores assimilation/entertainment categories and presents films organized by content. Those that return to the source present an easy category to understand as do those that confront the historical relationship between Africa and Europe. He calls his last category "Social Realist." These films employ a variety of genres to examine cultural issues and their impact on society, especially modern social problems. Such works may base their criticism in existing forms such as the oral tradition (1430–41). In addition to reflecting the various options for Third Cinema, the cinema of sub-Saharan Africa is the expression of many different cultures. But there are elements of these societies that transcend national boundaries. While the various colonial powers governed their colonies in their own styles and viewed their colonies according to distinct visions of their role on the continent, there are some constants. The importance of an oral tradition transcends national boundaries. The oral tradition helps define the structure of narratives and perceptions of time and space. By linking past and present, it makes history come alive, and it records the glories of ancient empires.

THE ORAL TRADITION AND FILM

The importance of the oral tradition to film can be seen in the number of works that take it as their subject. *Angano . . . Angano . . .* * (1989) documents the storytellers. *Keïta: Le Héritage du Griot* * (1995) demonstrates the importance of keeping the past alive through the griot, the traditional keeper of the oral record, especially in a modern world where the only history children learn is that of their European colonizers. Of course each society has its own version of the oral tradition that should be thought of as "traditions" rather than a monolithic system. The oral tradition also covers a variety of modes of expression from stories to epics, from poems to songs. The storyteller is not a passive conduit for the story. Teller and tale form a unit where performance is united with message.

The subjects of oral narrative are as varied as its expressions. Griots can present history, epic tales, folk lore, genealogy, and general knowledge in their stories. Tales can move from the real to the fantastic, from one era to another and express a union with the natural world where humans and animals can exist together. The oral tradition also expresses the collective values of the society. The story is of primary importance, but its telling is not necessarily linear. Digressions are common. And while they are connected to the main narrative, they do not function as subplots do in the Western tradition where they reflect the main plot. When characters are stereotypes and the story is known, the joy is in the telling and in the experience of listening. The audience is attuned to the details that refine the narrative.

When filmmakers invoke the oral tradition, they employ it in many different ways. Ousmane Sembene* turned to film as a means of conveying messages in an oral rather than written mode, and he claims the slow pace of his films reflect the presentation of time in the oral tradition. Other filmmakers attempt to identify the camera with the storyteller. Diawara describes scenes in *Tilaï* (1990), *Ceddo* (1976), and *Yeelen* (1987) that suggest the telling of the story by a third person through the position of the camera as an observer. In his essay "Oral Literature and African Film: Narratology in *Wend Kuuni*," Diawara demonstrates how this film's organization invokes the oral tradition at the same time that its structure counters the conservative impulses of that tradition. In this film, as in others, the character's lack of voice points out the importance of being able to speak and what happens to those who cannot. Malkmus and Armes point out how the importance of the group that is an element of society also reflected in the oral tradition shapes the African film. In several works the kind of character development found in the Hollywood style—where the individual's conflicts are central to the plot—is ignored in favor of concentration on the actions of the group (210–16). In all of these instances, the oral tradition contributes to a film style that sets African film apart from that of the Western dominant cinema.

AFRICAN FILM AND THE FANTASTIC

While one must take care in applying concepts of the oral tradition to all African films, it is generally understood that one is using a specifically African form when discussing this tradition. Problems in interpretation become even more complex when attempting to deal with the idea of the fantastic, the world that acknowledges the possibility of the supernatural. Much of the critical theory relating to the fantastic is based on Western literary theory, which is concerned with the individual in both social and psychological terms. An understanding of the fantastic is also tied to belief systems, especially those of Western religions. In order to begin to categorize possible examples of the fantastic in African film, one must be aware of the connections between the real world and the spiritual world in the context of African belief systems. Much of the time those of us operating in the Western tradition can define, through scholarly systems, the boundaries between the real and the fantastic by relying on shared cultural perceptions. Such distinctions are much more difficult when dealing with examples from African societies that have not been westernized. Just as the oral tradition presents a narrative that transcends the boundaries between past and present, this tradition also connects the spiritual to the everyday. One of the best ways to approach an analysis of the fantastic is to examine specific examples in several films and begin to determine both the connections and differences in Western views of the subject and those of the filmmakers and their primary audience.

The seven films, *La vie est belle** (1987), *Quartier Mozart** (1997), *Ta Dona** (1991), *Touki Bouki** (1973), *Wend Kuuni** (1982), *Yeelen**, and *Xala** (1974) all contain what Western viewers would consider to be elements of the fantastic. They also cover a wide range of approaches to Third Cinema and to a presentation of Africa from a recreation of precolonial society to analyses of postcolonial big city problems. Both *Wend Kuuni* and *Yeelen* re-create precolonial eras. *Wend Kuuni* turns to the pre-Christian and Islamic past of Burkina Faso to tell a fable that presents traditional Mossi values as a means of reaffirming these values for the present. Its story of a young boy who becomes mute at the death of his mother and is adopted by a family has a surface simplicity. But an examination of its narrative structure reveals its complex connections to the oral tradition. While its style represents an important stage in the development of African film, its depiction of rural life most closely resembles our preconceptions of Third Cinema. In his analysis of the film in "Oral Literature and African Film: Narratology in *Wend Kuuni*," Diawara shows how the director, Gaston Kaboré* plays with traditional storytelling techniques in order to incorporate a critique of tradition in this film. Events are presented in an order that might occur in the oral tradition where cause/effect relationships are not the primary organizing modes of the narrative. The film might qualify as fantastic because of its presentation as a fable. The story also does not rely on psychological explanations for Wend Kuuni's muteness or his regaining his speech. But it is difficult for the scholar to point to specific ways that such concepts are incorporated into the film since the film does not attempt to create a style that tells us directly through costume or decor that we are watching a nonrealistic re-creation of the past.

With *Yeelen* there is little doubt of the mythic context of the film or its magic. In addition to mythic symbols that appear in the film, cinematic special effects are also used to convey magical events. This critically ac-claimed epic of the Bambara people deals with the renewal that occurs when Nianankoro challenges his father, the leader of the reactionary *Komo* cult. Nianankoro sets out on a quest for knowledge about the cult pursued by his father. The *Komo* is the source of science and knowledge for the people that has been misused by its leader. The final confrontation between father and son is also a confrontation between their religious symbols. When the wing of Kôré, its stone, and the pestle are united they cause the flash of light that results in the destruction of the past. The future is represented by Nianankoro's son in a seamless transition from past to future. While the working of the *Komo* ritual, which was carefully re-created for the film, may be most understandable for those who recognize its music, we can all see the magic. In *Yeelen* viewers may have different appreciations of the fantastic elements and how they operate, but there is no doubt as to their presence. Both *Wend Kuuni* and *Yeelen* re-create a mythic past, but views of fantastic elements change with the way it is presented. In one the audience has to decide whether or not it is actually present while in the second traditional cinematic markers are among the clues that key our reading of the film.

Two contemporary films, *La vie est belle* and *Quartier Mozart* are also clearly marked as fantastic. *La vie est belle* combines social satire with farce in telling the story of a village musician who comes to Kinshasa to make his fortune. The "rags to riches" story is familiar to any audience. The Zairian audience would immediately recognize the poor musician as the legendary Papa Wemba. While the city scenes give the film realistic images, the many coincidences, repeated encounters with a strange dwarf, and the easy successes of the hero place the film in the realm of the mythic. In addition, traditional problems such as impotence are treated comically and religiously. This film combines fantastic elements that are recognizable to Western audiences with purely African moments.

Quartier Mozart is also set in modern Africa, Yaoundé, Cameroon. The entire film is based on the persistence of traditional magic in this modern setting where local characters are given mythic names. The Queen of the Hood joins forces with a sorceress, Maman Thekla, and is transformed into the body of a young man, My Guy, so she can experience the sexual politics of the quarter. The magical transformation takes place on camera when she enters a car and emerges as a man. Maman Thekla takes the form of Panka, a stock rural comic character. In this role she humbles arrogant men by making their penises shrivel up. The story uses modern images to update traditional figures from the oral tradition.

Ta Dona's visual style contains few clues to its mixture of the super-natural and the realistic. The film combines modern concerns for the environment with a quest for traditional herbal magic that has almost been lost. Sidy, the hero, fights the corruption of the ruling class for their mis-understanding of the need for controlled burning in the countryside at the same time that he seeks the Bambara cure, the seventh *canari* from an aged women in Dogon country. The cure works its magic, but he too works his own cure for the landscape, a cure of fire, the revolution that was needed to heal Malian society. In this film traditional ritual magic is connected to modern ecology not in a Western method of joining opposing forces but in a seamless transition from past to future.

In *Xala* one of the leaders of African cinema, Ousmane Sembene, uses a curse that causes impotence to examine some of the problems in post-colonial Senegal. The curse once again represents tradition in the face of change. The hero, El Hadji, is cursed by a beggar he has cheated. While he consults various marabouts (witch doctors or spiritual advisors) in cars to find a cure, his own downfall occurs in the world of modern business. The world of the curse is the world of tradition even though he drives to the marabouts and pays one with a check that bounces. In the business world Sembene shows us how the effects of colonialism linger. The world of the beggars alternates with El Hadji's marriage and business world until they are combined in his final destruction and humiliation.

While many of these films employ modern cinematic devices to present their modern themes, *Touki Bouki* goes the farthest in its exploration of cinematic communication to express the emergence of the fantastic in the modern world of Africa. Mory and his girlfriend Anta are characters who echo outlaw couples from many cultures. They see escape from Dakar to France as the solution to their alienation from their world. Djibril Diop Mambety,* the director, uses two kinds of techniques to introduce other worlds into their story. At key moments he intercuts timeless scenes of cattle herding and slaughter into the couple's love life and quest for money. He also inserts a dream sequence as the couple imagines a triumphant trip through Dakar. Through much of the film the couple ride around Dakar on a motorcycle with a cow's skull mounted on its handle-bars and a symbolic representation of the horns on its back. As Ukadike cautions, we should not read the various textual interruptions as "avant-gardist manipulation of reality" (173). Instead he suggests an analysis that "would attempt a reconfigurative reading that synthesizes the narrative components and reads the images as representing an indictment of contemporary African life-styles and sociopolitical situations in disarray" (173).

The question remains: Are there any constants that unite these explorations of areas that might be called "fantastic"? It is easiest to apply such a term when the cinematic text itself is marked through special effects. There are also those points that are marked through the text as religious moments, which carry people and events beyond the everyday. Even though religious moments move directly out of the everyday they are still marked by occurrences beyond the ordinary such as curses, magical cures, and mysterious transformations. There are also texts that are set in a mythical past marked by a timelessness, by a return to traditional living styles and values. But there are other elements of the text that come from oral traditions such as the comic techniques of *La vie est belle*. Are these too part of the African expression of the fantastic? Perhaps such a theory must deal with African views of time and space and situate the fantastic in the circular treatment of time and space that occurs frequently within these films. While this overview suggests some possible categories and means of representation, any definitive theory obviously requires detailed examination of each text.

The range and variety of topics covered in this introduction suggest some of the complexity in the analysis of African cinema. For those who have grown up outside of the various cultures of this continent, interaction with these films is a constant process of education. Too often Western educational systems either ignore this continent or subtly support the remnants of colonial attitudes. Such reference texts as atlases and world histories seldom allocate the same space to Africa as they do to other continents and their cultures. It is hoped that such texts as this guide will help to increase the information available about this critical area of the world.

Bibliography

Chirol, Marie-Magdeleine. "The Missing Narrative in *Wend Kuuni.*" *Research in African Literatures* 26 (Fall 1995): 49–56.

Diawara, Manthia. *African Cinema: Politics & Culture.* Bloomington: Indiana UP, 1992.

———. "Oral Literature and African Film: Narratology in *Wend Kuuni.*" *Questions of Third Cinema.* Ed. Jim Pines and Paul Willemen. London: British Film Institute, 1991. 195–211.

Gabriel, Teshome H. "Towards a Critical Theory of Third World Film." *Questions of Third Cinema.* Ed. Jim Pines and Paul Willemen. London: British Film Institute, 1991. 30–52.

Malkmus, Lizbeth, and Roy Armes. *Arab and African Film Making.* London: Zed Books, Ltd., 1991.

Shohat, Ella, and Robert Stam. *Unthinking Eurocentrism: Multiculturalism and the Media.* London: Routledge, 1994.

Tomaselli, Keyan, Arnold Shepperson, and Maureen Eke. "Towards a Theory of Orality in African Cinema." *Research in African Literatures.* 26.3 (Fall 1995): 18–32.

Ukadike, Nwachukwu Frank. *Black African Cinema*. Berkeley: U of California P, 1994.
Willemen, Paul. "The Third Cinema Question: Notes and Reflections." *Questions of Third Cinema*. Ed. Jim Pines and Paul Willemen. London: British Film Institute Press, 1991. 1–29

GUIDE TO AFRICAN FILM

A

ABOU SEIF, SALAH (Cairo, Egypt, 1915). Along with Yusuf Chahine,* Abou Seif is one of the defining figures in Egyptian cinema. He received a commercial degree from the Ecole Supérieure de Commerce (Upper Commercial School) in Cairo. He was always fascinated by the cinema. During the production of a documentary about the cotton mill where he worked, he made friends with the director and his staff and convinced them to influence his transfer to a film studio where he was hired as an assistant editor in 1934. He gradually worked his way up to head the department. By 1946 he convinced the studio he had enough training to direct a feature film.

Daiman fi qalbi/ Always in My Heart (1946) is an Egyptian adaptation of the American film *Waterloo Bridge*, the story of a romance between a soldier and a ballet dancer who meet on Waterloo Bridge, lose track of each other, and finally meet again on the bridge. While *Always in My Heart* might seem quite traditional to Western audiences, Abou Seif's realistic presentation of human emotions was not usual in the Egyptian cinema of that period. He retains a romantic theme in his second film, *Al-muntaqim/ The Avenger* (1947), the story of a marriage between a wealthy doctor and a poor young nurse. In his third film, *Mughamarat Antar wa Abla/ The Adventures of Antar and Abla* (1948), he fully establishes the basic elements of his style.

Guy Hennebelle presents this early style as a series of dualities relating to presentation of character, thematic development, aesthetics, and techniques (54–55). Abou Seif's characters come from two opposing worlds: the rich and the poor. These categories might be further developed beyond monetary privilege to such other attributes as the weak and the strong, the respectable and the disreputable, the just and the unjust. Whichever position he foregrounds in a particular film, Abou Seif remains on the side of the poor. Hennebelle indicates that Abou Seif's films always have a moral resolution that can often be generated by the cohesiveness of the poor in response to injustice. Abou Seif's concern for the poor permeates his style as well. His visual style and the performances of his actors appear much more realistic when set in the homes of the poor than in the palaces of the rich.

Hennebelle traces Abou Seif's developing concern for the lower classes and his progress from the Egyptian cinema's stylized melodramas to this filmmaker's stay in Rome in 1950 (57). His incorporation of elements of neorealism, an approach in Italian cinema that attempted to portray the world of postwar Italy realistically and which emphasized the lives of poor people and real settings, changed his career and greatly influenced the development of Egyptian cinema. With ten of the films he made from 1951 to 1966 (*Lak yawm ya Zalim/ Your Day Will Come*, 1950; *Al-usta Hassan/ Foreman Hassan*, 1953; *Raya wa Sakina / Raya and Sakina*, 1953; *Al-wahsh/The Monster*, 1954; *Shabab imra/ A Woman's Youth*, 1955; *Al-futuwwa/ The Bully*, 1956; *Al-tariq al-masdud/ The Alley*, 1958; *Bayn al-sama wal-ard/ Between Heaven and Earth*, 1959; *Bidaya wa nihaya/ Dead Among the Living*, 1960, and *Al-qahira thalathin/ Cairo '30*, 1966) Hennebelle sees Abou Seif combining the lessons of Italian neorealism with his own view of the world to create films that deeply explore contemporary Egyptian society.

Two of these films, *A Woman's Youth* (1955) and *The Bully* (1956), exemplify many of Abou Seif's stylistic and thematic concerns. As Lizbeth Malkmus and Roy Armes suggest, Abou Seif combines melodrama and comedy in *A Woman's Youth* where a young man who has been seduced by his landlady is saved through the intervention of family members both real and surrogate and by his true love (105). In *The Bully* the melodramatic plot examines the concept of *futuwwa*, which Malkmus and Armes explain is a chivalric term for brotherhood that has degenerated in modern Egypt into a name for a social system based on the power of a boss over his workers (101). In this film the central character comes to the city and tries to work with others to change the system. Unfortunately he becomes seduced by the lure of the very power system he has tried to subvert. While Abou Seif's concerns clearly lie with the poor in both of these films, he demonstrates the complexity of any moral position and the difficulty of maintaining such a stance when surrounded by temptation.

He continues to examine the difficulty of remaining moral in the midst of corruption in such later films as *Al-kadhdhab/ The Liar* (1975) where a reporter thinks he can escape the false world presented by the media. But he realizes his life in a poor neighborhood is no better. He lies when he hides his real identity, and his new neighbors are also liars. Again Abou

Seif demonstrates the fact that the poor are no more naturally good by reason of their poverty than the rich are naturally evil. The only way to really effect change is for the whole neighborhood to participate as they do at the end of this film.

Abou Seif has, for the most part, continued to explore contemporary Egyptian society. He occasionally presents historical periods as in *Fajr al-islam/ The Dawn of Islam* (1970) and the film made in Iraq, *Al-Qadisiyya* (1980). But Abou Seif's real contribution to Egyptian cinema is his successful integration of Western realism into his country's cinema.

Filmography:

Daiman fi qalbi/ Always in My Heart (1946)

Al-muntaqim/ The Avenger (1947)

Mughamarat Antar wa Abla/ The Adventures of Antar and Abla (1948)

Shari' al-bahlawan/ Street of the Acrobat (1949)

Al-saqr/ The Falcon (1950)

Al-hubb bahdala/ Love is Scandalous (1951)

Lak yawm ya Zalim/ Your Day Will Come (1952)

Al-usta Hassan/ Foreman Hassan (1953)

Raya wa Sakina/ Raya and Sakina (1953)

Al-wahsh/ The Monster (1954)

Shabab imra/ A Woman's Youth (1955)

Al-futuwwa/ The Bully (1956)

Al-wisada al khaliya/ The Empty Pillow (1957)

La anam/ Night Without Sleep (1957)

Mujrim fi ajaza/ A Thief on Vacation (1958)

Al-tariq al-masdud/ The Alley (1958)

Hadha huwwa al-hubb/ That Is What Love Is (1958)

Ana hurra/ I Am Free (1959)

Bayn al-sama wal-ard/ Between Heaven and Earth (1959)

Law' at al-hubb/ The Anguish of Love (1960)

Bidaya wa nihaya/ Dead Among the Living (1960)

La tufi' al-shams/ Don't Put Out the Sun (1961)

Risala min imra majhula/ Letter from an Unknown Woman (1962)

La waqt lil-hubb/ No Time for Love (1963)

Al-qahira thalathin/ Cairo '30 (1966)

Al-zaujat al-thaniya/ The Second Wife (1967)

Al-Qadiya 68/ Case 68 (1968)

Thalath nisa/ Three Women (1969) with others

Shayun min al-'adhab/ A Certain Pain (1969)

Fajr al-islam/ The Dawn of Islam (1970)

Hammam al-Malatili/ The Baths of Malatili (1973)

Al-kadhdhab/ The Liar (1975)

Sana ula hubb/ The First Year of Love (1976) with others

Wa saqatat fi bahr min al-'asal/ In an Ocean of Honey (1976)

Al-saqqa mat/ The Water Carrier is Dead (1977)

Al-mujrim/ The Assassin (1978)

Al-Qadisiyya (1980)

Al-bidaya/ The Beginning (1986)

Bibliography

Hennebelle, Guy. *Les cinémas africains en 1972*. Paris: Société Africaine d'Edition, 1972.

Malkmus, Lizbeth, and Roy Armes. *Arab and African Film Making*. London: Zed Books, Ltd., 1991.

Afrique, je te plumerai/ Africa, I Will Fleece You (1992: Jean-Marie Teno, Cameroon). This film is an outstanding example of how African cinema is experimenting with traditional documentary forms to communicate the complex reality of modern life on this continent. While many fiction films have addressed the colonial experience, *Afrique, je te plumerai* uses a variety of texts to restore a history of the past one hundred years in Cameroon, the only African country to have experienced colonialization by France, Great Britain, and Germany. Jean-Marie Teno, the director, reverses the usual direction of a historical documentary by moving backward from the present to reveal the sources of the current situation in his country. He combines elements of his own experience, as well as contemporary and older documentary footage to make his position clear.

In traditional nonfiction films, historical material is presented as evidence that helps the filmmaker re-create the past. Many documentaries use this method of the compilation of texts in a chronological order as a means of re-creating the past for the viewer. By disrupting the time frame, Teno calls attention to the footage he uses. This reversal of the normal order also juxtaposes the present reality with images which, when placed in this context, suddenly take on new meaning. Old newsreels lose their supposed objectivity when they are examined from a postcolonial perspective. This change in perspective also affects the audience. The variety of style and images that come together in this film push the viewers into a different interaction with the subject. Rather than merely sitting back and absorbing the historical flow of the information in a traditional format, the shifting tones and the changed chronology force the audience to become actively involved in the viewing experience.

The film begins with a summary of recent history. The first images are of the present. The film then cuts to the celebration of liberation. Cameroon became independent on January 1, 1960. The French, as the Belgians did with Patrice Lumumba, eliminated positive popular leadership in favor of a less confrontational bureaucracy. The film then moves forward to trace the two presidents: Ahmadou Ahidjo (May 5, 1960 to November 1982) and Paul Biya who took over in 1982 after the death of Ahidjo. While the government of Cameroon has remained stable and the country has avoided military coups, the film describes how Biya's presidency is actually a dictatorship. Teno dedicates the film "To all who have died for liberty." He relates liberty to ideas about education. School is promoted as the country's one hope to become like the whites. He shows that even in postcolonial Africa white is the color associated with success, and black is a sign of despair. Education continues to focus on the promotion of a Western ideology. France remains the center of the world. The film argues for a history of Cameroon and a concentration on the problems faced by a country where 98 percent of the urban population live in slums without any real liberty.

Teno traces true independence to freedom for all aspects of the press, books as well as newspapers. The film's presentation of different texts foregrounds the importance of language. In addition to the general problems of preserving an oral tradition that was never recognized by the colonists and that is now endangered by the introduction of Western media, Cameroon's culture was further assaulted by the three different countries that colonized it. The film's title is one of the ways that it plays with language and culture as it transforms the words of a traditional French song into an expression of the French attitude toward Africa. "Alouette" is a well-known French song about a lark. Teno transforms it into a commentary on the fleecing of Africa by European countries. He uses a visit to a library as an example of the continued operation of cultural imperialism by the West. Only a very small number of its volumes actually deal with Africa and even fewer are by Cameroon authors. Even African texts are often published by missionary presses and represent a Christian perspective. People have not really developed strong reading habits except for the daily newspapers that deal with problems they find relevant to their lives.

Teno indicates the problems that exist with the attempt to create an authentic African literature coming out of a historical situation where the technology was not available. In the present, financial control by the International Monetary Fund results in an economic situation that protects Western interests. If a culture, especially an oral culture, is denied access to literature it can mean the death of collective memory. Teno attempts to record some of these memories in his film, stories of colonialism from an African perspective, from his grandfather. Even the written language and the decision as to which language should dominate the country was decided by colonizing powers. French became the language of those who served colonialism or aspired to emulate their rulers. He also connects traditional skills to the oral tradition both of which are destroyed by the urbanization of the culture. The relationship between technology, money, and the exploitation of the country is demonstrated with images of the building of the rail system, which sacrificed many African workers to facilitate the removal of gold from the colony.

Teno explores many ways of communicating through cinema as he returns again and again to the way language controls culture. French speech and attitudes change dramatically when the speakers leave their own country and operate in a colony just as a song about a lark is radically transformed by altering the text so the bird becomes Africa. The French, who were seen as a great source of culture by other Western nations, only understand their own society when they attempt to civilize those they are destroying. Teno details the exploitation of the land as well as the people, the destruction of timber, the rubber plantations, and the use of African troops in France. The only anticolonial expression he can find among the French comes from the Communist party. The West feared communism in Africa as well as their own countries and fought it by killing people and destroying villages. Rather than allow anyone who might have a communist ideology to be part of the government, the colonial powers installed their own puppets at the time of independence. He supports these points with the example of Lumumba. He returns to the present and a mock conversation with the head of the country. But such imaginary dialogues only reconfirm the way the colonial heritage persists into the present.

Afrique, je te plumerai attempts to create a new documentary style that incorporates all kinds of sources and various types of filmmaking to present an African view of the colonial experience. Teno uses film as a means of questioning the present through images that connect a historical past, an oral tradition, and the excesses of postcolonialism into a complex picture. The different perspectives in the film demonstrate the fallacy of a single point of view as a means of understanding the African experience. In a country whose history has been fragmented by a succession of foreign powers, traditional documentaries are inadequate. Teno wants his film to bring his audience to an understanding of colonialism by challenging it to both relearn and recall a world that is in danger of being lost.

Bibliography

Chazan, Naomi, Robert Mortimer, John Ravenhill, and Donald Rothchild. *Politics and Society in Contemporary Africa*. Boulder: Lynne Rienner, 1988.

Ukadike, N. Frank. "The Other Voices of Documentary: *Allah Tantou* and *Afrique, je te plumerai*." *IRIS* 18 (Spring 1995): 81–94.

Allah Tantou / A la grâce de Dieu / God's Will (1991: David Achkar, Guinea/France). The filmmaker, David Achkar, creates a unique documentary as he explores his father's life and death and the larger questions of human rights in a dictatorship. While fiction film is most often used in African film to reclaim a precolonial past, this director employs a documentary methodology to re-create his personal history and that of a recent period in Guinea. Marof Achkar, David's father, toured many countries as one of the stars of the *Ballets Africains*. Guinea was the first French African colony to declare its independence in 1958. Sekou Touré was the leader at the moment of independence, and he was president until his death in 1984. Marof Achkar, at first, was an important member of the government of the new country. He was appointed U.N. ambassador and became a strong voice against apartheid. Without understanding what he had done, he was recalled and jailed in 1968. His family was exiled and did not know that he died in 1971 until after Touré's death.

Marof Achkar managed to keep a secret journal during his years in prison. David uses this written testimony, photos, pieces of old films, and his own reenactment of Marof's life in prison to reconstruct his father's life. The film moves from one kind of evidence to another, generating both an emotional and intellectual impact unlike the usual documentary experience. While the images of Marof's terrible treatment in prison stimulate a passionate response in the viewer, the rapid shifts, the contradictory texts, and the complex reflections create an atmosphere of intellectual inquiry. David does not provide a clear authoritative voice; such a voice would leave no room for the audience to make its own decisions. One might even argue that a single voice forces the kind of single-mindedness associated with the type of repressive government that imprisoned his father. Also, in a film of discovery, David himself searches for the reality behind the man who was his father.

As the film states, David only knew his father from prison. David was aware he was an important man who was arrested, but he did not understand the nature of Marof's heroism. Even Amnesty International was concerned about his imprisonment. After images of a family Christmas celebration, David begins the film by providing the viewer with the details of his father's involvement with the government and his imprisonment in Camp Boiro prison. He re-creates his father's early experiences in prison, the torture, and humiliation. His father did not betray anyone including himself. Humiliation is also described as the last weapon of the weak. After the detailing of the terrible conditions in prison, David moves backward into his father's past. Images of the *Ballets Africains* and a 1954 tour in Paris give a reality to a happier time. Other images present the ballet in the United States and the birth of a daughter in 1957.

But the comfortable reality of the photograph is destabilized by a series of conflicting statements about who is right and who is wrong in a political situation. In prison Marof is confronted with a state that wavers between life and death. He attempts suicide and writes about how the years in jail make him feel dead even though he is alive, another set of oppositions. The film moves back and forth between the images of his past, his journal, and David's re-creation of his prison experiences. The memories that make prison nights the hardest are the connections between these worlds. Marof's journal details the number of days he is in prison. He sees his wife after 510 days. He also details the further tragedy of his gradual loss of sight. He works through a major conversion from Islam to Christianity as he reflects on his relationship with spirituality and the grace of God. The rest of the family is exiled in 1971 and must live with the question of what has happened to their father and husband. Finally years later, they learn he was executed on January 26, 1971.

The distance between his father's death and their knowledge of it is another measure of the absence that David attempts to bridge by reclaiming his father's life and restoring the years that were hidden from the family and the world. All that remains of Marof's heroic struggle against intolerable conditions are the fragments David transfers to film. Traditional documentaries assert their authority through claims of authenticity in their presentation of the real world. They refuse to recognize the inherent bias in any choices made in the organization of the film and the attitude of the all-knowing voice-over narration. During the colonial period documentaries about Africa selected images that reinforced Western views of Africans and their culture. Even today Western films concentrate on the tragedies of civil wars and famines. Certainly the largest amount of footage shot in Africa and shown in documentary formats is not devoted to the people at all. Now that images of the strange practices of tribes are no longer acceptable, most documentaries about Africa focus on the animals. Achkar refuses both the technique and ideology of the traditional form, which can only recall a colonial presence. A single voice is not enough to present the complexities of his search for an understanding of his father's life. His reenactment of his father's prison existence moves beyond the confines of a simple photographic presentation of reality to the only contact possible with a man who can no longer speak for himself. The viewer is forced to confront a different reality in the dark, barren images of a man who is tortured, who is isolated from human contact, who fears he is going mad yet retains a humanity that those who placed him in prison lack. The film also stresses the irony of a man who headed a U.N. committee on South African Human Rights being subjected to the same inhumane treatment in his own country. It is yet another irony that the dictator who ordered his incarceration was admired throughout the continent for his Pan-Africanism and for leading the first French-speaking colony to independence in 1958. David dedicates the film to his father and to all prisoners. His father dedicated the journal of his prison experiences to David on his tenth birthday. By creating this document David provides everyone with knowledge that will hopefully prevent such events from occurring in the future.

Bibliography

Ukadike, N. Frank. "The Other Voices of Documentary: *Allah Tantou* and *Afrique, je te plumerai.*" *IRIS* 18 (Spring 1995): 81–94.

Angano . . . Angano . . . / Tales from Madagascar (1989: Cesar Paes, Madagascar/ France). Ethnographic filmmaking, a documentary form that aligns itself with an anthropological point of view, has a troubled history in Africa. For many years anthropologists objectified people and presented them in ways that only reinforced cultural stereotypes. Early Western impressions of Africans came largely from these distorted images. *Angano . . .* blends the techniques of ethnographic filmmaking with an understanding of the magic generated by the griot who is more than a storyteller. In countries where oral traditions are of primary importance, the griot is the guardian of the past, the preserver of African traditions in the face of colonial and postcolonial influences. Rather than pretending to record events from the position of the hidden observer who never intervenes in the action, the speakers are aware of the camera that is recording their tales. A strict ethnographic film might stay with the speakers or combine images of them with those of their listeners. At the same time *Angano . . .* acknowledges the presence of the cameras, and it uses this awareness to move beyond simply documenting the stories to images of the country, which serve to evoke the world of the storyteller.

The role of the teller is recognized at the beginning of the film. The first speaker says, "Tales, tales, nothing but tales. It's not me telling lies, but people of long ago, and that's how they heard it as well." Thus his story of the God of Earth and the God of Sky and the God's daughter who misses rice is placed in a mythical context. This context denies the responsibility of the narrator at the same time that it makes a necessary connection to a past. The story's continuity with the present is established through the images of rice cultivation. While the storytellers present versions of creation myths, the visuals demonstrate the tales' vitality in a living culture. But the narrators are also aware of the changes that have occurred. One remarks, "The earth is not as strong as it used to be like my teeth." These first stories emphasize how humans live between earth and sky in their path from life to death, relating the cycle of life to that of the earth.

The next set of stories expands the connections to the world of animals that both help humans in the field and provide sacrifices that assist humans in their relationships with each other and the gods—such as the removal of a taboo. Other sacrifices can confer blessings on a marriage or a child, cure illness, or ensure a good harvest. Various stories detail such events and the reasons for them. Images such as those of men attempting to ride a zebu become part of the narrative about how zebus acquired their sub-servient role by going against the wishes of God and drinking up man's share of the medicine God left with them.

The film depicts one of the most interesting of the Malagasy rituals, the turning of the dead that affirms the relationship between soul and life, mind and body. The *famadihana* entails both the exhumation and rear-ranging of the bones of ancestors. During the cool season people go to a familial tomb where they retrieve the bodies of their ancestors, which they wrap in silk shrouds. This is a joyful ritual; the participants dance with the bones, almost bringing them back to life as they connect the living and the dead. The observance of the ritual is important for the blessings it can bring and for the way the living and the dead are connected as the past comes alive.

The oral tradition is also an important source of the history of the group. Storytellers detail the effects of colonialism. Written history was always recorded by strangers. The French deprived the Malagasy of their own history and substituted a colonial identity that focused on Western ideol-ogy rather than indigenous culture. The griots were even more important during this period in maintaining knowledge that otherwise might have disappeared. Tales serve other important functions for the group. As one griot remarks, "Tales help form the mind." They are part of the education of children about the larger issues in their world, a philosophy of life. Even in this modern world people need time to remember. "Tales are the ear's inheritance."

Many African films deal with the role of the griot and the relationship between the storyteller and the oral tradition. A film like *Keïta** (1995) uses the griot to restore a lost past to a child whose postcolonial education is still focused on France. Fictional films have also attempted to re-create the style of the oral tradition in their narratives. *Angano . . .* documents the tradition with the voices and images of real storytellers. Such a film emphasizes the importance of these people in maintaining the cultural heritage of a society. But film as a record also carries with it another dimension. The very process of recording is a means of capturing some-thing that has happened and will never occur in exactly the same way again. Film itself records the present becoming the past. The older people who share their stories in this film are part of the very cycle of life they describe. The film momentarily pulls them out of this cycle, records them, and freezes them in time. The images that accompany their words are also a record that operates differently from their stories. The images are all inclusive in their presentation of the details of a ritual; the viewer sees details that a storyteller might omit. But they also represent the attitudes of the filmmakers rather than the storytellers; the filmmakers decide what to show, how much to show, and when to move on. *Angano* . . . never hides the complexity of its relationship with its subjects as it attempts to record both the reality and the myth that lies behind it. *Angano* . . . won the award for best documentary at the Cinema du Reel and Festival dei Popoli.

Bibliography

Loizos, Peter. *Innovation in Ethnographic Film: From Innocence to Self-Consciousness, 1955–1985*. Chicago: U of Chicago P, 1993.
Ukadike, Nwachukwu. Frank. *Black African Cinema*. Berkeley: U of California P, 1994.

ANSAH, KWAW PAINTSIL (Agona Swedru, Ghana, 1941). While Paintsil Kwaw Ansah has only made two feature films, he has achieved a reputation as an independent filmmaker who engages in important issues and whose films reflect a concern with the future of cinema in Africa. His interest in film can be traced back to his father's profession as a photographer. After becoming a draftsman and working in textiles, Ansah went to England where he enrolled in the Polytechnic of Central London and studied theater design. He took other courses at the American Musical and Dramatic Academy and received a film production grant at RKO Studios in California. One of his plays, *The Adoption*, was staged off-Broadway. His second play, *A Mother's Tears*, was produced after he went home. Upon his return to Ghana he became actively involved in the film industry as a production assistant for the Ghana Film Industry Corporation. He then produced short films for advertising companies. Finally he formed a production company with some friends in order to attempt the difficult task of making independent films. He has always struggled with the financing of films and has almost given up filmmaking at times because of the obstacles he faced in getting the money to make a film. Both of his features deal with problems of identity in a postcolonial context.

Love Brewed in the African Pot (1980) took ten years to produce because of financial difficulties. This love story of people from widely different backgrounds allows Ansah to develop themes relating to class and cultural differences and the modernization and loss of tradition that often accompanies wealth and upper-class status in postcolonial Africa. Aba Appiah, an educated seamstress, wants to marry Joe Quansah, an almost illiterate mechanic. He is the son of a fisherman, and her father, Kofi, a retired civil servant, wants her to marry a professional from the upper-middle class, like the lawyer he has selected. She remains insistent on valuing love over money and status. In presenting the problems the couple faces, Ansah introduces such cultural conflicts as the difference between the traditional African wedding Aba wants and the Western one her father dreams of. Kofi may believe he is a modern man, but he wavers when Aba becomes ill. He tries a range of religions from Christianity to traditional healing in his search for a cure. He also experiences a dream that reaffirms the importance of the fisherman's approach that asserts the importance of the past. But Aba also experiences a dream. She overvalues the fisherman tradition at the expense of her father's beliefs. Ansah shows the complexity of the interaction of past and present in Africa. In this film there are no easy solutions; each side has its positive and negative elements.

Heritage . . . Africa (1987), Ansah's second film, deals with actual historical events to examine the effects of colonialism. This narrative employs a complex structure of dream sequences and flashbacks to trace the shifting cultural stances taken by its central character. Kwesi Atta Bosomefi marks his entry into the colonial system by Westernizing his name to Quincy Arthur Bosomfield. Throughout his education he trades elements of his African identity for the British system that he hopes to adopt. When his mother comes to visit him, he hides her from his guests by seating her outside his house like a servant. She entrusts a precious family heirloom to him, and he gives it to the governor who admires its construction and sends it to England. These acts reverberate with symbolic meaning expressing the abandoning of "mother" Africa by many who were attracted by the false promises of the colonizers. Ansah exposes the colonial impact on every aspect of native life. In addition to the political and educational systems that erase social structures and knowledge of the past, religion is shown to be a hypocritical missionary intervention that was only concerned with conversion and the destruction of traditional beliefs and not with the real welfare of Africans. In another sequence that is rich in symbolic overtones, Bosomfield catches his son watching a forbidden native dance. He take him to a minister who beats the boy so that he eventually dies from his wounds. The same minister buries the boy. As the narrative develops, Bosomfield begins to sense the conflicts in his position. When it is too late he finally attempts to return to his roots. While his journey takes place under colonialism, Ansah suggests many Bosomfields still exist in modern Africa, and the poisoning of the society that began in that era continues into the present.

Ansah's two films demonstrate his ongoing concern with effects of the past on the present and the need for an appreciation of a heritage that is in danger of being lost. Under colonialism, African history was attacked to promote foreign interests and to demonstrate the inferiority of indigenous practices. But in modern times, Africans themselves ignore their heritage as they seek to become exactly like the very colonialists that have been ejected from Africa. In his films, Ansah demonstrates how these themes operate in his country and how they mirror similar situations around the continent.

Filmography:

Love Brewed in the African Pot (1980) Peacock Award Eighth International Film Festival of India, Oumarou Ganda Prize FESPACO 81.

Heritage . . . Africa (1987) Grand Prize FESPACO 89, FESPACO Institute of Black People's Award.

Bibliography

Diawara, Manthia. *African Cinema: Politics & Culture*. Bloomington: Indiana UP, 1992.

Malkmus, Lizbeth, and Roy Armes. *Arab and African Film Making*. London: Zed Books, 1991.

Shiri, Kenneth, comp. and ed. *Directory of African Films*. Westport, Conn.: Greenwood P, 1992.

Ukadike, Nwachukwu Frank. *Black African Cinema*. Berkeley: U of California P, 1994.

B

BALOGUN, OLA (Aba, Nigeria, 1945). Ola Balogun is considered one of Africa's most prolific filmmakers. He is a Yoruba, and his father was a lawyer. As with many African filmmakers, he received his formal training at IDHEC (Institut des hautes etudes cinématographique). He later completed a doctoral dissertation on documentary film at the Université de Nanterre. He worked in various capacities for the Nigerian government including scriptwriting for the Federal Film Unit and acting as a press attaché for the embassy in Paris. He also became a research fellow at the University of Ife when he returned to Nigeria and an audiovisual specialist with the National Museum in Lagos. After making several documentaries, he was able to finance a feature film *Alpha* (1972). Many of Balogun's early features are stylistically innovative as he explores elements of the Nigerian culture, but these experiments did not always lead to financial success. He has had to balance his interest in testing the boundaries of cinematic communication with the need to be economically viable so he can continue to make films.

For the most part, Balogun's early documentaries explore elements of traditional life in his country. However his first, *One Nigeria* (1969), was made in response to his impressions of the civil war that was going on when he returned home. Two later documentaries return to the area affected by the war, *Eastern Nigeria Revisited* (1973) and *Nigersteel* (1975). *Fire in the Afternoon* (1971), *Thundergod* (1972), and *Owuama, a New Year Festival* (1973) are among the shorts he made to document traditional festivals. With most of these films he believes in allowing the images to speak for themselves without voice-over commentary for the power of the rituals to be communicated.

Balogun's early features explore various cinematic techniques as he gradually discovers his own voice. His first feature, *Alpha*, is an examination of his artistic beliefs. The central character, Alpha, wanders around Paris meeting with other African émigrés until he finally reaches the point where he decides to return home. This film is experimental and somewhat episodic. Its lack of appeal for the general public forced Balogun to realize he needed to communicate in a more accessible manner. *Amadi* (1975) his next feature was much more popular. This semidocumentary makes innovative use of Ibo, the language of the region where it was filmed. The film tells the familiar story of a young man, Amadi, who returns to his village from the city. He works with the village to modernize their agricultural methods at the same time that he advocates the restoration of traditional religion. The film argues for a reconsideration of the relationship between the old and the new in which both have value.

Balogun's next feature *Ajani-Ogun* (1976) turns to the Yoruba tradition and is considered the first musical to come out of black Africa. Balogun collaborated with Duro Ladipo who is the master of the Yoruba traveling theater. Lapido's theatrical group became the cast of the film and contributed greatly to its popularity. Ajani-Ogun, a young hunter, pursues a corrupt politician who has stolen his dead father's land and wants Ajani-Ogun's love. The music and dance convey the atmosphere of village life at the same time they contribute to the thematic concerns of the film. Balogun continues to examine ways to combine important elements from the past in the context of modern life. He also demonstrates the way the colonial heritage is the source of postcolonial corruption.

Balogun followed *Ajani-Ogun* with a film that he hoped would have even wider appeal, *Musik-Man/ Music Man* (1976). He turned to English and pidgin English to make the film accessible to a larger audience. But there were considerable problems during the making of the film. Balogun wanted to complete *Music Man* for entry in a festival. It was difficult to film in Lagos at that time because of numerous bottlenecks, and some of the technicians who worked on it were not as adept as they might have been. The film was not a success, and the director returned to work with the Yoruba theater. He worked with the actor who played the lead in *Ajani-Ogun*, Ade Folayan, and adapted a novel by Adebayo Faleti into the film of the same name, *Ija Ominira/ Fight for Freedom* (1977). The narrative deals with a tyrannical king who is deposed by his people. The film was very successful despite clashes between Balogun and Folayan.

When he received an offer of financial support from Brazilians who were impressed with the success of *Ajani-Ogun*, Balogun agreed to a coproduction. *A deusa negra/ Black Goddess* (1978) was shot in Brazil. Balogun was interested in this project because his mother was descended from Afro-Brazilian slaves who returned to Nigeria after being liberated. After having to deal with financial problems in Brazil, Balogun was able to make this film about a love that transcends time through supernatural intervention. An African prince is transported to Brazil as the result of tribal warfare. After two centuries, another African returns to Brazil to trace his roots. A trance reveals his kinship with the prince who had become a slave. The young man realizes his guide is the reincarnation of the prince's love. The two young people understand they are destined for each other. The film achieved great commercial and critical success.

Balogun returned to Nigeria and agreed to work with another important veteran of the Yoruba traveling theater, Chief Hubert Ogunde, and adapted his play as a film. *Aiye* (1979) is a classic story of the struggle between good and evil in which good is represented by a healer priest and evil by sorceresses in a Yoruba village. The film used many Yoruba theater actors. Once again there were difficulties between the two men who were working together on the production. But, just as with his previous collaborations with the theater, this film was also a tremendous success.

Balogun wished to make a more significant film and deal with deeper subject matter. He decided to make a film about the struggle for liberation and found inspiration in a novel by the Kenyan author Meja Mwangi, *Carcass for Hounds*. He shot *Cry Freedom* (1981) in Ghana once again in the face of tremendous difficulties. He wanted to present a specifically African perspective of colonialism and those who fought it. The film deals with the activities of a guerrilla group and a colonial army both led by young men of the same age who have grown up together—one as master and the other as servant. While the film appealed to intellectuals who were impressed with its serious considerations of important issues, the general public, accustomed to Hollywood-style action adventure films, largely ignored it.

With this failure Balogun returned to the safety of the Yoruba theater and yet another collaboration with a famous actor known as Baba Sala. *Orun Mooru* (1982) is the story of a credulous villager who has been fooled so many times he decides to commit suicide. When he travels to the land of the dead he discovers that his time has not yet come. As has been true of Balogun's other theatrical collaborations, this film was also very successful. But the problems he encountered in dealing with theatrical people during each production led him to abandon this area. Instead, he made the two-part film *Money Power* (1982), which deals with the corruption associated with money in Nigeria. Balogun has been both praised and criticized for the direction of his recent films. Some think he needs to worry less about pleasing the public and more about working toward a more cinematically fluid style. Others find his work with the theater a positive development on the road to an authentically African cinema.

Filmography:

One Nigeria (1969)

Les ponts de Paris/ The Bridges of Paris (1971)

Fire in the Afternoon (1971)

Thundergod (1972)

Alpha (1972)

Nupe Mascarade (1972)

Owuama, a New Year Festival (1973)

Eastern Nigeria Revisited (1973)

Vivre/ To Live (1974)

Nigersteel (1975)

Amadi (1975)

Ajani-Ogun (1976)

Musik-Man/ Music Man (1976)

Ija Ominira/ Fight for Freedom (1977)

A deusa negra/ Black Goddess (1978) International Catholic Office of Cinema prize, Best Film Music Carthage Film Festival 1980

Aiye (1979)

Cry Freedom (1981)

Orun Mooru (1982)
Money Power (1982)

Bibliography

Armes, Roy, "Culture and National Identity." *Cinemas of the Black Diaspora: Diversity, Dependence, and Oppositionality*. Ed. Michael Martin. Detroit: Wayne State UP, 1995. 25–39.

Balogun, Françoise. *Le cinéma au Nigeria*. Brussels: OCIC, 1984.

Diawara, Manthia. *African Cinema: Politics & Culture*. Bloomington: Indiana UP, 1992.

Malkmus, Lizbeth, and Roy Armes. *Arab and African Film Making*. London: Zed Books, 1991.

Shiri, Kenneth, comp. and ed. *Directory of African Films*. Westport, Conn.: Greenwood P, 1992.

Ukadike, Nwachukwu Frank. *Black African Cinema*. Berkeley: U of California P, 1994.

La Battaglia de Algeria/ The Battle of Algiers (1966: Gillo Pontecorvo). This Algerian/Italian co-production was one of the first films to gain an international reputation for its presentation of a colonial revolution from the point of view of the colonized people. Gillo Pontecorvo and his script writer Franco Solinas consulted with Algerians and rewrote the script to incorporate their suggestions. *The Battle of Algiers* uses the locations and people of the actual events to re-create the battle for the liberation of this city and the rest of the country from French colonial rule. Before the film begins, a title proudly proclaims the total absence of documentary footage. Pontecorvo uses black and white photography and documentary techniques to re-create the impression of screening real events at the same time that the script is carefully constructed to draw the viewers into the story and control viewer identification with the revolutionaries. While the film deals with different personalities, the various stories are united around the character of Ali-la-Pointe. The narrative begins with his betrayal, moves back in time to trace his involvement in the revolution, and returns to his death and then to the birth of a free country.

The actual struggle in Algeria began in the countryside in November 1954 and moved actively to the capital in 1956. The film opens by indicating both time and place: Algiers, 1957. French soldiers surround a small defeated man who has just betrayed his comrades. Pontecorvo deliberately begins with what seems to be the defeat of the FLN (National Liberation Front). The soldiers quickly move into the Casbah and surround the remnants of the opposition who are hiding behind a wall. The camera moves behind the wall and pans along the faces of a handsome young man, a beautiful woman, a youth, and finally stops on the arresting image of a young man, Ali. While the officer tells them of the hopelessness of their situation, the film moves back in time to 1954.

The director immediately establishes the opposition between the two worlds of the film: the French and the Algerian. In the flashback, the camera moves from the European city to the Casbah. As the FLN broadcasts their first communiqué declaring their goals for their country, the camera rests on Ali who is running a version of the old shell game with cards. His spiel in Arabic contrasts with the French of his European customers. A European calls the police, and when he runs, a young French man trips this Arab who is obviously out of place in their Algeria. The crowd that forms when Ali punches the young man turns so angry and violent that this incident leads the viewer to believe subsequent attacks on the French justified responses to racism.

Pontecorvo uses this introduction to Ali as a means of demonstrating how the revolution grew. Like many other leaders Ali learns about politics and becomes converted to the cause in prison when he witnesses the execution of an Algerian patriot. The early part of the film traces his growing involvement in the revolution. The viewer learns about the FLN and how it operates as Ali rises in the organization. Through identification with Ali and his conversion, the viewer is drawn into sympathy with the revolution. However, by following Ali, the film concentrates on the violence of the movement to gain freedom for Algeria rather than its ideology, which is also an essential component.

The next date in the film, April 1956, marks the twenty-fourth communiqué from the FLN directed toward erasing such degrading effects of colonialism as alcoholism, prostitution, and gambling. The film moves back and forth from Ali's growing role in the organization to the effect of the FLN on the community: children attack a drunkard, Ali kills a former friend who is still a gangster, and people celebrate the first wedding performed according to the FLN rather than French law. The wedding is both an act of war against the French and a unifying moment for the community as the camera pans up from the house across the Casbah.

The growth of the FLN is demonstrated through a series of individual attacks on the police. A new pattern emerges: a series of attacks on one side brings reprisals as the film moves into a cycle of ever-escalating violence. The increasing division between the two sides is defined by the fencing off of the Casbah and directives from the governor of Algeria and the police. The size of the FLN is demonstrated by the organization behind a series of killings and the different people involved in each one. Just as the opening of the film is marked by the crowd's attack on Ali, this section is marked by a group of French women's reaction to a street cleaner. Finally, the French respond to individual acts by going into the Casbah and destroying a whole house. While the FLN has only attacked police up to this point, the French are the first to kill women and children indiscriminately with a bomb. Once again, community is emphasized as the people of the Casbah deal with the effects of the explosion, and the FLN prepares its own response.

In one of the most moving sections of the film, Pontecorvo shows how several women sacrifice their religious garments transforming themselves with Western clothing and hair styles so they will not be searched carrying bombs out of the Casbah into the European part of the city. The soldiers let the women through the barriers because these men are blinded by their own preconceived ideas of who might be a terrorist. The film increases the impact of the bombs by showing the audience each place and the people in it. While the previous shots of the bodies of small children after the Casbah explosion make the FLN's response understandable, the fact that both sides kill the innocent is not ignored.

The French answer this new level of violence with paratroopers, one of whose leaders, Lieutenant Colonel Mathieu, has experience both against the Nazis and insurgents in Indochina and Nigeria—a real representative of France's colonialism. He devises the plan that will destroy the leadership of the FLN. He drives the action of the film to the beginning of the flashback, Ali and the others trapped in the wall of a house. He knows that in order to get the information they need, the paratroopers must treat Algeria like a battlefield and use any means necessary, including torture, to gain this information. While the voice-over narration discusses the need for a general strike required by the FLN, the film shows how the daily life of the city is affected by the strike and how the French respond. At this point in the film, Ali conducts one of the FLN's leaders to a safe house, and this man explains revolutionary theory both to Ali and to the viewers. Ali only understands the need for terrorism; the leader explains the need for a general strike to involve more people and to get a sense of the strength of popular support. He also tells Ali that the most difficult stage in a revolution comes when they win.

Gradually, through arrests made easier by the strike—which helps the paratroopers identify FLN supporters—and torture, Mathieu identifies members of the organization. He explains that as long as the French want to remain in Algeria, all kinds of force are necessary. Pontecorvo insists that the viewers see the torture and continued response of the FLN of bombs and attacks. Ali is the last of the FLN leadership to remain free in the Casbah. When the film shows Ali with the others, the viewers remember from the beginning that they know their capture is near. The film recounts the opening from their perspective. Once more, Ali's connection to the community is reaffirmed. Before the French explode the bomb that kills him, the camera moves to rooftops of the Casbah and the people who watch and wait. The French are satisfied that at last the battle is over in Algiers.

The film jumps ahead two years to the end of December and a massive demonstration of crowds with thousands of Algerian flags. When the people attempt to enter the European section, many are shot, but the distinctive sounds made by the women continue through the night and into the next day. In a final show of force, the French bring tanks up against the crowds. This time the numbers and intensity of demonstrations influence French public opinion. On December 21, 1960, the last day of the demonstrations, women dance in the street for the freedom of Algeria. The film ends with these images while the narrator explains that two more years of fighting take place until Algeria is finally free on July 2, 1962. While the film gives the audience heroes as a focus and as points of identification, its ending provides its political focus. Individuals are necessary for a revolution, but ultimately the force of all of the people was necessary to win the battle of Algiers. Its international reputation made it one of the first films to promote a worldwide understanding of an anticolonial struggle.

The Battle of Algiers was nominated for an Academy Award as best foreign film in 1966. In 1968 Pontecorvo was nominated for best director for the film and shared the screenplay nomination with Franco Solinas. The film won the Golden Lion at the Venice Film Festival in 1966.

Bibliography

Hennebelle, Guy. *Les cinémas africains en 1972*. Paris: Société Africaine d'Edition, 1972.

Shohat, Ella, and Robert Stam. *Unthinking Eurocentrism: Multiculturalism and the Media*. London: Routledge, 1994.

BOUAMARI, MOHAMED (Sétif, Algeria, 1941). Unlike many of his colleagues in the ONCIC (Office national du commerce et l'industrie cinématographique/The National Office for Cinematic Commerce and Industry). Bouamari had no formal training in film. He gained experience by working as assistant director on such films as Ahmed Rachedi's* *Fajr al-Mu'adhdhabin/ Dawn of the Damned* (1965), Mohamed Lakhdar-Hamina's* *Rih al-Awras/ Wind from the Aurès* (1966), and Jean-Louis Bertucelli's *Remparts de Argile/ Ramparts of Clay* * (1970). He also aquired further training by making several short films during the seventies.

Bouamari's first two features deal with agrarian reforms. These films were very successful and greatly enhanced his reputation. *Al-Fahhâm/ The Charcoal Burner/ Le charbonnier* (1972) traces the fate of the title character who can no longer make a living when gas is brought into his area. In addition to the difficulties he faces trying to find work in the city, he must also contend with a wife who wants to pursue the opportunities offered to women by the new government. Bouamari's use of sound in this film suggests the further cinematic explorations he pursues in subsequent work. Both natural and artificial noises depict the way the modern world changes the charcoal burner's life. In *Al-irth/ The Inheritance/ L'héritage* (1974) the wife is also an important force. She works to restore the sanity of her husband who has become deranged as a result of French torture during the fight for independence. Belkacem, the central character, is able to resume his role as a teacher and join his wife in rebuilding their village, which was destroyed by the French. They are successful because he can identify important elements of their past, Roman ruins, which indicate the direction of the reconstruction.

Bouamari's next film furthered his exploration of cinematic techniques that attempt to unite revolutionary form and content. The *Al-khutwat al-ula/ First Step/ Premier pas* (1974) opens with the explanation of the roles of the various cast members as they step forward and present themselves. The film combines its depiction of the growing importance of the wife and the conflict her liberation creates with images of archetypal heroes and heroines from the past. As is often the case with cinematic experiments, neither *First Step* nor his next film *Al-raft/ The Refusal/ Le refus* (1982) were as popular as his earlier films. But Bouamari's career is an example of that which attempts to find unique means of expression and one that takes film beyond the conventions of Western cinema.

Filmography

Conflit/ Conflict (1964)

L'obstacle/ The Obstacle (1965)

La cellule/ The Cell (1967)

Le ciel et les affaires/ Heaven and Business (1967)

APC-école de la démocratie/ APC School of Democracy (1978)

Charte nationale/ National Charter (1978)

Al-Fahhâm/ The Charcoal Burner/ Le charbonnier (1972)

Al-irth/ The Inheritance/ L'héritage (1974)

Al-khutwat al-ula/ First Step/ Premier pas (1974)

Al-raft/ The Refusal/ Le refus (1982)

Bibliography

Armes, Roy. *Dictionary of North African Film Makers*. Paris: Editions ATM, 1996.
Malkmus, Lizbeth, and Roy Armes. *Arab and African Film Making*. London: Zed
    Books, Ltd., 1991.

C

Camp de Thiaroye/ Camp Thiaroye (1988: Ousmane Sembene* and Thierno Faty Sow, Senegal). In this film, which he co-directed with Thierno Faty Sow, Ousmane Sembene returns to a period and theme he explored in the earlier film, *Emitai** (1971): real events occurring during World War II that expose the effects of colonialism in Senegal. Sembene has personal knowledge of this period because he served in the French army during this era. *Camp de Thiaroye* is both a broader and deeper condemnation of the actions of the French and their attitudes toward Africans. He also continues his recovery of the lost history of Africa as in *Ceddo** (1976). The directors present a wide variety of characters in their exploration of the events that occurred in a repatriation camp in Senegal.

The film opens with the disembarkation of African troops who have served in Europe. At first no specific characters emerge as the men march down the gangplank to the music of the band that forms part of the group welcoming them. A comment from one of the French officers alerts the audience to the fact that these soldiers are not wearing regulation uniforms. They have been clothed by the Americans because there were no French uniforms available. One soldier emerges to greet his waiting relatives who seem reluctant to meet his white commanding officer, a captain who is very friendly with this sergeant. The troops march through Dakar to the transit camp on the edge of town. Colonial attitudes emerge immediately as one of the officers claims that the huts they will stay in are better than their own homes in their villages. As the men arrive the directors begin to distinguish the characters who will play important roles in the film. Among the Africans Sergeant Diatta has already been introduced and stands out even more because of his education. Corporal

Diarra, who serves under him, is less clearly presented, and he is depicted mainly through his actions with little attention to his background. The most moving introduction is that of the man called Pays (which means country). He was a prisoner in Buchenwald, one member of the African troops abandoned and left to be captured at Dunkirk. Pays can no longer speak. He has gone mad as a result of his experiences. He walks up to the barbed wire that surrounds Camp de Thiaroye. He touches the wire unable to understand why he is once again in prison. The corporal pours dirt on his hand, explaining things are different; this is African soil. Pays is calmed, but spends much of the film wearing his Nazi helmet, a symbol of his past.

Various events establish life in the camp. One man tries to learn how to ride his bike. A tailor sets up his shop as he waits to return to his village. The Muslims follow their prayer rituals. The men complain about the terrible food. While most of the white officers ignore the men, the captain, who fought with them in Europe, appreciates them and their request for decent food. When the sergeant's uncle visits him he learns that his parents were killed by French soldiers when their village refused to give up their rice, the story of *Emitai*. The sergeant is separated from the rest of his countrymen by his education, his love of French literature and classical music, which he shares with the officers. Even his uncle is put off when he realizes his nephew has married a French woman and has a daughter with her. But he agrees to get coffee for his nephew to send back with the captain to the sergeant's wife in France.

The first part of the film alternates between life in the camp and life in Dakar or the countryside around the camp. The directors gradually accelerate the events that demonstrate how colonial attitudes dominate life. The sergeant goes into town still wearing an American uniform. He is about to be served at a brothel until they realize he is not an American but an African, and Africans are not allowed in that place. Americans think he is falsely wearing their uniform and beat him and carry him off. One of his men watches the incident, and when he does not return to camp he forms a commando unit that captures an American who they hold to exchange for the sergeant. Once again the captain intervenes and effects the release of both men. The other officers are upset at an instance of insubordination among the Africans. For the French, order and discipline are more important than what happened to the sergeant. They are unable to understand how the men feel when they must trade in their American uniforms for the traditional uniforms of African colonial infantrymen, *tirailleurs*. The sergeant loses a badge of his office when no one provides the proper hat for him. While the men appreciated the distinction of wearing clothes and shoes comparable to their European counterparts, their colonial officers see their change in attire as still better than what they would wear in their villages.

The final incident, which precipitates the violent ending of the film, concerns the back pay the men are to receive before they leave for their homes. The French refuse to exchange money at the correct rate and want to give the men half of what their money is really worth claiming times are difficult and money is short. The captain argues for a fair exchange and is isolated from his fellow officers at the army headquarters, which becomes the only location outside of the camp presented during the last part of the story. The men capture the general who promises to pay them at the correct rate. The men have a party to celebrate their victory. Pays climbs into one of the watch towers placed around the camp. He wakes up to the sound of the tanks that surround the camp. When he tries to explain what he has seen, the others believe he thinks the Germans are attacking. Suddenly, at three in the morning of December 1, 1944, the tanks fire on the camp. The directors alternate long shots of the men trying to avoid being shot and the buildings being destroyed with close-ups of the tanks firing until nothing is left. The camera then pans along the bodies at ground level, mute evidence of the destruction. Five hours later, after sunrise, men bury the dead. Only a piece of the sign that was over the gate to the camp remains. The officers at headquarters are pleased with their actions and justify them by claiming approval at higher levels.

But the film does not end with the massacre and its results. The directors return the viewers to the location of the opening of the film. But this time now *tirailleurs* leave for service in France. Their relatives come to see them off. The camera passes over the captain, who is about to leave with these men, and stops on the sergeant's uncle and niece. She is holding the coffee for his wife and a doll for his daughter, but the boat leaves without these gifts. The sergeant is dead. The final image is a close-up of the coffee and the African doll.

In addition to reclaiming events from Senegal's past Camp de Thiaroye refers to the continuing effects of colonialism in the present. The *tirailleurs'* experiences in Europe teach them that they are comparable to the French when it comes to fighting. Their observation of the German occupation of France and their experiences in German concentration camps makes them aware of the similarities that exist between the German and the French and of their connection to other victims in the concentration camps. They return to Africa aware of the effects of colonialism and are empowered by their experiences in combat. But their newly discovered power leads to their rebellion and destruction. The final images of the film make the viewers aware of the continued reliance on colonial structures in modern Africa. The big ships continue to dock in African ports today and take away African resources. Colonial ties have not been completely broken. The African doll lies on top of the sack of coffee, symbolic of the African products that are exported without any real change in the attitudes of those who continue to exploit Africa. *Camp de Thiaroye* won the Special Jury Prize at the Venice Film Festival and the Carthage Film Festival in 1988, as well as a prize at FESPACO in 1989.

Bibliography

Cham, Mbye. "Official History, Popular Memory: Reconfiguration of the African Past in the Films of Ousmane Sembene." *Ousmane Sembene: Dialogues with Critics and Writers.* Ed. Samba Gadjigo, Ralph Faulkingham, Thomas Cassirer, and Reinhard Sander. Amherst: U of Massachusetts P, 1993. 22–28.

Diawara, Manthia. *African Cinema: Politics and Culture.* Bloomington: Indiana UP, 1992.

Ghali, Noureddine. "An Interview with Sembene Ousmane." *Film & Politics in The Third World.* Ed. John D. H. Downing. New York: Praeger, 1986. 41–54.

Malkmus, Lizbeth, and Roy Armes. *Arab and African Film Making.* London: Zed Books, Ltd., 1991.

Ukadike, Nwachukwu Frank. *Black African Cinema.* Berkeley: U of California P, 1994.

Ça twiste à Poponguine/ Rocking Popenguine (1993: Moussa Sene Absa, Senegal). This film of life in a Senegalese village uses a period in the recent past to comment on what it is like to grow up in an emerging country. The teenagers in *Rocking Popenguine* share attitudes with young people everywhere at the same time they must deal with problems that are unique to their situation. The universality of the teenage life makes this film accessible to the novice viewer of African cinema, but the viewer must still be aware of the specifics of a country that had recently achieved independence (August 20, 1960). The film is a perspective of events in December 1964 told from the viewpoint of an unspecified current time. The narrator, a character in the drama, provides a voice-over account to accompany the events and give them the panorama of the present.

The film opens with the quotation, "If you seek happiness bring back your best years," a statement that sets the tone. While the film will not make light of the conflicts faced by the young people, the statement suggests all will end well. After these words, the narrator sets the scene by introducing the seaside Popenguine, "in the heart of Senegal," as the mail truck approaches. The truck's trip through the town allows the introduction of the various characters and situations and sets the tone for the episodic narrative that moves from group to group recounting the stories of each. Bacc, the voice-over narrator, runs out of school to follow the truck. He is ten years old, a parentless child who lives with his grandmother and survives by doing odd jobs. The camera also introduces the two rival teenage gangs, neither very large, which are defined by their allegiance to two different cultures. The Kings are dominated by their love of African American music and have adopted such names as Jimi Hendrix,

Ray Charles, Otis Redding, and James Brown. They possess the only record player in Popenguine, but they have attracted no girls. The other group, the Ins, short for Inseparables, have taken the names of French pop stars. They have no record player, but they do have the attention of the few girls in the village.

If the two gangs represent opposing attitudes toward modern Western culture, two adults establish the opposition of African and European education. Mr. Benoit, the local teacher, a Breton, is well liked. For Bacc he is nicer than the tyrannical teacher of the Muslim school he previously attended. But his lessons about the fables of Jean de la Fontaine contrast with the African stories Madame Castiloor tells the younger children. *Rocking Popenguine* introduces both cultures and the methods used to teach the students, but it is more concerned with how diverse cultural elements can be integrated into the lives of the characters in a modern world rather than advocating what would be an impossible task, the rejection of outside influence. Even the most critical member of the community, the storekeeper El Hadj Gora, who constantly attacks his son's activities with the Ins, buys a television at the end of the film, an act that will culturally alter the village. El Hadj Gora also represents another pairing of opposites in the village: the two major religions, Christianity, led by a local priest, and Islam, led by a marabout.

Rocking Popenguine focuses the various conflicting circles in the village around the actions of the two teenage groups. The Ins attempt different money-making schemes culminating in a party that leaves them in debt to the girls who have prepared the food and angers the Kings who burn down the Ins' club house. However the Kings are no more successful. When they set fire to the Ins' club, they also burn their own record player and records. The girls abandon the Ins who try to restore their fortune by going fishing only to take a boat that sinks, necessitating a nighttime rescue by villagers who are disgusted with them. Their downward spiral is mirrored by that of the French teacher, who desperately wants to return to France on a leave but never manages to go. The fate of the teenagers and Mr. Benoit are connected by two musical events at the end of the film.

The villagers are so concerned about their teacher's depression that the priest gets the village choir led, by Madame Castiloor, to join in a song praising him. This tribute unites the French and African religious traditions. The Ins strike up a relationship with a French rock star who throws a party for the whole village bringing together the French and American pop traditions, a union forecast by a French version of "The Twist" earlier on the sound track. African and French life are also united when one of the villagers introduces Mr. Benoit to a Senegalese woman. The final moments of the film demonstrate the possibilities of an approach where cultures blend and where the positive in each is adopted by the group.

While *Rocking Popenguine* promotes the blending of various traditions, it does not avoid criticism of the negative elements in each. Mr. Benoit may be loved by the village, but he sees no value in the indigenous culture. Students who speak their native language instead of French in school must keep a stick. The person left with it at the end of the day gets beaten. But this situation leads to a moment of generosity, when a teenager deliberately speaks Wolof so a younger child won't get hit. El Hadj Gora, the local storekeeper, is religious as evidenced by his name (which indicates the completion of a pilgrimage to Mecca), but he is intolerant of the young. He likes the status of the modern world, a car, and a television but not the ideas. He beats all of the teenagers to punish them and is stopped by Mr. Benoit who tells him he is beating the future. The teacher defends the children's dreams. El Hadj Gora thinks he protects his tradition when he is really attacking it, and Mr. Benoit supports the very culture he attempts to erase at school. The afterword, which tells of the future of the teens, suggest a further blending and perhaps a loss of both cultures. The girls marry managers in the city, further reducing the number of women in the village. One has joined the army; another is in Gambia; Bacc, presumably the filmmaker, is somewhere is Paris. Only El Hadj Gora's son remains in the village running his father's business.

Rocking Popenguine examines the dreams of many of the members of this village. It shows the complexity of desire in the modern world where reality allows for no easy answers. Rather than an easy condemnation of colonialism, the film explores the impossibility of avoiding cross-cultural influences. The outside world enters the village easily through newspapers, records, magazines, and the letters brought by the mail truck. Villagers are constantly leaving as evidenced by the children without parents. The film suggests such change cannot be avoided. What is important is to build an environment where all can live together. The teenagers' gaudy sixties clothes blend with the party clothes of the rest of the villagers at the party at the end of the film. When the television is turned on in El Hadj Gora's house for the first time, the audience sees a French version of a Greek myth. Moussa Sene Absa, the director, recognizes the inevitability of change, and he acknowledges the difficulty of movement into a modern world. He does not gloss over both the losses and the gains of such transitions. These views present a positive attitude toward the inevitable effects of the modern world in all lives.

Ceddo (1976: Ousmane Sembene,* Senegal). Sembene continues the examination of the African past that he began with *Emitai** (1971). This time, rather than dealing with a specific historical incident, Sembene exposes the way basic elements of modern Senegalese life are the result of outside intervention. In a period vaguely set in the seventeenth or eighteenth centuries, he exposes the introduction of Islam as an element of exploitation similar to the later colonialization of the country by the French. Sembene also continues to reject the Western film style and instead employs cinematic techniques that convey African traditions. Mbye Cham lists the ways Sembene presents an African view of history by using popular memory, revisiting both the Euro-Christian and Arab-Islamic past, demonstrating how these two traditions have used similar tactics to conquer Africa, and restore the importance of women's roles (24). In place of the conventional reliance on causality and individualism that dominates the Hollywood film, Sembene substitutes a storytelling mode that draws its power from the oral tradition. In *Ceddo* he tells of events in the history of his country by breaking with colonial filmmaking techniques and exposing a form of cultural imperialism that has been ignored by Africans.

Ceddo examines the conversion of Africans to Islam at the same time that traditional society is also being approached by Christian missionaries and attacked by slavers. The film opens with images of the slave trader and the Catholic missionary, the expected figures in an attack on a colonial past. But they are not central to the narrative. The missionary has little impact on the film and is killed after he experiences a vision of a Catholic Africa in the future. The slave trader disappears before the end of the film. The film's real focus is the kidnapping of the king's daughter, Dior Yacine, by one of the ceddo, the traditional people who wish to retain their native gods, to protest the Muslim incursion into the kingdom. The king and members of his court have already converted to Islam. The imam wants the entire kingdom to become Muslim. The imam is shown to be the real threat to the unity of the community. The kidnapping is a response to the Islamic intrusion.

The rest of the film examines the responses to the imam's imposition of Muslim beliefs on the community. One of the king's nephews who converted, assured that the traditional matrilineal line of succession would be maintained, learns he is no longer an heir to the throne. Instead the king's son, who is now the heir, is the first selected to rescue the princess. When the ceddo kill him through trickery, the champion warrior is sent and is also killed. The king, who is a weak ruler and cannot make decisions, disappears as a result of actions of the imam who then declares a holy war on the ceddo. The ceddo are defeated and forced to accept Islam; their heads are shaved, and they must adopt Muslim names. The imam has the princess freed. But she has sided with the ceddo during her captivity. At the end of the film she shoots and kills the imam. But the audience senses this triumph is only temporary. Senegal is a Muslim country.

Through *Ceddo* Sembene shows how Islam is not an inherently African religion but rather a faith violently imposed on Africans that radically changed their lives by banning alcohol, and the representation of human images in art and by destroying older beliefs. In order to demonstrate the relationship between the two opposing forces in the film, Sembene establishes two spaces: the village with its clearly defined ceremonial space is associated with the Muslims, an open space outside the village is the location associated with the ceddo. The imam operates in his space with authority appropriated from the king, and he abandons ceremony when it suits his purposes—such as the killing of the kidnapper. The ceddo follow ancient tradition. The kidnapper communicates with the princess through a griot. The ruthless nature of the imam is revealed through his actions and his willingness to do anything to make certain Islam triumphs. Sembene uses the film to show the indigenous traditions that are lost with the Islamic conquest of Africa.

Many Africans did not accept easily the ideas presented in *Ceddo*. The film was banned in Senegal. While it is easy to blame the Europeans for cultural imperialism, Sembene takes an important if less popular position when he demonstrates how the Muslim influence is also a foreign imposition on native cultures. He also challenges tradition by presenting a film with a female heroine for a patriarchal culture. In many of his films, Sembene is concerned with restoring the roles of women in the history of the country. While the princess is not physically present during much of the film, the picture is organized around her. Hers is the final image of the film; she represents a hope for the future. The audience knows that Islam has triumphed over the ceddo, but her image suggests the possibility of continued resistance. The knowledge of her actions, which the film conveys, gives the viewer an understanding of the past that can be used to reevaluate the present.

Bibliography

Cham, Mbye. "Official History, Popular Memory: Reconfiguration of the African Past in the Films of Ousmane Sembene." Ed. *Ousmane Sembene: Dialogues with Critics and Writers*. Ed. Samba Gadjigo, Ralph Faulkingham, Thomas Cassirer, and Reinhard Sander. Amherst: U of Massachusetts P, 1993. 22-28.

Ghali, Noureddine. "An Interview with Sembene Ousmane." *Film & Politics in The Third World*. Ed. John D. H. Downing. New York: Praeger, 1986. 41-54.

Malkmus, Lizbeth, and Roy Armes. *Arab and African Film Making*. London: Zed Books, 1991.

Mpoyi-Buatu, Th. "Sembene Ousmane's *Ceddo* & Med Hondo's *West Indies*." *Film & Politics in The Third World*. Ed. John D. H. Downing. New York: Praeger, 1986. 55–67.

Ukadike, Nwachukwu Frank. *Black African Cinema*. Berkeley: U of California P, 1994.

Vieyra, Paulin Soumanou. "Five Major Films by Sembene Ousmane." *Film & Politics in The Third World*. Ed. John D. H. Downing. New York: Praeger, 1986. 31-39.

CHAHINE, YUSUF (Alexandria, Egypt, 1926). Yusuf Chahine is one of Egypt's most important and most prolific filmmakers to emerge in the early 1950s. While he graduated from Victoria College in Alexandria, he also studied in California at the Pasadena Playhouse. Some critics feel his contact with the Western world has led to his inclusion of thematic and formal complexity in his work (Malkmus and Armes 222). His career has gone through several different stages as he developed his own approach to filmmaking.

The fifties, a time of great change in Egyptian history, was also the period where Chahine found the themes that define his career: his concern for the workers and their problems. From 1950 to 1953 Chahine made five films that can be considered his apprenticeship (*Baba Amin/ Papa Amin*, 1950; *Ibn al-Nil/ Son of the Nile*, 1951; *Al-muharrij al-kabir/ The Big Buffoon*, 1952; *Sayyidat al-qitar/ The Woman on the Train*, 1952; *Nisa bil rijal/ Women Without Men*, 1953). With these films he developed his interest in nature, the lives of the poor, and social criticism. *Sira' fil-wadi/ Struggle in the Valley* (1954) is the first film to demonstrate his mature style. Its story of a young man (played by Omar Sharif), who brings modern agricultural methods to his village causing violent reactions from a traditional landowner, can also be seen as an allegory of life in Egypt during the time of the 1952 revolution against Farouk.

The next period in his career leads to his first major film. While Chahine does not like *Shaytan al-sahra/ The Demon of the Desert* (1954), the film that followed, *Sira' fil-mina/ Struggle in the Port* (1956) is his first to deal directly with the problems of workers in the city. After his next two films the musical melodramas, *Inta habibi/ You are My Love* (1957) and *Wadda' tu hubbak/ Goodbye to Your Love* (1957), Chahine made *Bab al-hadid/ Cairo: Central Station* (1958), which is considered one of the great films in Egyptian cinema. In this film the train station is the location that unites the many stories of the lives of the poor in modern Egypt. The central narrative concerns the love of two very different men for a soft drink vendor who is always in trouble with the authorities for not having a license. One of the men is a cripple (played by Chahine) who tries to attract the young woman with stories of the beauty of a peaceful country life. She is already engaged to a strong, wealthy porter who represents the attraction of city life. He is often occupied by his union duties. Chahine avoids the easy emotions of traditional melodrama by making the cripple a complex character whose interest in young women has an unhealthy edge to it demonstrated by his mutilation of their photos. The cripple goes crazy at the end of the film and is carried away in a straightjacket. Stylistically Chahine combines the influences of Italian neorealism with surrealistic elements associated with the work of Luis Bunuel to present the exterior and interior world of his central characters.

While the film was well received abroad, Chahine was not well known or accepted at home. He followed *Cairo* with a film about the Algerian revolution, *Jamila al-jazairiyya/ Jamila* (1958). The film focuses on the transformation of a young teenager, Jamila, into a tortured victim of the struggle. He seems to have had a run of bad luck with his next few films, *Hubb lil-abad/ Yours Forever* (1959), *Bayna aydik/ In Your Hands* (1960), *Nida al-'ushshaq/ Call of the Lovers* (1961), and *Rajul fi hayati/ A Man in My Life* (1961). Finally in 1963 he took over the direction of *Al-nasir Salah al-Din/ Saladin* from a sick colleague. Much of the production had been set before Chahine encountered the project. But the constant parallels between Arab victories during the Crusades and the French and English aggression toward Egypt after the nationalization of the Suez Canal can be attributed to his political views. He also added a level of theater to the confrontation by placing the opposing forces on the same stage, which breaks up the film's linear presentation of its events.

Chahine was still not satisfied with the filmmaking situation in Egypt. He was pleased with his direction of his next film, *Fajr yawm jadid/ Dawn of a New Day* (1964), which mixes melodrama and symbolism in its story of a woman's unhappy marriage as it analyzes the relationship between modern Egypt and its prerevolutionary past. He moved to Beirut, Lebanon, to avoid the irritations of working in Egypt and made *Bayya' al-khawatim/ The Seller of Rings* (1965), a film in the style of an American musical comedy with the Lebanese singer, Feyrouz. After *Rimal min dhahab/ Golden Sands* (1966), another film shot abroad, he returned to Cairo and made *Al-nas wal-Nil/ People and the Nile* (1968). He faced censorship with his critique of Egypt, which came after the country's defeat in a conflict with Israel. He reworked the film and framed the story with the Soviet/Egyptian partnership in the building of the Assouan dam.

When Chahine returned to themes and styles that had been central to his work he made another great film, *Al-ard/ The Earth* (1969). Chahine revisits the people of the countryside in a story set in 1933 with contemporary overtones. Once again, his characters are both people and symbols of the various social classes. With this film he wanted to give a voice to the people of Egypt and their concerns. In *Al-ikhtiyar/ The Choice* (1970) he uses the intelligentsia of Egypt to explore the same societal splits he examined in *Cairo* between individual liberty and social conduct. He continues to examine these themes in subsequent films at the same time that he continues to explore stylistic innovations. Sound is important in both *Al-'usfur/ The Sparrow* (1973) and *Iskandariya leeh?/ Alexandria Why?* (1978). In the latter he also connects the theater of war with a production of Hamlet. Singing and dancing also have an important place in *'Awdat al-ibn al-dall/ Return of the Prodigal Son* (1976), where he makes his usual connections between the lives of individuals and their symbolic representation as aspects of the state. He continues to examine various versions of a single story in *Hadutha masriyya/ An Egyptian Story* (1982) where a film director reviews his life during an operation. In his most recent films, *Al-wida' a Bonaparte/ Farewell Bonaparte* (1985), *Al-yawm al-sadis/ The Sixth Day* (1987), and *Iskandariya, kaman wa kaman/ Alexandria, Again and Again* (1990), Chahine works in Cairo with those themes and concerns about people, their lives, and their relationship to the state, which have been his life work as in the recent film *Cairo As Told by Yusuf Chahine* (1991).

Filmography

Baba Amin/ Papa Amin (1950)

Ibn al-Nil/ Son of the Nile (1951)

Al-muharrij al-kabir/ The Big Buffoon (1952)

Sayyidat al-qitar/ The Woman on the Train (1952)

Nisa bil rijal/ Women Without Men (1953)

Sira' fil-wadi/ Struggle in the Valley (1954)

Shaytan al-sahra/ The Demon of the Desert (1954)

Sira' fil-mina/ Struggle in the Port (1956)

Inta habibi/ You are My Love (1957)

Wadda' tu hubbak/ Goodbye to Your Love (1957)

Bab al-hadid/ Cairo: Central Station (1958)

Jamila al-jazairiyya/ Jamila (1958)

Hubb lil-abad/ Yours Forever (1959)

Bayna aydik/ In Your Hands (1960)

Nida al-'ushshaq/ Call of the Lovers (1961)

Rajul fi hayati/ A Man in My Life (1961)

Al-nasir Salah al-Din/ Saladin (1963)

Fajr yawm jadid/ Dawn of a New Day (1964)

Bayya' al-khawatim/ The Seller of Rings (1965)

Rimal min dhahab/ Golden Sands (1966)

Al-nas wal-Nil/ People and the Nile (1968)

Al-ard/ The Earth (1969)

Al-ikhtiyar/ The Choice (1970)

Al-'usfur/ The Sparrow (1973)

'Awdat al-ibn al-dall/ Return of the Prodigal Son (1976)

Iskandariya leeh?/ Alexandria Why? (1978)

Hadutha masriyya/ An Egyptian Story (1982)

Al-wida' a Bonaparte/ Farewell Bonaparte (1985)

Al-yawm al-sadis/ The Sixth Day (1987)

Iskandariya, kaman wa kaman/ Alexandria, Again and Again (1990)

Cairo As Told by Yusuf Chahine (1991)

Bibliography

Hennebelle, Guy. *Les cinémas africains en 1972.* Paris: Société Africaine d'Edition, 1972.

Malkmus, Lizabeth, and Roy Armes. *Arab and African Film Making.* London: Zed Books, Ltd., 1991.

Sadoul, Georges. *Dictionary of Films.* Trans., ed., and update Peter Morris. Berkeley: U of California P, 1972.

CISSE, SOULEYMANE OUMAR (Bamako, Mali 1940). Souleymane Oumar Cissé comes from a large Muslim family of the Sarakholé ethnic group. He developed a love of cinema as a child. His film-going interfered with his studies, and he was expelled. When his family moved to Senegal, he went to school there. They returned to Mali after its independence in 1960. He won a scholarship to study projection in Russia and also studied photography. He remained in Moscow for eight years, eventually studying filmmaking with Mark Donski at VGIK. When he returned to Mali, he worked on many nonfiction films on such varied subjects as the relationship between modern and traditional medicine and an annual festival of fishermen in the Sanké region. Cissé's early documentary experience influences his later style. Even when he is working with myth, he maintains a realistic approach to the narrative. He also works as a socially committed filmmaker who is concerned with both the current situation and the connections between past and present.

Cissé's early work demonstrates the connection between reality and fiction in his worldview. *Cinq jours d'une vie/ Five Days in a Life* (1972) is Cissé's first longer documentary and his first film in Bambara. Its story provides a connection between his fiction and nonfiction. The film details the life of a young man who leaves school, becomes a thief, and is sentenced to prison for three years. After he is released, his uncle convinces him to return to the simple life of the village. His first fiction film, *Den muso/ La jeune fille/ The Young Girl* (1974) deals directly with social conflict. Sékou, who is fired from his job for asking for a raise, goes out with a mute young woman named Ténin. She becomes pregnant and is totally rejected by her parents who hold on to traditional beliefs about marriage. Sékou, too, abandons her. When she goes to see him, he is with another woman. With no place to turn she commits suicide by setting fire to her house. This film turns to a topic that concerns many African filmmakers, the situation of young women who must confront tradition while living in a modern world. The mute Ténin represents all of those African women who have been denied a voice.

Baara/ Le travail/ Work (1978) Cissé's next film continues to examine the problems of daily life, especially for those who wish to improve life by advocating change. As Lizbeth Malkmus and Roy Armes point out, the film's complex organization can best be understood as a series of events that take place in an "interaction of contrasting spaces" (194). The film deals with two men with the same name, Balla. The first man is a worker who meets the second, an engineer, in a factory. After the first man's arrest for not having the correct papers, the second Balla gets him a job in the factory. The action moves from the out-of-doors to the factory and the work and living space of the owner, and the focus shifts to the engineer, and his relationship with the factory workers and his boss. The engineer is involved with organizing the workers in the factory into a trade union and is strongly opposed by the boss. At the end of the film, the boss murders his wife and has the engineer killed. But the workers react to the engineer's death by revolting. The factory owner is finally arrested. In this film, Cissé demonstrates the kind of action possible when various social groups unite for the good of all. He is countering the tendency for professionals to isolate themselves from the workers. He shows how many of the problems in modern Africa come from Africans themselves. *Baara* won the Grand Prize at FESPACO 1978.

Finye/ Le vent/ The Wind (1982) continues Cissé's examination of internal African problems. This film examines the sources of student unrest and the relationship between postcolonial and traditional authority under a military regime. It opens with a statement about the wind awakening man's thoughts. Batrou, the daughter of the governor, Sangaré, falls in love with Bah. The students become involved with a protest against the repressive government. Batrou must confront her father, who is both a parental as well as military authority figure. Sangaré faces resistance on many fronts in addition to the conflict with his daughter. His third wife confronts his abuse of authority as does Kansaye, Bah's grandfather and the traditional leader who has been overthrown by the governor. While Cissé presents these stories, he is really concerned with the larger implications of the narrative, the way the characters represent the larger concerns of society. This film also won the FESPACO Grand Prize in 1983.

Cissé's next film, *Yeelen/ Brightness** (1987) is one of the most celebrated of recent African films. This narrative is set in an undefined mythic past. Cissé reclaims a culture that is in danger of being forgotten by a postcolonial world often more concerned with learning about Western ideas than valuing its own customs. Cissé employs a cinematic style influenced by the oral tradition as he reproduces secret rituals of the *Komo*, a repressive society of the Bambara, in his story of the conflict between father and son. Soma rejects his son, Nianankoro, and attempts to kill him because he fears his son will surpass him. Nianankoro engages in his own quest for knowledge as he escapes from his father. Finally the two confront each other with powers so strong they are both destroyed. But Nianankoro is survived by a wife and a son who will carry the positive elements of the tradition into the future. Cissé experiments with narrative and thematic elements in this film as he attempts to find an authentic means of expression that will present an African film in a style that also reflects its origins.

While *Yeelen* is the only film to actually return to the past, Cissé's work is repeatedly concerned with the relationship between past and present. He does not accept blindly either tradition or the modern world as the answer to Africa's problems. The past can be repressive as in *Yeelen*, but it can also be a reminder of values that should not be lost as in *Finye*. His most recent film *Waati/ Time* (1996) traces the story of a women in apartheid South Africa as her life develops from poverty to an advanced degree and inclusion in the decision-making groups of her society. Through his films Cissé demonstrates the complexity of life in Africa and problems that must be faced if there is to be any true progress.

Filmography

> *L'homme et les idoles/ Man and Idols* (1965)
>
> *Sources d'inspiriation/ Sources of Inspiration* (1966)
>
> *L'aspirant/ The Candidate* (1968)
>
> *Degal a Dialloube/ Degal at Dialloube* (1970)
>
> *Fête du Sanké/ The Sanké Celebration* (1971)
>
> *Cinq jours d'une vie/ Five Days in a Life* (1972)
>
> *Dixieme anniversaire de l'OAU/ Tenth Anniversary of the OAU* (1973)
>
> *Den muso/ La jeune fille/ The Young Girl* (1974)
>
> *Baara/ Le travail/ Work* (1978), Grand Prize FESPACO
>
> *Finye/ Le vent/ The Wind* (1982), Grand Prize FESPACO 1983
>
> *Yeelen/ Brightness* (1987)
>
> *Waati/ Time* (1996)

Bibliography

Bachy, Victor. *Le cinéma au Mali*. Brussels: OCIC, 1983.

"Cissé, Souleymane." *Dictionnaire du cinéma africain*. Vol. 1. Paris: Editions Karthala, 1991. 191–94.

Dauphin, Gary. "Continental Divides." *Village Voice*. 16 April 1996: 82.

Diawara, Manthia. *African Cinema: Politics & Culture*. Bloomington: Indiana UP, 1992.

Malkmus, Lizbeth, and Roy Armes. *Arab and African Film Making*. London: Zed Books, 1991.

Shiri, Kenneth, comp. and ed. *Directory of African Films*. Westport, Conn.: Greenwood P, 1992.

Ukadike, Nwachukwu Frank. *Black African Cinema*. Berkeley: U of California P, 1994.

E

Emitai/ Dieu du tonnerre/ God of Thunder (1971: Ousmane Sembene,*
Senegal). With this film Ousmane Sembene turns to a historical event to
explore the conflict between colonialism and tradition in an African village. The filmmaker uses a real incident to begin the process of reclaiming
African history in African films. The film is set in Effok, a village in the
Casamance region in southern Senegal near the border with Guinea Bissau, whose inhabitants speak Diola. Sembene used actual villagers for
much of the cast: The main portion of the film is in their language. Only
the French soldiers and the Africans conscripted into the army speak
French or pidgin French. This use of an indigenous language is one of the
breaks Sembene makes with European filmmaking. He also continues to
develop a narrative structure different from the Hollywood model that
depends on cause/effect relationships, the importance of individual action,
the development of complex narrative structures that combine several
plots, and extensive use of suspense.

Emitai's structure is based on the oral tradition, which is central to African narrative. African films often move at a pace different from that of
their Western counterparts. The slow movement of the story is a reflection
of the progress of life in a village, a world connected to the passage of
events in the natural order rather than one dominated by clocks and
schedules. The adoption of narrative techniques consistent with the lifestyles of the people it depicts gives *Emitai* an authenticity absent from
those Western films that claim to present accurate pictures of African life.

The subject of the film also distances *Emitai* from the Western tradition.
While the story of a rebellion may be universal, Sembene's film not only
deals with an incident in the struggle against colonialism, but also exam-

ines the role of traditional values in such a conflict. He does this in the context of a narrative that also restores women's history to a place of importance. The film presents the story of the conscription of men and the demand for the rice harvest by the French in the context of the responses by both the men and the women of the village.

Emitai opens with individual episodes as the French conscript the young men into units called *tirailleurs,* African soldiers, forced to serve in the French army. In one incident, an old man is tied up to force his son out of hiding. The women in the family convince the son to give himself up. But these episodes are not developed as they might be in a Western film. The consequences of these actions for the people involved are not pursued. The early episodes serve to introduce the conflict between the opposing sides in the film.

The film then moves forward one year as the French return to claim the majority of the rice harvest (67 pounds per person) as the villagers' contribution to a war they don't understand. The film also shifts to an emphasis on the group, which is more important in the African tradition than in the Western world. Sembene wants to make a film that reflects the importance of the community. There are no individual heroes and no concern for the problems of the solitary person. The confrontation with the French occurs at the same time as the death of the chief of the village. The men cannot act because they have lost their leader and because they must follow tradition and bury their chief according to ritual before they can do anything else. The women become involved because the rice is under their care. They grow the rice and are responsible for it.

The women refuse to give up the rice, and the French surround them in the village square. While they are being held captive in the strong sun the French prevent the men from performing the burial ritual to place added pressure on them to give up the rice. Sembene does not stop at this confrontation between the villagers, the French, and the *tirailleurs* who assist their colonial masters. The men in the village call on the gods to help them resolve the conflict, but the gods do not respond. Sembene indicates some aspects of tradition must be reevaluated. Not all that is traditional is good for the community; some conventions should adapt as the world changes. The women act when a small boy is killed; they go on to attempt to perform the burial rituals. While the women act together the men are not united. One group gets the hidden rice to appease the French. The men hand the rice over but then decide to revolt by not carrying it for the French. But their decision comes too late, and the French shoot them down.

The revolt of these villagers may not have been successful, but mere existence of opposition to colonial rule is a significant episode in the development of a national consciousness. When Sembene reproduces these events, he reclaims a heroic incident from his nation's past. But *Emitai* does more than merely recall the past. This film examines the past in an African context by foregrounding such events as the extended attempt to gain a response from the gods, an episode that lacks the dramatic structure necessary for its inclusion in a Western film. Sembene's use of different languages is also a refusal to concede accessibility over honesty. While many prospective viewers would not understand Diola or be able to read the French subtitles that translate it (all transformed into English for distribution in the United States), Sembene uses the multiple languages to expose the French methods of colonialization. The French viewed the colonies as part of the French world, and the *tirailleurs* speak pidgin French rather than their own language.

Emitai continues Sembene's complex examination of various aspects of life in Senegal. In this film he deals with history, politics, and religion in his re-creation of a tragic episode from that nation's past. The film won a silver medal at the Moscow Film Festival in 1971.

Bibliography

Gadjigo, Samba, Ralph Faulkingham, Thomas Cassirer, and Reinhard Sander, eds. *Ousmane Sembene: Dialogues with Critics and Writers.* Amherst: U of Massachusetts P, 1993.

Ghali, Noureddine. "An Interview with Sembene Ousmane." *Film & Politics in The Third World.* Ed. John D. H. Downing. New York: Praeger, 1986. 41–54.

Malkmus, Lizbeth, and Roy Armes. *Arab and African Film Making.* London: Zed Books, 1991.

Ukadike, Nwachukwu Frank. *Black African Cinema.* Berkeley: U of California P, 1994.

Vieyra, Paulin Soumanou. "Five Major Films by Sembene Ousmane." *Film & Politics in The Third World.* Ed. John D. H. Downing. New York: Praeger, 1986. 31–39.

Everyone's Child (1996: Tsitsi Dangarembga, Zimbabwe). This film grew out of a desire to deal with an increasingly difficult problem in Africa, the number of orphans created by AIDS. People working in the field and with the Media for Development Trust joined to create a community training project that developed into a feature film. A Zimbabwean novelist, Shimmer Chinodya, was added to develop the script. Tsitsi Dangarembga was hired and became the first black Zimbabwean woman film director. While there is a long tradition of political filmmaking in Africa, *Everyone's Child* is an experiment in the attempt to affect social change through fiction. Most often documentary films such as *Femmes aux yeux ouverts/ Women with Open Eyes** (1994), which deals with some of the same topics, are used to address issues and promote community action. This film thoughtfully balances its fictional story of the two older children in a family who must face adult responsibilities with its larger social message. The characters are carefully developed and the situations, while representative of more general problems, take on individual tone through the skill of the actors.

The film opens by introducing the children. Tamari, the older daughter, begs her boyfriend Tabiso, an aspiring musician, to take her away from her family. He has no money and is determined to achieve a musical career. Her home life is bleak. Her brother, Itai, works to mend the plow, and she must take care of the two younger children and their dying mother. No one in the community helps them because of their fear of AIDS. The storekeeper seems to want to assist them, but he is only interested in seducing Tamari. When the mother collapses as they attempt to plow a field, no one comes to help them finish the job. The children manage to get their mother to the clinic. She is treated in the ox cart, and the children are told she will do better at home. These early scenes set the pattern for the film. The children struggle to maintain the life they have learned from their parents, but there is always an edge to this existence; something that sets them apart. They visit their father's grave. Their mother's cough gets worse. There is little money left. They owe at the store. When the mother dies, the rest of the family appears, but their father's brother, Uncle Ozias, does not even wait for the funeral to take away the two oxen as a payment for their father's debts. He makes a speech about how he is the last member of the clan, and he will become their father. He takes their plow as he leaves, and claims it is also debt payment.

The children struggle on alone. There is no money for school when Tamari begs the headmaster to at least let Nora, her younger sister, attend. Itai has hopes of finding a job in the city and goes off to Harare where he cannot escape involvement with a gang of young men who share his situation. Finally there is no money for food, and the storekeeper promises much to Tamari if she will agree to satisfy him. When she goes to the church for help the minister has her pray and takes her to a meeting where she is offended at being called an orphan. The film cuts between the two teenagers as they each face impossible situations. Tamari becomes the shopkeeper's mistress in order to survive. The other women in the village shun her and call her a prostitute. Itai is forced into a robbery, captured, and sent to a kind of reform school where he is further tormented by a boy who calls his mother names. Tabiso returns, but he only wants Tamari and does not have the money to take care of the younger children. As the children become more and more isolated from the adults who condemn and exploit them, but also refuse to help, the film moves toward its climax.

Itai, in trouble for fighting at school, finally confides in a social worker who tells him that he can go home if that is what he really wants. Tamari tries to take a stand against the storekeeper but he forces her to come with him one night. She must leave Nora in charge of Namu, the youngest boy who wants to fly and walks around all day with a helicopter toy. At the dance Tamari continues to resist the shopkeeper's drunken kisses. Tabiso is a surprise performer, and she is moved when he sings in public a song he had written for her. When the shopkeeper tries to drag her away she breaks a beer bottle and threatens him. As Tabiso comes to help her, she manages to stop the shopkeeper. But as Tabiso and Tamari return home they see the fire. The children's home is destroyed. The film suggests Nora was not able to control Namu's interest in a candle. The young boy loses his life in the fire, and his death finally mobilizes the community. Itai arrives the next morning as the relatives reappear for the funeral. The uncle makes another speech about responsibility. He once again acknowledges them as his children, but he says Namu's death makes him realize the boy was everyone's child and no one helped. The film ends with the community finally responding by rebuilding the house and bringing household items. The uncle even returns the oxen and the plow. That night as Tamari and Itai stand outside, the rains come promising a renewal of life.

While the story ends on a hopeful note in the lives of the children, the words on the screen that close the film explain the extent of the problem. By the turn of the century more than 10 million African children will be orphaned as a result of AIDS. *Everyone's Child* presents what may be considered a typical story of some of these children, a story that audiences will recognize. The filmmakers want their primary audiences, those directly involved in these problems, to identify with Tamari and Itai. They may even see themselves in the less than sympathetic roles of the villagers or the residents of Harare. The filmmakers want people to realize the extent of the problem by watching the tragedies that overtake this family and think of ways to deal with similar situations in their own lives. But the film is effective as a narrative outside of its didactic message. Tamari and Itai's stories come to life through the careful construction of the film and the attention to small details of plotting and characterization. When Tamari finally accepts a dress from the shopkeeper it is a symbol of her inability to resist anymore and not a sign of vanity as she is not a self-involved character. Itai's attempts to exist outside of the gang are touching examples of both his naiveté and his basic goodness. These children may be trapped in a situation that they cannot control, but it is their struggle to make the right decisions in these impossible situations that makes *Everyone's Child* so moving.

F

FAYE, SAFI (Dakar, Senegal, 1943). Safi Faye is considered to be the first female black African filmmaker. She comes from a traditional background as one of numerous children of a village chief from the Serer ethnic group who practiced polygamy. She became involved in film through encounters with Jean Rouch, the French ethnographic filmmaker, who worked for many years in Africa, and she even appeared in some of his films. The contact with Rouch influenced her to go to France and study ethnography at the Ecole Pratique des Hautes Etudes. She pursued her filmmaking interests by enrolling at the Ecole Nationale Louis Lumière. She began her work in cinema with short films and was gradually able to finance a feature film. While she began to make films as a exile, she returned to Senegal and has been able to apply the insights she gained to provide a new perspective on that country. She is generally concerned with themes that have involved many African directors, the conflict between the past and present, between tradition and change. As a female filmmaker, Faye provides her own perspective on these problems although she claims to view these situations from an ungendered position.

Her short film *La passante/ The Passerby* (1972–75) already demonstrates some of her concerns. Faye examines the sexism of European and African men in her narrative about the life of a young African woman in Paris. Faye plays the role of the young woman. By providing a variety of shots and altering the point of view, she shows the multiple meanings inherent in men looking at women. *Kaddu Beykat/ Lettre paysanne/ Letter To My Village/ Peasant Letter* (1975) is her first feature and marks her return to her origins in Senegal. This semidocumentary is framed as a letter with Faye providing the voice-over narration and a perspective on the visuals. She carefully documents the daily routines in her village as a means of preserving a passing lifestyle. At the same time she critiques government policies that have led to single-crop farming of peanuts and poverty for the villagers. Ngor wants to marry Coumba, but he does not have the bride price. He must go to the city where he is unsuccessful. When he returns, his experiences do add to the villagers understanding of the world when he shares them and with the others at the daily ritual meeting of the men. Faye provides a critique of current government practice, which is validated by both the fictional and documentary elements of her film. Her understanding of village life and familiarity with the people gives the film a powerful combination of observed life and the impact of such a life on the individual.

Her recent films demonstrate her continued growth as an artist. Faye's next film, *Fad'jal/ Grand-père raconte/ Come and Work* (1979), pursues her interest in village life. She deals with the importance of the oral tradition in this examination of the difficulty of agriculture in an arid land. The opening statement of the film contends the loss of an old man is comparable to the destruction of a library. The importance of oral history is demonstrated by an educational system that is still concerned with teaching French history. Faye has followed this feature length documentary with many shorter films. *Les âmes du soleil/ Souls Under the Sun* (1981) deals with the roles of women in the village and the variety of difficult tasks they must accomplish. With *Man Sa Yay/ Moi, ta mère/ I, Your Mother* (1981) she returns to France to chronicle the life of a first-year African student who is being pressured to return home. *Selbé et tant d'autres/ Selbé and So Many Others* (1982) follows the daily life of one woman in a village. Her husband has left for the city, and she must cope on her own. *Mossane* (1991) is a fictional account of the conflicts faced by a beautiful young woman who is promised to one man but loves another. Faye continues to pursue her concerns for village life and the changes traditional communities must face. Her films chronicle both the positive and negative elements of tradition, the need to record the past, and the need to consider carefully economic development so the past is not destroyed.

Filmography

La passante/ The Passerby (1972–75)

Ravanche/ Revenge (1973)

Kaddu Beykat/ Lettre paysanne/ Letter To My Village/ Peasant Letter (1975), International Critic's Prize Berlin 1976, Prix Georges Sadoul 1976, Special Jury Mention FESPACO 1976

Goob na nu/ The Harvest Is In (1979)

Fad'jal/ Grand-père raconte/ Come and Work (1979)

3 ans 5 mois/ 3 Years 5 Months (1979–83)

As Women See It? (1980)

Ambassades Nourricieres/ Food Missions (1980)

Les âmes du soleil/ Souls Under the Sun (1981)

Man Sa Yay/ Moi, ta mère/ I, Your Mother (1981)

Selbé et tant d'autres/ Selbé and So Many Others (1982)

Mossane (1991)

Bibliography

"Faye, Safi." *Dictionnaire du cinéma africain.* Vol. 1. Paris: Editions Karthala, 1991. 287–90.

Malkmus, Lizbeth, and Roy Armes. *Arab and African Film Making.* London: Zed Books, 1991.

Reid, Mark A. "Dialogic Modes of Representing Africa(s): Womanist Film." *Cinemas of the Black Diaspora: Diversity, Dependence, and Oppositionality.* Ed. Michael Martin. Detroit: Wayne State UP, 1995. 56-69.

Shiri, Kenneth, comp. and ed. *Directory of African Films.* Westport, Conn.: Greenwood P, 1992.

Ukadike, Nwachukwu Frank. *Black African Cinema.* Berkeley: U of California P, 1994.

Femmes aux yeux ouverts/ Women with Open Eyes (1994: Anne-Laure Folly, Togo). This documentary film explores the implications of a poem by a Burkinabe woman that defines the role of a respectable woman. She "should learn from her husband/ She shouldn't read,/ She shouldn't have her eyes open." In this film many women have opened their eyes to their problems in modern Africa. *Women* presents a frank evaluation by those involved of seven important issues: excision, forced marriage, AIDS, the revolutionary struggle, survival, the economy, and politics. None of these are problems that are easy to discuss or that have convenient resolutions. The director, Anne-Laure Folly, acknowledges both the complexity of the issues and the difficulty of dealing with them at the same time she demonstrates how critical it is to examine them. While it might seem there is no order to the presentation of these problems, in fact, the film is carefully organized to connect the issues and move from the most controversial to the one that will effect lasting change in all of the rest. The film uses voice-over narration to give some basic facts about the status of African women who have no choice, own nothing, are given in marriage but must do everything acting as wife, educator, farmer, and the life of the community. While women may be the majority of the population in a country like Burkina Faso, they do not control their own bodies, and they are not free to speak about their concerns.

Female excision, or female genital mutilation, is one of the hardest problems facing the African woman because it divides them into those who want to eradicate it and those who still support it. The film gives a voice to all women. The filmmaker does not replicate the structure of the patriarchal society by only allowing a voice to the side she obviously supports. Women tell of their own experiences, and activists explain why the best approach is as a health issue thus avoiding direct confrontation with tradition. The emphasis on health seems to convince women who might otherwise continue to support the action. But even more frightening than the stories women tell of their own encounters with the process are the words of a woman who performs it. She demonstrates her technique and asks the person behind the camera if it is clear. Otherwise, she says, she can bring in a young girl and show exactly how it is done. In a rare moment of interaction the response of the filmmaker is heard on the track quickly stating she understands perfectly. When this supporter of the ritual explains how she uses fireplace ash on the wound and alcohol if it's available, the film shifts to another woman's story about a girl in her group who died as a result of the process. This section ends with an emphasis both on the health issue and on the larger issue of women's control of their bodies. But the women are realistic about their ability to alter attitudes. In the present situation, they recognize the need for men to be involved for changes to occur.

The topic of control of one's body is directly related to the next problem, that of forced marriage. The film presents two types of forced marriage, the promising of very young women to older men and widows who have to marry their husbands' brothers. The viewer meets young women who have run away to a convent to avoid marriage to an older man creating family conflicts because those who have arranged the marriage have already become connected. The girl cannot go home. A widow's forced marriage is part of the larger problem of women and ownership. Once the husband is dead the widow has no right to anything from his estate. She is considered a minor, and only a man can control the family assets. Even if a woman follows tradition and marries her brother-in-law there is no guarantee this man will take care of her and her children. He may simply take control of the inherited property, or the dead man's parents may also take his property. In these cases the woman is left to struggle with her children, a situation that results in an increasing number of children living on the street.

A woman's lack of control of her own life, especially in male/female relationships leads to the next large issue: AIDS. One woman explains how men are not interested in their wives' pleasure, only in having children. Husbands see no problem in finding additional partners outside of the marriage. She recounts a woman saying she is certain she will die of AIDS; she is just waiting for the symptoms to appear. In a wonderful scene, the camera shows an activist demonstrating the use of a condom in a market. Men must also be drawn into this issue since they must take the precautions. The film explains how, in addition to the usual AIDS concerns about catching the disease, transmitting it to children, or having to care for sick relatives, the African woman also risks contamination through forced marriage. If the widow of an AIDS victim is forced to remarry, the disease will be transmitted to the other wives in the new family. This section of the film concludes with a repetition of everything a woman is forced into without being asked.

The film then moves to an examination of the ways in which change can be effected. First the film focuses on the events of the revolution in Mali in 1991. The narration gives the background and explains how women united to attempt to halt the slaughter of their children. A woman tells her story of first taking victims to the hospital, then being drawn into the peace march. The government attacked these marchers. The woman discovers her own twenty-one-year-old daughter wounded. She is unable to get her treated in time, and the young student dies eight days later. She would have graduated from the university in eighteen months. This segment ends with pleas for increased education for women and more involvement of women in politics. A female provincial governor cites statistics about the importance of concentrating on women's problems.

The next sections deal with aspects of economics moving from women who work hard but have little control over their situations to those who have become successful and who control major aspects of the markets and trade in their cities. Just as the health and human rights issues end with a woman in a leadership position, the film moves from the powerless workers in the fishing and tanning industries and those farming to the small entrepreneur and finally the major success. One voice tells of men converting to Islam so they could marry more women and have more workers in the rice fields. But the successful women actually provide work for the unemployed men in their families. The business associations these women form are comparable to the grass-roots political organizations they create. In Benin women feel they are reclaiming their rights because their heritage goes back to the Amazon warriors.

While *Women with Open Eyes* traces the appalling problems West African women face in their daily lives, Folly is careful to present possible solutions. The film acknowledges the difficulty of altering fundamental social structures. Many of the images foreground women who have little control over any aspect of their lives. The director controls the images and narratives so the film builds toward examples of change and the political and economic structures necessary to further advance this change. The women who speak are able to articulate methods to promote progress. The film does not hide from present reality, but it shows what can happen and what must happen once women open their eyes.

Finzan/ A Dance for the Heroes (1990: Cheick Oumar Sissoko, Mali). This recent film is an important and controversial presentation of some of the problems facing modern African society. *Finzan* focuses on the lives of African women and the restraints that control their lives and prevent their full liberation. Cheick Sissoko uses a combination of realism based on careful observation of village life and stock characters from the *Koteba* theatrical tradition to examine such topics as the inheritance of wives and female genital mutilation. While Sissoko condemns practices that deny women basic human rights, he finds positive as well as negative elements in the traditional culture. In *Finzan* he explores a culture and the complexity involved in change.

The film opens with the sounds and sights of childbirth, conception, and nursing in the animal world intercut with a statement about the status of women from U.N. documentation. They "receive a double blow both inside and outside of the family because of their sex and social conditions. As fifty percent of the population they do two-thirds of the housework and receive ten percent of the income and own less than one percent of the property." The film then turns to images of morning in the village, which emphasize the role of the women. Just as the film introduces birth at the beginning there is also a suggestion of death as the women discuss the condition of their husbands and the reactions of Nanyuma, the youngest. She starts her day by caring for her two young sons. She was forced into the marriage at fifteen and has no love for her dying husband. Once he dies Nanyuma's mother criticizes her lack of sorrow at his death. The widow reminds her mother of her eight years of hell with this man. Her mother represents an older generation when she tells her daughter women give birth to the world but they must be resigned to the mistreatment they receive. Her words are echoed in a discussion between the village chief and one of the men of the village. The man adds the statement that women have no rule over the world. The chief takes the position that women should be kept from the secrets that control society even though the other man suggests there may have been a time in the distant past when women ruled. With these statements Sissoko sets up the traditional positions he wants to expose and erase with his film.

The narratives the film presents deal with several types of rebellion and the effects of the rejection of tradition on the society. Nanyuma attempts to escape a customary marriage with her brother-in-law Bala that is approved by the chief. Bala is infatuated with her, and he insists on invoking the old custom of the brother of the deceased husband marrying the widow. At the same time that she runs away from him, the men of the village must deal with demands for their grain from the district commissioner who wants them to sell it to a buyer for far below its real value. While the men can see the importance of rebellion against the official, they refuse to understand Nanyuma's comparable protest against unreasonable authority. All ages agree with the refusal to sell the grain, but only younger people support the widow. When she runs to the city another brother-in-law ties her up and returns her over the protests of his son. This man also sends his daughter Fila back to the village so she won't pick up the more modern ways of the town. But even this man is not monolithic in his approval of all tradition. He opposes his daughter's clitoredectomy because his wife hemorrhaged and died during child birth. Sissoko's position on all of these issues is clear throughout the film, but he uses the various attitudes of the characters to demonstrate the complexity of the issues and to show a person can support change in one instance but remain rigid in another.

Once Nanyuma is returned to the village all of the events accelerate. Even though she is forced to submit to a civil ceremony Nanyuma refuses Bala conjugal rights and defends herself with a knife. Her children lead the others in attacks on Bala. In one instance they use a powder in his drinking jug to create diarrhea. As one child explains, they use the same powder his grandfather used to deal with the white tax collector years ago. The oppression of women is linked to colonialism.

When Bala forces Nanyuma to put her fingerprints on the marriage certificate, the district commissioner gives him a summons to take to the village chief. The official holds the chief hostage for the grain. At the same time, members of the village discover Fila has not be excised. The entire village and the surrounding area support the refusal of the men to trade their grain for their chief, and he is finally set free. But only the women come to the chief to discuss the cases of Nanyuma and Fila. The chief listens reluctantly. The women threatened to withhold conjugal rights from all of the men unless Nanyuma is freed, but even they are divided on the subject of Fila's clitoredectomy. The younger women have sided with Fila, but the chief rejects their plea. At the end of the film the older women capture Fila and perform the operation. Her father arrives in time to rush her to the hospital because they can't stop her bleeding. Nanyuma does leave the village with her children. But the film ends with her stating the same words about the role of women that opened it.

The director uses various techniques to make his points about the position of women and the importance of their emancipation. As Nanyuma leaves the village Sissoko replaces the image of the tethered goats, the male chasing the female in an endless circle, with an image of several goats together in a stall, free to make their own choice of a mate. Bala is depicted theatrically as a traditional buffoon and is played by an actor trained in the *Koteba* theater. His exaggerated actions reflect poorly on the actions of all men whose possessiveness and domination are seen as just a matter of degree. The other men of the village are just more dignified versions of this buffoon.

While Sissoko may treat aspects of Nanyuma's problem comically, Fila's genital mutilation is clearly marked as a tragedy. This is the story of a single example of this operation, which is practiced in various parts of the

world. For some, a debate exists about people outside a tradition condemning a practice mandated by custom and religion. They claim those
against these operations are practicing a form of imperialism, the forcing
of Western views on non-Western societies. But Sissoko clearly places
himself with those who see this controversy as one where older ideas must
give way to more modern ones, and where such genital mutilation is part
of a larger culture of oppression of women. He also places the act in the
context of the health issues it creates, an area that cannot be debated.

In *Finzan*, Sissoko criticizes many aspects of African life. His focus on
the need for female emancipation in all areas of society challenges those
who support traditional institutions because they are indigenous to the
people. Sissoko takes the more radical position that freedom must be total
and that all oppression must be abandoned. He is not afraid to condemn
outmoded ideas no matter what their source. At the same time, he shows
just how difficult it is to change. *Finzan* is a "dance for the heroes," but
the steps in the dance are difficult and the cost to the dancers is great.

Bibliography

Diawara, Manthia. *African Cinema: Politics & Culture*. Bloomington: Indiana UP,
    1992.
Malkmus, Lizbeth, and Roy Armes. *Arab and African Film Making*. London: Zed
    Books, 1991.
Ukadike, Nwachukwu Frank. *Black African Cinema*. Berkeley: U of California P,
    1994.

G

GERIMA, HAILE (Gondar, Ethiopia, 1946). Haïlé Gerima is a filmmaker who lives and works in the United States. While only two of his films use African settings, he still maintains close ties with the continent and its filmmakers. He grew up in Ethiopia with a father who wrote plays and worked as a teacher. Gerima has expressed the cultural ambiguity of young people growing up in Africa when he tells of cheering for Tarzan rather than the Africans (Malkmus and Armes 18). He began his education studying drama both in Addis Ababa and in Chicago at the Goodman School of Drama. When he decided to turn to cinema he attended UCLA (the University of California at Los Angeles), and he graduated from this school in 1975. While in Los Angeles he was a member of a black film-making collective. He currently teaches film production at Howard University in Washington, D.C. Gerima's films deal with the oppression of marginalized people, and he believes that the treatment of themes that lie outside of the dominant cinema, as exemplified by Hollywood, should develop techniques that match their themes. Some of his films incorporate documentary footage or dream or fantasy sequences. They all challenge traditional narrative techniques.

Mirt sost shi amet/ Harvest 3000 Years (1975) was made while Gerima was still a student at UCLA. He filmed it with a crew and equipment from the school at a point of transition in the history of his country from Emperor Haile Selassie's government to a military administration, which was led by a succession of officers. Gerima chose to shoot the film in Amharic, his native language and the dominant language in the country as one of the ways in which the film becomes a uniquely African production. He combines a variety of documentary and fiction techniques to examine the endless oppression and hopelessness of those who work the land. As in his later film, *Ashes and Embers* (1981), a deeply disturbed veteran becomes the moving force, the person who kills the landlord who stole his land. Gerima joins other African filmmakers in exposing the excesses of postcolonialism where the colonialists have been replaced by black middle-class oppressors. *Harvest* has become an influential model of how a film can reproduce the rhythms of the oral tradition as a means of creating an epic presentation of recurring problems that trouble all of the continent.

Gerima's next two feature films, *Bush Mama* (1976) and *Ashes and Embers* (1981), use fiction to depict aspects of the African American experience. The first film tells the story of a woman's struggle to survive in the Los Angeles ghetto with a daughter while her man is in jail for a crime he didn't commit. The central character has to deal with the conflicting influences of the defeatist philosophy of her friend and the revolutionary attitude of her daughter. Gerima presents this film from the perspective of a woman, which was rare at this point in time. The second film deals with a Vietnam veteran who cannot adjust to life back in the United States. Gerima connects this man to his past by opening the film with images from *Harvest*. The film is told in flashback as the young man and his friend are arrested by the police in Los Angeles. When the hero visits his grandmother, she attempts to unite him with his past by telling him stories, an example of the need to keep the oral tradition alive. In both of these films, African Americans are marginalized and become comparable to the poorer Africans in *Harvest*. Gerima finds the same range of classes and attitudes in the African American community as he did in Africa.

In the recent *Sankofa* (1993), Gerima traces the slave experience from Ghana to Jamaica and Louisiana in the United States. The film deals with memory as the attempt to restore what has been lost in the tradition of many African films that work at the act of recuperating the past. Gerima uses an allegorical form that transforms a modern model, who is shown in front of a slave fort, into a house slave who has been raped by her owner. Gerima directly employs the oral tradition as the slaves tell stories of their past from Africa through the Middle Passage and the transition to life on a plantation. The title comes from an Akan figure, a bird that looks backward, a means of going back to retrieve the past. Just as he moves from continent to continent uniting different spaces in *Sankofa*, Gerima also uses many of the techniques he has developed in his earlier films to present a story that unites his concerns about Africans and African Americans.

Filmography

Hour Glass (1971)

Child of Resistance (1972)

Mirt sost shi amet/ Harvest 3000 Years (1975)

Bush Mama (1976)

Wilmington 10—USA 10,000 (1981)

Ashes and Embers (1981)

After Winter: Sterling Brown (1985)

Nunu (1991)

Sankofa (1993)

Bibliography

Brown, Georgia. "*Sankofa.*" *Village Voice* 12 April 1994: 56.
Diawara, Manthia. *African Cinema: Politics & Culture*. Bloomington: Indiana UP, 1992.
Malkmus, Lizbeth, and Roy Armes. *Arab and African Film Making*. London: Zed Books, 1991.
Shiri, Kenneth, com. and ed. *Directory of African Films*. Westport, Conn.: Greenwood P, 1992.
Ukadike, Nwachukwu Frank. *Black African Cinema*. Berkeley: U of California P, 1994.

Gito L'Ingrat/ Gito the Ungrateful (1993: Leonce Ngabo, Burundi). The director Leonce Ngabo presents a humorous view of the effects of colonialism in *Gito L'Ingrat*. Rather than attacking the French for their ongoing influence over modern Africans, Ngabo exposes the fallacy of attempting to emulate the old colonial regime. Gito, the central character, thinks his French degree in international law will be all he needs to ensure his future when he returns home. While many films explore the conflicts that arise when Africans attempt to continue the educational traditions established under colonial rule, in this film Gito is alone in believing in the importance of his French education and his love of modern consumer goods. His French girlfriend, his parents, and his other friends in Burundi have no illusions about the value of Gito's experiences in Paris. While the film does not deny Burundi's past, Ngabo indicates people like Gito must take responsibility for their own problems. In order for Gito to be successful he has to retrieve his African identity unlike the other characters in the film who have already located themselves in their worlds.

The film opens with establishing shots of Paris, Sacre Coeur, and a view of the city from this landmark. Gito's voice-over narrative informs the viewer he is abandoning his work making clothes because his law degree should assure him at least a minister's position when he returns home. The visuals show him selling his sewing machine and the clothes he has made.

He uses the money to buy gold chains and electronic equipment. His girl-friend Christine thinks he is stupid to sell his sewing machine and buy a television. They have agreed he will go ahead and get settled and she will follow in a month. He has made a red dress for her, which he takes with him to have finished. He must leave the television with her at the airport because he packed so many things and has exceeded his baggage allowance. She says she will bring it when she comes. He is only worried he will look stupid with a VCR and no television.

He concern about appearance is emphasized when he arrives in Burundi. The plane lands to the sound of drums on the sound track, but Gito sprays himself with cologne as one way of keeping a European identity. He is alone as he steps off the plane, confident of his important future. His total self-involvement is demonstrated in his treatment of those who come to greet him after an absence of four years. He rejects his friend André's offer of a place to stay and ignores his parents. He is only concerned about his image, which must be maintained by staying in a hotel where he can receive important people in the appropriate style. He even uses an ointment that he hopes will lighten his skin. His alienation from his own culture is demonstrated as he visits the market with André and covers his nose when they pass the butcher. Others treat him like an outsider. Children beg from him, merchants see him as a foreign customer, and he even has his wallet stolen.

Ngabo constantly demonstrates the fragility of Gito's facade. He gets in to a ministry and thinks his application is being taken seriously. But after he leaves the room, the viewer sees another stack of applications placed on top of it. He falls helping André push his car and hates being laughed at by bystanders. He gives Christine's dress to his old girlfriend Flora because he is unable to correct her when she thinks it is a gift. Even when his world begins to disintegrate he refuses to abandon his pretenses. He cannot accept his Uncle Adrian's information about the lack of government jobs. He avoids dealing with Christine's calls. He is finally thrown out of the hotel when he can no longer pay for his room, but he retains his belief in the importance of his diploma. He rejects his past by refusing to visit his parents in their village.

His problems accelerate when Christine suddenly appears in Burundi with his television. In addition to his financial problems, he must now juggle the two women in his life so that they are not aware of each other. He constantly makes excuses to keep them apart. Also, Christine wants to meet his parents. As they visit the village, he remains the outsider who refuses to participate in life in the countryside. Gito sprays for mosquitoes and cannot stand the lack of modern comforts. Christine, the European, quickly adapts and is more comfortable with his parents than Gito. His father is concerned about the survival of the family line and the fate of the lands he has so carefully accumulated. Gito is the one who makes some excuse for them to leave and return to the city. No matter how hard he tries, the two women finally find out about each other. They decide to play a trick on Gito. They get him to the hotel. He undresses and then is forced out of the room. He only has the red dress to put on and has to walk down the street with everyone laughing at him wearing a dress and high heels.

This crisis finally makes Gito face his situation. He sets fire to his diploma and breaks down and cries. He waves good-bye as Flora sees Christine off at the airport. There is nothing left for him after he is thrown out of a bar and bandaged so he can't even talk. He is suddenly inspired when he sees a friend who wants to sing professionally who is badly dressed. In a voice-over commentary that mirrors the opening of the film, he says one can live well without being a minister. He will live by sewing. But he does not totally abandon his dreams. He will open a boutique. In a reversal of the opening, he sells the electronics he bought in France, paints the store, and purchases sewing machines and African fabrics. In the final shots he photographs his new creations, modern versions of traditional dress.

In Gito Ngabo shows the viewer one way of reconciling the old and the new. Gito's alienation from his culture is a facade that must be removed. But his need for this false appearance is not a result of his relationship with Christine. It is not his experience in France that forces him to value Western consumer goods. Christine is not impressed when he buys the television to take to Burundi. He buys things because he thinks they will support his status. His choices are made only on the basis of the impression he thinks they will make. But the audience shares the views of his friends who like him in spite of the false attitude he presents. While the film does not make sweeping statements about the lingering effects of colonialism, it does suggest that those pretentious people who return home with false values will only find happiness when they recognize the importance of their own culture.

This film won the Emile Cantillon Youth Award, Namur International Festival of French Film; Hani Jawharia Award, Carthage Film Festival; City of Amiens Award/Gold Unicorn Award of the Official Jury, Amiens International Film Festival; Oumarou Ganda Award for Best First Film/ Best Actor, FESPACO.

Le Grand Blanc de Lambaréné/ The Great White Man of Lambaréné (1995: Bassek ba Kobhio, Cameroon/France). Albert Schweitzer's life in Lambaréné forms the basis for this film about the interaction of well-meaning colonialism and an African population. Not a biography, *The Great White Man* uses the daily events of Schweitzer's life in the years leading to his death to examine the disparity between the doctor's Western image as a Nobel Peace Prize winning humanist and the reality of his treatment of his patients and his staff. The director, Bassek ba Kobhio, does not use this film, shot in Gabon at the site of the hospital, as an exposé of the horrors of colonialism. He shows how Schweitzer's patriarchal attitudes not only affected those he dominated, but, as is the case with such oppression, damaged his life as well. Rather than the torture, beatings, or shootings often associated with colonialism in recent African films, *The Great White Man* shows the result of pride, self-involvement, and a belief in the innate superiority of Western culture on both the colonizer and the colonized.

The film opens with close-ups of hands pulling teeth, shots that will be repeated later. The African patient screams. The film shows a shot of the shoes of the one pulling the teeth. Someone comes to get the doctor. The next shots are of the river that becomes one of the focal points of the film, the major highway connecting the hospital to the rest of the world. The beautiful shots of boats on this river contrast with the brutality of the opening and establish one of the basic oppositions of the film. As Bissa, the concubine given to him by a chief who he rejects, tells Schweitzer when he claims to have loved the land, "You should have loved the men and women." The beautiful shots of the river are part of his love of the land. The pulling of teeth without concern for the pain he causes show his desire to cure without real concern for the feelings of the patient.

The film also begins a point of crisis for the hospital. The opening is set in 1944, toward the end of World War II. Few medical supplies remain. Schweitzer attempts to do the best he can with the help of his staff, especially the native male nurse, Lombi. An encounter with Koumba, Lombi's son, sets the tone for the doctor's attitude toward those Africans who work with him. When Koumba tells him he wants to be a doctor Schweitzer laughs and tells him he should be a nurse like his father; Africa doesn't need doctors. But, as the film demonstrates, patriarchal colonial attitudes extend beyond the Africans. The Great White Man, as he is called throughout, does not treat his own wife much better. When he fails to appear to eat the cake she baked to celebrate their wedding anniversary, her secondary status is made clear.

Schweitzer's encounter with a great chief provides the key to understanding his unease in the face of local customs and establishes essential relationships for the rest of the film. The doctor, desperate for any kind of medicine, wants to learn the secret of an indigenous drug that he has tried in the hospital. The film details his meeting with the medicine man and the chief whose permission he needs. He is uneasy at these meetings, especially when the chief gives him the gift of Bissa, which he cannot accept. Schweitzer can barely force himself to drink the local wine. When he does dance with Bissa after becoming drunk he has her waltz to the African music.

The film moves forward from event to event. The dates between episodes are not stated, and the viewer is expected to follow narrative clues to understand the passage of time. But the next major event is easy to follow, the end of the war. Supplies arrive at the same time as the few remaining African soldiers to have fought with the Allies. Mikendi, one of these veterans, must tell the waiting parents their sons are all dead. His experiences during the war have turned him against all whites. He becomes the focus for a revolutionary spirit that gradually overtakes the region. Koumba listens as Mikendi tells stories of his encounters with colonialism during the war. Later, in a key scene, Lombi angers Schweitzer who knocks him down as Koumba watches. Lombi has told the chief that he is dying because he should die like a chief. Schweitzer thinks it's better to hide this knowledge from the patient. Mikendi tells Koumba he must leave immediately, study to become a doctor, and come back and direct the hospital. Mikendi looks toward the future; he states that the days of the chiefs are over. It is time for education and politics.

Schweitzer's resistance to other kinds of change is demonstrated in the sequence dealing with an assistant, Mr. Altmeyer, who is never allowed to be called doctor, a title reserved for the Great White Man. Altmeyer's awkward attempts to make friends with the Africans are dismissed by Lombi whose has a different view of the whites after being hit. Finally Altmeyer can no longer take Schweitzer's treatment of the Africans as children. He protests the doctor's refusal to enforce good hygiene in the hospital and in the worker's huts at the same time the white staff's quarters reek of disinfectant and soap. He also cannot understand why Schweitzer has withheld electricity from the hospital and the workers, as his supporters, have sent many generators. The only time they have electricity is after a Christmas celebration where the Great White Man rewards the carolers and the others with food gifts and a display of electric light.

The next white visitor, a journalist, is even more critical. She obliges Schweitzer by waiting for him to set up carefully staged photographic opportunities. But, at dinner where the chef grandly details the menu, she asks questions that anger the rest of the European staff, and the Great White Man refuses to answer. The staff defends him by stating the imminent Nobel Prize has caused many to be jealous of the good doctor. When she raises accusations about his throwing out medicines because "primitives," as he calls Africans, have different bodies or that he uses his patients as guinea pigs, he responds by telling her she must leave.

The film moves on toward its close at the same time the criticism of Schweitzer accelerates. Independence in 1960 highlights the changes he cannot accept. Koumba has returned after studying law and medicine. He is elected a deputy because he believes working for change in the new Africa is more important than practicing medicine. He corrects Schweitzer when he still calls him little Koumba. The doctor sees the hospital and the gifts he has received to run it as his possessions, and he is unable to understand his staff's request to participate in its management. When he tells them everything is his, Koumba points out Schweitzer is nothing without the Africans. He tells the doctor that emancipation was never his goal. "You shared our hell to gain your heaven."

The tragic cost of Schweitzer's refusal to enter into the African culture is expressed in the scenes between him and Bissa just before he dies. She explains his missed opportunity. "You came closer than any white man before you. The path to the nation's heart lay open to you, but you chose to walk its edge." The night he dies is the only night she lies next to him in bed. Only on his death does he really experience Africa. He has asked Koumba to arrange his funeral, and Schweitzer is given the rites of a great chief. The film ends with a quotation from his own writing which reverberates ironically backward over the narrative: "All we can do is allow others to discover us as we discover them."

Ba Kobhio's view of the effects of colonialism is complex. While elements of Schweitzer's attitudes are shared by many of the Europeans who came to Africa, this film does not examine the great excesses of these encounters. Instead, *The Great White Man* examines the way oppression damages the oppressor as well those who are oppressed. The film does not negate Schweitzer's contribution to the physical health of the people he treated. It mourns the lost opportunity for a much greater and deeper exchange between two cultures.

Guelwaar (1992: Ousmane Sembene*, Senegal). With *Guelwaar* Ousmane Sembene returns to a view of African life he explored in *Xala** (1974), a presentation of the combination of comedy and tragedy that is central to the social life of the community. In this film, he places his criticism of life in Senegal in the context of a funeral and the complications that occur when the dead man's body is misplaced. While Sembene's narrative technique is similar to that of earlier films, he re-creates the life of the deceased through a series of flashbacks and the voice-over memories of his widow. The film also presents a rich vision of funeral customs that incorporate both African and Christian traditions.

The film opens with the younger son, Aloys, announcing his father's death to his mother. Guelwaar, the noble one, Pierre Henri Thioune, has died from injuries, but the cause of his death is gradually revealed during the film. The other son, Barthélémy, is at his hotel. The mother recalls her wedding, introduced by the sound of church bells, which place the memories in their Christian context. While the priest is told that Thioune wanted a Latin Mass, they discover the body has disappeared. The older brother, who has returned from France, goes to the police. He encounters African bureaucracy and treats officials with contempt. He blames every difficulty on being in Africa and implies that nothing like this situation would occur in France. He accompanies the policeman on a search for the body at the same time people arrive at his parent's home for the ceremony. Through his interaction with the police the cause of his father's death is revealed; Thioune died from a beating. Guelwaar's death is also connected to concerns about foreign food aid, which he opposed. At the same time he introduces the central situation of the film and most of the important characters, Sembene also establishes the theme of his social criticism, the reliance on foreign aid. The policeman figures out Guelwaar's body has been claimed by a Muslim family and has been buried in the village cemetery. The family refuses to allow the body to be exhumed.

Once the central conflict has been established, Sembene develops an important secondary theme, the role of women in modern Senegal. A young woman who is the friend of Guelwaar's daughter and who has accompanied her to the funeral from Dakar attracts attention because of her revealing dress. When the priest talks to her, she thinks he is attacking her lifestyle. She defends herself by explaining why she must work as a prostitute to support her family including a brother in medical school. Guelwaar's daughter has been supporting his political activities and other members of the family the same way. The priest is not concerned about her profession; he just wants her to understand her clothing is not appropriate for the occasion. In the Muslim village the young widow of their deceased body decides she will no longer put up with the sexual abuse of her husband's relatives and returns home leaving her children behind. Another theme that Sembene continues to explore is Barthélémy's alienation from his African roots. He waits impatiently by the truck while the policeman negotiates the village social structure to attempt to find a solution to the problem of the misplaced body. In a flashback presented by his friends Guelwaar is remembered for the time he dressed like an old woman to gain access to a married woman in the village. The young women's prostitution can be connected to the reliance on foreign aid, which creates a society that would rather receive from others than work. But the other sexual infidelities present a critique of African traditions that do not contribute to the welfare of the community.

The loss of traditions can also cause conflict. When the Christians arrive at the village to reclaim the body, they are attacked, and the priest is hit on the head. The imam apologizes by saying things didn't use to be this way. This conflict is the result of the loss of traditional ways. The men who have taken over from the French don't even speak native languages. Guelwaar was killed because he spoke out at a rally against the acceptance of foreign aid, which has destroyed the dignity and independence of the people. One of the officials at the rally sent someone to silence Guelwaar. The two sides continue to confront each other at the cemetery. There are individual acts of kindness. One of the Muslims gives the priest a hat; the women of the village give the widow something to sit on. The major arrives and is more worried that his Mercedes be parked in the shade than in resolving the situation. He presents the position that the Muslims have native tradition behind them. Barthélémy point out neither religion has African roots or why would Muslims go on pilgrimages to Mecca and Christians to Jerusalem. Security forces arrive to prevent violence. But Sembene does not see this kind of confrontation as the solution to the problem.

The policeman negotiates a resolution. He will remove the body from the cemetery so Christians will not enter Muslim holy ground. He carefully deals with the problem of locating the body assisted by the major's bribe to the village of more food aid. Sembene does not romanticize the exhumation process. Once the body is unearthed, the difficulty in dealing with the odor is obvious. The Muslims refuse to leave the coffin with a cross on it in the cemetery. Finally the body is returned to the widow. The funeral party leaves with an understanding that even if they are on opposing sides they must learn to work together. As the funeral procession meets the aid truck coming toward the village the children attack it. Guelwaar's message will live on in the new generation.

Even though *Guelwaar* deals with a dead body and a funeral, it is more hopeful than many of Sembene's films. Guelwaar's voice may have been silenced, but his message survives. A conflict between opposing religions, which could have spread and become a holy war, is averted through accommodation and understanding. The feud between Barthélémy and the policeman is also resolved, and Guelwaar's son gains an understanding and appreciation of African tradition as he watches the officer operate with the Christians and the Muslims. Sembene makes his points about foreign aid through the traditional means of Guelwaar's speech. But the effects of this aid are forcefully presented through the lives of the prostitutes and the breakdown of the moral structure of society caused by a lack of self-reliance. As in the rest of his work, Sembene does not locate Africa's problems in a single source. Colonialism is responsible for a lack of independence and a tradition of official corruption. But African society is not entirely innocent. Guelwaar's infidelity is not caused by the French. While Christianity and Islam may have come from outside of the country, they can be positive forces. In order for lasting change to occur people must acknowledge the sources of the problems that trouble the social structure and work together to resolve them.

Guimba un tyran, une époque/ *Guimba a Tyrant in his Time* (1995: Cheick Oumar Sissoko, Mali). Cheick Oumar Sissoko's earlier film, *Finzan** (1990), uses contemporary situations to deal with problems stemming from African traditions. In *Guimba*, the director returns to a fictional past to create an allegory about the present. Sissoko is concerned about the role of power and its abuse in modern Africa. He calls *Guimba* a political film that is a fable about power. The director's own experience of the misuse of authority come from his involvement in the recent coup to overthrow the dictatorship in Mali in 1991. *Guimba* explores the relationship between the personal and the political. While tyranny affects the entire community, individuals must decide to take action either alone or as a part of the group in order for resistance to be effective. The film demonstrates how the tyrant's power arises from his ability to attack his enemies individually; he also maintains his position by isolating himself from the people. Guimba wears a mask in public and appears on horseback, a position of strength, mobility, and speed. If Guimba uses the physical symbols of power and the force of magic to maintain his position, Sissoko uses the pageantry and magic of the cinema to create his vision of the corruption that comes with such force. The pageantry of the film also establishes the allegorical relationship with Africa, a continent whose beauty and wealth has been overperverted by exploitation and empty pomp.

The film opens with a griot, or storyteller, walking along the shore introducing a tale that happened once upon at time in the city of Sitakili. The griot's delivery of his lines sets the tone for a narrative that uses two types of Malian truth-saying speech: the satiric street theater or *kotéba* and the public oratory or *baro*. The griot establishes the basic events that set the narrative in motion. Guimba is the wicked ruler. His neighbors gave birth to a baby girl, Kani, who they betrothed to Guimba's dwarf son, Janginé. The story opens with Kani a beautiful adult, and Guimba even more of a tyrant, a man who shot his own daughter when she left home to marry. The film moves from the griot to Guimba's appearance as he exits the palace forcing people out of his way. Back in the ceremonial throne room he both demonstrates and explains the secrets of power to his son. But it is evident the son is more concerned with satisfying his sexual needs and behaving cruelly to all than learning from his father.

Janginé is an example of the decreasing power of the tyrant. His refusal to marry Kani sets in motion the events that eventually lead to his destruction and that of his father. Once the other men learn she is not to marry the dwarf they all come riding into town on their horses eager to impress her. Guimba bans them by threatening castration. He then decides he wants to marry Kani, and Janginé is convinced he must have her mother, Meya. He tells his father to force the divorce of Meya and her husband so he can marry her. When Meya's husband refuses Guimba banishes him. He joins the rebels who wait outside of the town. Guimba gradually descends into madness as there are further events that defy his power. When he follows a man out of town on foot, he must resort to magic, creating darkness through an eclipse to escape.

Kani's father enlists the help of a great hunter, Siriman, who has his own magic. He first uses his personal magic to demonstrate how the gods have forsaken the king. The king's own guards realize he does not care for them. Kani's father recalls how Guimba came to the throne by killing everyone else. Since that time Guimba has hidden his face, and Janginé has not grown. Siriman then uses the king's own lust against him. An enchanted woman leads the king to his humiliation and eventual suicide. Before he dies Guimba kills Janginé because he desires the same enchanted woman and leaves the palace to get her. Siriman does not allow the others to kill Guimba because he recognizes a kinship with the tyrant. But he does make the rope and noose for Guimba's suicide. The film cuts from a close-up of Guimba's face and the noose to the griot by the river. He completes the narrative by reciting what happens to the rest of the characters. Kani's father is elected chief of the city thus restoring a democratic government. She marries a knight. Siriman, who has not married before, goes off with the woman who lured Guimba out of the city. The last shot is of the two of them.

The narrative of the film closely follows the style of the oral tradition. Griots are key figures in both the central and framing stories. The use of the oral tradition is just one of the ways *Guimba* revives important aspects of Africa's past. The film was shot in Djenné, a legendary city whose homes, walls, and gates are examples of an architectural style that has also been lost in the modern, Westernized cities of the continent. The costumes also contribute to the visual splendor of the film. The beautiful colors and textiles revive an artistry in danger of being lost. The settings and costumes exist both as a testament to past glory and as a suggestion of the potential for future greatness.

The story uses the contrast between past and present in an even more complex manner. Guimba's rule correlates with the kinds of government many countries are currently forced to endure. Dictatorships in Africa are one of the tragic legacies of colonial regimes that refused to believe independence would come and refused to prepare for it. Colonialism never recognized the glory of Africa's past, and it, too, was a tyrannical rule like that of Guimba. Current dictators and colonial governments strip Africa of its wealth in similar manners. *Guimba*, which is dedicated to Africa, uses its sweep and grandeur to recall a past. The film takes on the role of the griots it features; it is a living record of what has been. In its message of the overthrow of tyranny and the restoration of order and democracy it is a story of what can be. *Guimba* won the Grand Prize at FESPACO 95.

H

HONDO, MED (Abid Mohamed Medoun Hondo, Atar, Mauritania, 1936). Born in Africa to a Mauritanian mother and a Senegalese father, Med Hondo has lived in exile in France since 1958. While he has never had any formal schooling in cinema he studied theater under a French actress, Françoise Rosay, and eventually formed his own theater company, *Shango*. He hoped to showcase African and West Indian performers in works by authors from such areas as Africa and South America and also present the work of African American writers. He acted in various media and turned to films as a means of getting a large audience for his message.

He began with two short documentary films in 1969: *Balade aux sources/ Ballad to the Sources* and *Partout ailleurs peut-être nulle part/ Everywhere, Nowhere, Maybe*. His real breakthrough came in 1970 with his first feature, *Soleil O/ O Sun*. This film combined theater, songs, documentary footage, fictional scenes, and interviews into an examination of the life of the marginalized exile in France. All the material is played against a historical background that deals with African history and the present situation of blacks from various countries. The credit sequence features an animated puppet ruler being deposed by the same colonists who put him in power. While the film rejects conventional organization and is termed a pamphlet by its director, it does concentrate on the life of an African immigrant accountant whose frustrations represent those of the many workers who come to France. Hondo examines the racism that crosses economic and social strata. But he does not just deal with prejudice in the white community. He also demonstrates how class and race operate among Africans. Hondo deals with these issues in a film that challenges traditional style. *Soleil O* is his first attempt to find a form that accurately reflects his subjects. He is among those African directors who believe their world must be portrayed by a cinema that divorces itself from the dominant Western tradition as exemplified by Hollywood. He moves from point to point in an episodic structure motivated by ideological content rather than the demands of the narrative.

For the next few years, Hondo made both fiction films and documentary. He uses the same techniques as *Soleil O* in his next film, *Les bicots nègres vos voisins/ Arabs and Niggers, Your Neighbours* (1974) where he continues to deal with the situation of immigrants and the causes of immigration. This film won the Gold Tanit at the Carthage Film Festival. *Sahel la faim pourquoi?/ The World's Hunger* (1975) which he co-directed with Théo Robichet turns to the problems of famine. The directors connect Third World hunger to politics and multinational companies whose exploitation makes peasants more and more dependent on the industrialized world. His next two documentaries, *Nous aurons toute la mort pour dormir/ We Have the Whole of Death for Sleeping* (1977) and *Polisario, un peuple en armes/ Polisario, a People in Arms* (1978), support liberation struggles by the Polisario against the Moroccans and the Mauritanians and examine how such a war affects the Saharawi people involved.

Hondo returns to his experiments with fiction in his next two films. *West Indies or the Nigger Maroons of Freedom/ Les nègres marrons de la liberté* (1979) is a musical drama based on *The Slaves*, a play by Daniel Boukman that Hondo staged in 1972. This film, which takes place in a slave ship, covers the period from the seventeenth to the twentieth centuries. "Maroons" in French means escaped slaves, and the film focuses on the role of slavery in the Antilles. The different levels of the ship correspond to social organization; the higher a person's social position the higher the deck. Slaves live in the hold, the middle class on a deck below the colonial class, which rules from the bridge. Hondo's historical approach demonstrates how little oppression has changed over the centuries. He uses a musical form but works to separate it from the Hollywood musical tradition and instead returns to the Caribbean music that accurately reflects the lives of the characters. He also uses language to characterize the different people on the ship from the French of the rulers and those who collaborate with them to the peasant Creole of The Ancestor who brings a tribal memory to the film.

From the large panorama of historical era presented in *West Indies*, Hondo turns to a specific incident in his next film although he uses this episode to comment on African history. *Sarraounia* (1986) is based on the novel by Abdoulaye Mamani from Niger. The film is grounded in a historical event, the confrontation of a French colonial army with Sarraounia, an African queen of the Aznas of the Niger. The film traces two stories: Sarraounia's development into a forceful ruler and the French army's conquest and destruction of the territories it traverses. She is an excellent queen and a powerful sorceress who knows how to fight the French, under the command of Captain Voulet, through skillful engagement and withdrawal. The final destruction of the army comes from the African soldiers, the *tirailleurs*, who mutiny and kill their colonial officers. Hondo draws from many historical sources in his restoration of lost history. He also joins such directors as Ousmane Sembene* in presenting women in important and powerful roles. *Sarraounia* was filmed in cinemascope, and Hondo uses a realistic style to give credence to the events he portrays. The film won the Grand Prize at FESPACO 1987.

Hondo remains a major force in modern African cinema. His feature films are highly respected and have generated a great deal of critical interest. His devotion to political positions and the presentation of them through a cinematic style that reflects an African point of view have served as models for other filmmakers.

Filmography

Balade aux sources/ Ballad to the Sources (1969)

Partout ailleurs peut-être nulle part/ Everywhere, Nowhere, Maybe (1969)

Soleil O/ O Sun (1970)

Les bicots nègres vos voisins/ Arabs and Niggers, Your Neighbours (1974), Gold Tanit Carthage Film Festival

Sahel la faim pourquoi?/ The World's Hunger (1975)

Nous aurons toute la mort pour dormir/ We Have the Whole of Death for Sleeping (1977)

Polisario, un peuple en armes/ Polisario, a People in Arms (1978)

West Indies or the Nigger Maroons of Freedom/ Les nègres marrons de la liberté (1979)

Sarraounia (1986) Grand Prize FESPACO

Bibliography

Diawara, Manthia. *African Cinema: Politics & Culture*. Bloomington: Indiana UP 1992.

Hennebelle, Guy. *Les cinémas africains en 1972*. Paris: Société Africaine d'Edition, 1972.

"Hondo, Med." *Dictionnaire du cinéma africain*. Vol. 1. Paris: Editions Karthala, 1991. 215–217.

Hondo, Med. "The Cinema of Exile." *Film & Politics in The Third World*. Ed. John D. H. Downing. New York: Praeger, 1986. 69–76.

Malkmus, Lizbeth, and Roy Armes. *Arab and African Film Making*. London: Zed Books, 1991.

Mpoyi-Buatu, Th. "Sembene Ousmane's *Ceddo* & Med Hondo's *West Indies*." *Film & Politics in The Third World*. Ed. John D. H. Downing. New York: Praeger, 1986. 55–67

Shiri, Kenneth, comp. and ed. *Directory of African Films*. Westport, Conn.: Greenwood P, 1992.

Ukadike, Nwachukwu Frank. *Black African Cinema*. Berkeley: U of California P, 1994.

Hyènes/ Hyenas (1992: Djibril Diop Mambety,* Senegal). *Hyenas* is the long-awaited second feature film by Djibril Diop Mambety. *Touki Bouki** (1973), his first film, was a stylistically and thematically impressive debut. His second feature more than fulfills the promise of the first. Mambety transposes Frederich Dürrenmatt's play, *The Visit*, to an African setting and creates a complex narrative about postcolonial life on the continent. He uses the story of the wealthy woman who returns to her village to buy revenge as a comment on the consumerism and lack of initiative of his countrymen who are willing to sacrifice a life for televisions and air conditioners. Mambety is fond of animal imagery, and in this film both the title and repeated shots of hyenas represent the scavenging inhabitants of the village of Colobane. The use of animals is also an example of the intricate connections among the themes the director presents. The hyenas have human equivalents, but in Africa scavengers cleanse the land of sources of contamination; they are part of the ecology of the land. Scavengers also exist because of death; they benefit from the weakness of others. If Mambety compares his characters to hyenas, he raises many questions about these people and the choices they have made about how to live.

The film opens and closes with shots of elephants wandering around a land with little vegetation, another complex animal image. In the film animals usually precede their human counterparts. At the beginning this shot is followed by a shot of a ragged group of inhabitants of Colobane who are going to the local bar to try to get free drinks. Close-ups of the elephants' feet are followed by shots of human feet walking on the same dry soil. The elephants never find their water, but these men, who may have helped to destroy the land, are the human hyenas who will later benefit from a death. By the end of this film the animals seem doomed. Their wandering follows shots of bulldozers destroying whatever habitat existed. The film traces the events that lead to the triumph of the hyenas and suggests the various interpretations the narrative proposes.

The deceptively simple story chronicles the return of Linguère Ramatou, a former inhabitant of Colobane. The townspeople try to create a positive past for this woman who was forced out of town. She has become one of the wealthiest women in the world, and they hope she will give money to revive the town. The current mayor promises Draman Drameh, her former boyfriend, his position when he retires, and the people agree because they feel Draman will be able to get the funds from Linguère. Draman is the owner of the almost bankrupt local bar/grocery store. At

first, all seems to go well. The town prepares flowery speeches and ceremonies to welcome the wealthy woman. However, Mambety inserts shots
of vultures into the preparations. And the town council meets in the rubble
of a building called the Hyena Hole. The teacher recalls how someone
who received a zero in math is now richer than the World Bank, an association that brings up ideas about the distribution of wealth in the world
and the problems faced by debtor nations into this microcosm of the large
problems faced by the entire continent. The men continue to remember
those traits that would be most likely to assure them of her sharing her
wealth and restoring the village to a vision of lost splendor.

When Linguère finally arrives she causes the train to halt at a place
where it no longer stops. She immediately suggests her past relationship
with Colobane might not be that suggested by the rest of the town. Linguère and Draman visit scenes from their past. He must help her because
she has lost a leg and replaced it with a gold one. They recall their old
names for each other; she was the wild cat and he the panther. She also
reveals a gold hand, a replacement for another limb lost in a plane crash,
which suggests a person gradually turning into metal and losing her human
side. The viewers learn that their love affair was not as idyllic as has been
suggested. She became pregnant, and he abandoned her to marry a rich
woman, an action he justifies for her own good. A vulture again appears
during their conversation. And his wife is told to sacrifice a black bull.
Shots of the bull are also intercut in this sequence.

Linguère reveals her plan at the town's reception. She will give the
people a trillion dollars if she can buy Colobane's court. She introduces
the former chief justice who presided over her paternity trial. She wants
to clear her name. Draman had been able to deny paternity by getting
two men to swear that they had also had sexual relations with her. The
two witnesses appear. She found them and had them castrated. They now
have been transformed into women. The child only lived a year, and, as
a result of Draman's actions and the court's lack of justice, she roamed
the world as a prostitute. Now she will give the town the money if someone
kills Draman. The mayor immediately protests the drought has not turned
them into savages. But Linguère knows she will just wait.

It does not take the people long to make up their minds. Customers
appear at the grocery buying expensive foreign items on credit. Everyone
is suddenly wearing yellow boots from Burkina Faso. When Draman goes
to the police to complain that people are going to kill him, the policeman
also has new boots. More consumer goods arrive as part of Linguère's
payment. Significantly, the most prominent items are those most difficult
to sustain in a struggling economy—appliances and cars that consume important resources. Each time Draman tries to get help, he finds someone
who has already been corrupted. Even in church he is counseled to take

the train out of town as a new chandelier is uncovered. Fireworks replace the stars in the sky as carnival rides appear to amuse the village. When more and more people claim their goods, Mambety connects a series of shots making complex relationships between the people, Linguère, and all of their actions. He cuts from shots of the fireworks to her face to an owl, hyenas, and finally people with torches who surround Draman as he makes a feeble attempt to leave town.

The next day he still tries to leave. An image of a hyena with a large scrap in its mouth foreshadows his ultimate disappearance where only a scrap of his clothing is left. The villagers learn Linguère has bought up the town's factories and closed them as part of her revenge. She states, "The world made me a whore. Now I'll make the world a brothel." The villagers attempt to avoid a decision by suggesting Draman commit suicide. They then make an appointment with him to arrive at the final determination of his fate. In an open area bounded on one side by a large cliff, he faces the men of the town who are all wearing imitations of judge's wigs and robes. The mayor declares their decision is based on justice. The money does not influence them. They are only interested in fairness. Draman rejects an offer to pray for him and suggests the man pray for Colobane. He is surrounded by his judges. When they pull back he has disappeared. Only his coat remains. The shots of Draman's end are intercut with images of Linguère by the sea. As he vanishes, she walks down stairs into the darkness below. The film closes with shots of a bulldozer preparing the ground and a long shot of a city of high-rises and the sound of an airplane. A ballad dedicated to Frederich (Dürrenmatt) plays over shots of the elephants. The song tells of a person who has traveled the world and seen everything and ends by telling people to get up and start working. If there is no work it is not possible to find freedom.

The words of the ballad form another element in the thematic complexity of the film. The people of Colobane may have been exploited. They may not actually be responsible for the loss of their factories, but they are not innocent. Like their compatriots they have accepted the goals set by colonialism, the attraction of a Western lifestyle. Rather than determining their own postcolonial direction they have remained dependent, accepting aid and credit. While Draman must bear the responsibility for his actions, his acceptance of the past allows him a certain dignity. The larger community must live with its actions. Linguère has revenge, but she has not found happiness. Mambety suggests there are many different hyenas in the film. The animals represent various human counterparts at the same time that they exist as a part of the African culture that has been attacked by both colonial and postcolonial periods. The hyenas, who also exist as tricksters in African folklore, reign in all of their various guises as long as the people accept them.

Bibliography

Porton, Richard. "*Hyenas*: Between Anti-Colonialism and the Critique of Modernity." *IRIS* 18 (Spring 1995): 95–103.
Rayfield, J. R. "*Hyenas*: The Message and the Messenger." *Research in African Literatures* 26 (Fall 1995): 78–82.

I

In a Time of Violence (1994: Brian Tilley, South Africa). This film is actually a three-part television series that is distributed as a single film. *In a Time of Violence* presents a controversial version of the period immediately preceding the end of apartheid in South Africa. The film's central characters are members of the ANC (African National Congress), and this focus greatly angered members of the Inkatha Freedom Party because of the negative depiction of their point of view. The original telecast of the series was halted briefly as a result of the controversy. The distributor's catalogue (California Newsreel) gives examples of the reaction to the series in South Africa. The film's political position is evident from the beginning, and each viewer can make an independent judgment about whether or not it is biased. Even though the film does take a stand on recent history it also demonstrates the complexity involved in each side's stance. The film's real importance lies in its examination of issues that have not been widely viewed in the media, especially in the world outside of its country of origin.

The Line is the title of the first part of the film. It opens with images of a train and a young man, whose voice-over poetic words about the winter wind that blows more harshly than ever before, set the mood. The train and other modes of transportation become important symbols as the film progresses both connecting and separating the various locations. This particular train ride establishes the major event that motivates the entire plot. The young man, Bongani, an ANC member, is the sole witness to a train massacre by Duma, a member of the Inkatha Party. Bongani, who lives in Soweto, fights with Duma and finally pushes him out of the train. He knows he must find a safe place to live after this incident and moves to his uncle's apartment in the Comiston Court complex in Johannesburg with his girlfriend, Mpho. He and Mpho live next to each other in Soweto. This place represents a complex mixture of tradition and change. The couple is involved with a group of revolutionary young people based in the township. They work for a future that is different from the present. The couple's fathers are angry because their children have gone off to live together without a traditional marriage. The mothers are willing to accept their children's lifestyle.

Bongani and Mpho's move to Comiston Court brings them into contact with his Uncle Zakes, who is happy to be out of the political morass he sees in the township. His wife shares his liberal views, but his mother, who also lives with them, does not approve of the young couple. Comiston Court also represents a changing image of South Africa. The large apartment complex houses a multiracial, multicultural group of people. Uncle Zakes lives on the edge of the law trading in electrical goods acquired through shady transactions and sold directly to customers around the city. The first part of the film concentrates on the two different locations, establishing the characters associated with each. While the parents deal with understanding and accepting their children's departure, the residents of Comiston Court learn that their building has a new owner who wants to make changes in their lives. The Afrikaner caretaker is the first to meet the new boss, an African who raises the rent and threatens his employees with the loss of their jobs. Back in Soweto, the couple's friends warn their parents there may be violence that night. Later, a van does drive through the neighborhood firing a machine gun. Bongani's friends respond with Molotov cocktails. The white van is later associated with Duma and his political party.

At the same time that the various characters are introduced, the film also presents their attitudes toward life. Bongani and Mpho disagree about how to respond to the increasing violence they encounter. Bongani is against their group getting guns, while Mpho wants them to be able to react. When Bongani reluctantly agrees, Mpho begins to explore sources of weapons. Their interest in guns is contrasted with that of Duma who is a regular weapons customer of Pedro from Mozambique, a former revolutionary in his own country, who has become disillusioned with political positions. When the tenants meet to deal with the rent increase, Bongani's leadership skills help them decide on an action. They will boycott the increase but not endanger their rights by withholding all of the rent. That night Bongani, who cannot sleep, discovers the business relationship between Duma and Pedro when Duma comes to the apartment to negotiate for guns.

The second part, *All on Edge,* opens with two contrasting meetings. Bongani speaks to his supporters about how to bring about change. Duma, on the other hand, incites his followers to violent action. They all have some kind of weapon that they raise to show their bravery. Mpho and Bongani continue to argue about guns. He is still concerned about answering violence with violence. He works within the system when he goes to talk further with a police officer about the train massacre. The honest policeman is contrasted with another officer who gives Duma guns in exchange for information. This middle section traces the increasing tension in the various plots. The landlord fires the cleaning help to retaliate for the boycott. On a lighter note, the caretaker forms a relationship with a prostitute who lives there. Another aspect of male/female relations is revealed when Bongani becomes jealous as Mpho negotiates with Pedro for guns. Visser, the policeman connected to Duma, tries to track down Bongani. He grabs him as he and Mpho return from the grocery store. She runs back to the apartment where the owner has cut off the electricity.

All of the various stories come together in the last section, *Fire with Fire*. A street child writes down the license number of the car that took Bongani. The family contacts the good policeman who puts pressure on Visser's boss to find him. Visser wants Bongani to give him addresses of his associates. Uncle Zakes gets Pedro to take him to Duma, but the meeting only results in an argument. Duma and Visser meet, and the police break into Pedro's apartment but don't find the guns. Visser threatens to give Bongani to Duma, which affirms the Inkatha connection with the police. The owner threatens to evict the tenants if they don't pay the rent increase, but they know their rights. There can be no eviction without a notice. Visser releases Bongani after taking a photo that he thinks will convince people that the young man took a bribe. But this tactic is so well known that Bongani later jokes about it as he tears up the money. When Uncle Zakes and Mpho take the young man back home so his mother can see he is free, he experiences violence in the township when a neighbor becomes a victim of a drive-by shooting.

They decide Duma must pay. Bongani agrees about the need for weapons, and Uncle Zakes takes them to an old friend who can supply them. When both sides are armed, it seems that a confrontation is inevitable. At a road block, Bongani and his side successfully hide the gun, but Duma is arrested on Visser's pretense that he will be safer inside. When the tenants go to the landlord's office they discover bank officials there. The landlord bought the building with improper financing, and he has left town. Visser arranges Duma's death in prison. Pedro, who has seen these kinds of events before in his own country, predicts things will only get worse. The film closes with Bongani on a train with Mpho. His voice-over narration is just as pessimistic as he tells his countrymen it is too late; time has run out. The train passes Duma's body, which is lying on the ground next to the tracks.

The train at the end brings the film full circle. In the opening Duma's body also lies by the side of the tracks, but he is alive, pushed out by

Bongani. A great deal has happened by the time the film ends. Bongani learns he may have accepted violence, but his release comes because his friends apply pressure to the police. Duma dies because he has gone too far for even a corrupt officer. The law works for the tenants who know their rights and don't give in to the new owner whose house of cards comes falling down. The film demonstrates the effectiveness of legal actions. Those who act outside of the law are those who are the most severely punished. The series does more than just present the ANC point of view. The film argues against violence and demonstrates the peaceful solutions that are still possible even in the heated atmosphere of modern South Africa. The film's multicultural, multiracial, multilingual narrative also gives hope to those who work for a country where all can live and work together like the inhabitants of Comiston Court.

J

Jit (1990: Michael Raeburn, Zimbabwe). This first major feature produced in Zimbabwe is a comedy that demonstrates a way for traditional beliefs to survive in a big city. The hero was named UK (United Kingdom) at school because his classmates thought he would go far. He has come to the city to make money to send back to his family. The film follows his adventures as he deals with both an ancestor and a future wife. UK lives with his Uncle Oliver who is played by the musician Oliver Mtukudzi. The film's music, which is featured throughout both in the sound track and in live performances, is called "jit-jive," the source of the title. *Jit* makes no attempt to deal with some of the larger issues that are often central to African cinema. But it does provide an entertaining story of the improbable achievements of an improbable hero. It examines the uses and abuses of tradition and ritual in the modern world. The film's style also combines the old and the new. Along with modern music and city life, it features a humorous version of a character who connects the past with the present. UK is watched over and directed by an ancestral spirit or Jukwe only he can see. This elderly woman, dressed in traditional clothing, appears at any time, has a piercing scream that can blow people down, and an unquenchable thirst for beer. UK must appease her and control her in order to gain what he wants, a task that has larger implications for the accommodation of the past and present.

At the beginning of the film, when UK drives through the city and picks up records from a company, the viewer understands this young man is going to be important in the film. But, when he almost knocks over a man and a strangely dressed older woman reacts, the viewer is puzzled. It is even odder when this woman appears under a table trying to get UK's attention. She is only visible to him and warns him that someone has stolen one of his records. She screams to help him catch the thief, but she breaks the record in the process. She humorously admits to the mistake and tells UK she doesn't like it because she doesn't have a beer. The audience later learns that this strange person is a Jukwe who wants UK to get a real job so he will start sending money back home. Both of these characters are introduced with a comic tone even though the problems they deal with have an underlying seriousness. The rest of the film balances the humor with real life problems just as many folk tales do. UK is very like a folk hero who does not seem to have a chance of succeeding but who manages to overcome the odds through work and wit.

UK lives with and helps his Uncle Oliver, a singer. When UK assists his uncle at a nightclub where he performs, the Jukwe appears in search of a beer. She is angry seeing people dance with no ceremony. The city resists her influence; no one except UK even sees her. But she also will not accommodate herself to the modern world. She only wants him to return to the country. She threatens UK. If he doesn't do what she wants she can cut his life like a string. She causes his uncle to find him a job as a waiter, but it is the first of a series of employment disasters he experiences. He falls in love with a young woman, Sofi, who he meets by chance. But she is already involved with a wealthy, shady character named Johnson. UK talks to her father who demands a bride price, a $2,000 radio and an additional $500 in cash. The Jukwe does not approve of Sofi and threatens UK by causing him to fall down in pain. He loses his job when Johnson leaves without paying the bill at the night club, and the ancestral spirit laughs at him. She intervenes more directly when he takes a delivery job to earn the bride price by knocking him off his bicycle.

He moves further into a downward spiral when Johnson tricks him into delivering a package that results in UK getting beaten. The Jukwe causes him to crash a car at his next job. He finally confronts her and bargains with her to reach a mutual agreement. He will make $375 to take home in addition to the bride price. From this point he is successful in all of the different jobs he takes on. He buys the radio console and delivers it to Sofi's father with the cash. But her father knows Sofi is not particularly interested in UK, and he strings UK along to get more from him. He decides he would also like a refrigerator. UK does return to a happy family with money and gifts. The honest reception and traditional dancing in the country contrast with the modern dances at the night club. While both dances are recognized as a constructive element in the culture, the people who live in the country are positive images compared to Sofi's father and Johnson. Not everyone who lives in the city is corrupt. Uncle Oliver is a positive character; the children who play soccer across from his house repay UK's kindness by helping him get money for the bride price.

By the end of the film even Sofi and her father become impressed with

UK. As in the traditional folk story, the comic character triumphs over evil. Johnson thinks he has tricked UK into delivering a stolen refrigerator to Sofi's father. The viewer is concerned because the police wait and it is possible UK has taken the bait. But UK sees through the scheme, and the police are present to arrest Johnson. UK also tricks the Jukwe into no longer thwarting his attempts to make money. He adds vodka to her beer; a drunken Jukwe happily watches him work. She even accepts Sofi and toasts them with champagne. The film ends like a fairy tale. UK has a job in marketing and his love, Sofi. The evil are punished and the good rewarded. *Jit* shows the viewer how opposing sides can learn to live together. A hard working hero can unite the old and the new, the city and the country, tradition and the modern world.

K

KABORÉ, JEAN-MARIE GASTON (Bobo Dioulasso, Burkina Faso, 1951). Gaston Kaboré is one of a group of filmmakers who emerged from the small country of Burkina Faso with feature films in the late seventies and early eighties. He is one of the rare filmmakers to go on to make more than one film. Kaboré comes from a large Catholic family and from his country's largest ethnic group, the Mossi, whose past he presents in his first feature-length film. He received his primary and secondary education in Burkina Faso. He then began studies in history at the Centre d'Etudes Supérieures d'Histoire d'Ouagadougou, which he finished in Paris with an MA. He developed and pursued an interest in film studies at the Ecole Supérieure d'Etudes Cinématographiques. When he returned to Africa, he became involved in film as a teacher and administrator. He became director of the Centre National du Cinéma and taught at the Institut Africain d'Education Cinématographique. His first films were documentaries. His features gained him an international reputation as a filmmaker, and he became the general secretary of FEPACI (Fédération panafricaine des cinéastes). In this capacity he promoted the organization's goals of working with other African filmmakers to improve the conditions for cinema on the continent.

His first film, for which he shares the credit, *Je reviens de Bokin/ I Come From Bokin* (1977), was made by students of INAFEC (Institut africain d'education cinématographique) collective under his direction. The story suggests topics that will be of concern to him in later films such as the relationship between the country and the city. A young tailor, who lives in the country, decides to go to the capital for more opportunities. After a series of adventures, he ends up in jail for a crime he didn't commit.

The documentaries he made next are concerned with practical problems related to the land or, as in the case of *Regard sur le VIème FESPACO/ A Look at the 6th FESPACO* (1979), connected with his work promoting African film.

None of these early works give a real indication of the quality of his first feature film, *Wend Kuuni/ God's Gift** (1982). This film has become an example of the kind of film that represents the best of African cinema. It is set in the past before colonialism, at the height of the strength of the Mossi Empire and filmed in Moré, the dominant language of Burkina Faso. Wend Kuuni is the name of a young boy who is found in the bush. He is adopted by a family that has a daughter but no son. The young boy is mute and cannot explain his past. He settles in with his adopted family and becomes good friends with his new sister. He experiences a traumatic event when he discovers a dead body and recovers his voice. He is able to explain how his father, a hunter, disappeared. His mother was expelled from her village when she refused to remarry and died in the bush. While on the surface the film seems to tell a simple story, it is really a complex narrative that interacts with the oral story-telling form and both presents and criticizes tradition. The film actually opens with shots of the mother, whose story frames the main narrative, adding complexity to the film's structure. The film also demonstrates the failure of tradition to give rights to women and the destruction of lives that occurs when women are re-pressed. In addition to the mother's death, Wend Kuuni's sister has her choices limited by her gender. She is confined to the home area while he works freely in the fields.

The use of space to present themes carries over into his next feature. In-between his first and second feature, Kaboré made a short film about the problems of African cinema, *Propos sur le cinéma/ Reflections on the Cinema* (1986). He has two important filmmakers—Med Hondo* and Sou-leymane Oumar Cissé*—discuss the difficulties of making films on this continent that include such topics as promotion, production, and finances. In his next feature film, *Zan Boko/ Homeland** (1988), Kaboré turns to modern Africa to deal with the problems of modernization in postcolonial society. In *Zan Boko* the lives of villagers are disrupted as is their con-nection to the land when the encroaching city swallows up their homeland. The disparity between the needs of the poor and the desires of the rich is underlined when wealthy neighbors want land for a swimming pool with-out thinking about its importance to the people who live on it. Kaboré explores the role of the media when the villager is invited to share his point of view on a television show. Corrupt officials shut down the show when they realize its topic. By focusing on the land and its meaning, Ka-boré takes a creative approach to the topic of the role of the bourgeoisie in modern Africa. While there are a few people with integrity, the majority of the members of the middle class and government officials are not really any different in their tactics from the colonialists they replaced.

While Kaboré's films explore the current situation in Africa—either by retrieving the past or examining the present—he is also concerned with the more specific question of the position of film on the continent. He recognizes the importance of Africans having their own images on the screen. His work with FEPACI is his means of attempting to ensure the existence of such representation as he states in an essay he wrote for a FEPACI collection ("L'image de soi, un besoin vital" 21–22). In the same collection he talks about how cinema is central to his view of reality. He feels his film work allows him to share his view of truth with others and share his view of the world with them ("Mon rapport au cinéma" 373–74). Kaboré contributes to African cinema—both in his role as a filmmaker and in his work promoting the work of others.

Filmography

    Je reviens de Bokin/ I Come From Bokin (1977)

    Stockez et conservez les grains/ Store and Conserve the Grain (1978)

    Regard sur le VIème FESPACO/ A Look at the 6th FESPACO (1979)

    Utilisation des énergies nouvelles en milieu rural/ The Use of New Energy in Rural Areas (1980)

    Wend Kuuni/ God's Gift (1982)

    Propos sur le cinéma/ Reflections on the Cinema (1986)

    Zan Boko/ Homeland (1988)

    Madame Hado (1991)

Bibliography

Diawara, Manthia. *African Cinema: Politics & Culture*. Bloomington: Indiana UP, 1992.

"Kaboré, Gaston." *Dictionnaire du cinéma africain*. Vol. 1, Paris: Editions Karthala, 1991. 48–51.

Kaboré, Gaston. "L'image de soi, un besoin vital." *Africa and the Centenary of Film*. Ed. Gaston Kaboré. Dakar: Présence Africaine, 1995. 21–23.

———. "Mon rapport au cinéma." *Africa and the Centenary of Film*. Ed. Gaston Kaboré. Dakar: Présence Africaine, 1995. 373–74.

Malkmus, Lizbeth, and Roy Armes. *Arab and African Film Making*. London: Zed Books, 1991.

Shiri, Kenneth, comp. and ed. *Directory of African Films*. Westport, Conn.: Greenwood P, 1992.

Ukadike, Nwachukwu Frank. *Black African Cinema*. Berkeley: U of California P, 1994.

Keïta: Le héritage du griot/ The Heritage of the Griot (1995: Dani Kouyaté, Burkina Faso). This film combines the present and the past to retell a major African epic, the thirteenth-century *Sundjata Epic*, and demonstrate its relevance to modern life by explaining the history behind a young boy's name. The director is the son of a griot, a storyteller, who uses film to continue his inherited task of keeping stories alive. The film deals with the reintroduction of the past into the life of a child who must learn the meaning of his name, but the child's story parallels that of the tale he hears. Both are narratives about origins and the difficult road to fulfilling one's destiny.

The present and the past are combined at the beginning of the film. Djéliba Kouyaté lies in his hammock as a voice-over recounts a creation story. The voice describes the emergence of a new world from chaos. One man emerges and tells the others that the world cannot continue in chaos and proclaims himself king. When the others respond with "konate" ("no one hates you") he takes that name and becomes the king of the Mandé. The beginning of the telling of the story coincides with Djéliba's call to his destiny as the mysterious figure of the hunter, who reappears at critical moments in both stories, wakens him. The griot's journey is the first of many in this film. As he later tells the boy, he traveled from Wagadu where the world began, where the boy's ancestors rose up to command men, to the city where such stories are no longer valued.

Mabo Keïta, the boy, is involved in the knowledge of the modern world at the beginning of the film. He studies evolution as he reads, in French, about his ancestors developing from gorillas. The griot arrives and hangs up his hammock at Mabo's house, setting up the confrontation between two different lifestyles: his connection with the natural world and tradition and Mabo's parents who speak French and embrace the modern. As Djéliba begins his telling of a portion of the epic, the film moves from the present into the past. The different reality of the past is announced by the appearance of the same hunter who summoned Djéliba to his task at the beginning of the film. The epic nature of the ancient story is emphasized through the appearance of magical events in everyday life. The hunter has the king consult the cowry shells to learn of the king's future. The interpretation of the cowries introduce a key element in the story: A young girl will arrive, and the king must marry her to produce the future ruler of the Mandé.

The telling of the story is continually interrupted by the mundane events in the life of Mabo and his family. Djéliba's first dinner with the family is both humorous and instructive. Mabo's mother serves spaghetti. Djéliba is unable to eat this foreign food with the strange implements she provides and finally washes his hands and eats with his fingers in the traditional mode. He also refuses to stay in the house, preferring to sleep outside in his hammock. While the adults accept him initially, Mabo's mother expresses reservations that increase as Mabo neglects his studies to listen to the story. Mabo's mother is contrasted with the women in the epic. They represent the magical powers of the natural world as both the mother and grandmother of the future king transform themselves into powerful animals. Mabo's mother aligns herself with the schoolteacher and modern knowledge. The exact nature of that knowledge is demonstrated by a lesson about Christopher Columbus and the discovery of America, a myth that is legitimized because it is part of the European tradition.

Keïta continues to alternate episodes from the ancient epic and the growing problems its telling creates in the modern world. As many African films demonstrate, the process of reclaiming the past is essential to the creation of an authentic African present and future, but it is not an easy task. Just as the characters in the epic perform heroic acts to achieve their goals, so those who want to learn these stories must defeat those who do not understand why these narratives are so important. Mabo must deal with his mother, his teacher, and finally the parents of his friends when he begins to tell them what he has learned. The distance between battles with a buffalo—who is also a woman (an ugly woman who becomes the mother of the future king)—and the future king (who is cursed and must crawl on the ground) are a strong contrast to the arguments between parents, teacher, and child. The ancient stories are necessary because they provide a counter to the pettiness of modern life.

Djéliba ends his telling of the portion of *The Sundjata Epic* at a moment of conflict. Sundjata has just overcome the curse and begun to walk, but he and his mother are expelled from the kingdom by another one of the dead king's wives who has made her son king. Since everything predicted in the story has come true, there is no doubt Sundjata will eventually triumph. But by ending in the middle of the story Djéliba demonstrates the enduring nature of the oral tradition. There is no real beginning or end to his story. He leaves because there is also conflict in the modern story as Mabo's parents argue about the griot and the boy's education. The griot knows he has accomplished his task, the initiation of Mabo. He leaves the boy with a final parable about the importance of the oral tradition. Djéliba tells Mabo the hunter wins over the lion because he tells the stories. Maybe if the lion told the story the lion would win. The final images reinforce the point made at the end. The future comes from the past. The mystical hunter appears to Mabo. Djéliba may be gone, but the hunter assures Mabo that he will find other griots to tell him the rest of the story of his name.

Kouyaté effectively combines the past and the present to demonstrate the importance of reclaiming authentic traditions. Mabo's sense of self-worth can only come from his African past, not from stories about Columbus. The director does not reject modern life; he uses film as a means of capturing and recording what might be lost from the past. But he does suggest modern priorities are skewed. The everyday facts are not enough. If young Africans are to accomplish great deeds, they need to be inspired by the past.

L

LAKHDAR-HAMINA, MOHAMED (M'sila, Algeria, 1934). Lakhdar-Hamina originally went to France to study agriculture. He eventually attended film school in Prague in the former Czechoslovakia. While he never graduated, he acquired practical experience in camera work at the Barrandov studios. He then worked as a cameraman in Tunis. In the early sixties he made several documentaries on issues surrounding Algerian independence. Lakhdar-Hamina returned to Algeria and joined others in forming the OAA (Office des actualites algeriennes /Algerian Newsreel Office), which he headed from 1963 until its dissolution in 1974.

In 1966 he turned from documentaries to feature films with *Rih al-Awras/ The Wind from the Aurès/ Le vent des Aurès,* the first of three films produced by the OAA. With this work Lakhdar-Hamina developed the style he employs in all his feature films. He uses a Western-style dramatic narrative to relate a revolutionary story of the tragic destruction of a family during the fight to free Algeria from French colonial rule. He skillfully blends the history of the family into the larger concerns of the entire country by incorporating images of many Algerians into his presentation of a mother's search for her imprisoned son. With this first film, he demonstrated his power as a director of feature films and assumed a leadership position in Algerian cinema. The film won the prize for the best first film at the Cannes Film Festival.

Lakhdar-Hamina continues to develop his skills in his next two films. He changes direction in *Hassan Terro* (1968), a comedy. This film is the first in a series about Hassan, a comic figure always played by the Algerian actor Rouiched, who also writes the films that are directed by many different people. The central character is an unassuming man who wants to stay out of politics but does get involved and eventually becomes a hero.

Lakhdar-Hamina's third film, *Décembre/ December* (1972), marks a return to serious subjects as he examines the conscience of a French officer who tortures Algerians during the war.

Lakhdar-Hamina joined the ONCIC (Office national du commerce et l'industrie cinématographique/ The National Office for Cinematic Commerce and Industry), the nationalized company that controlled all aspects of film production and distribution in Algeria. He headed this organization from 1981–84 when he formed his own company. The ONCIC financed his next three films.

Waqai' sinin al-jamr/ Chronicle of the Years of Embers/ Chronique des années de braise (1975) is his most famous film. As its title might suggest, this film covers many years in the history of Algeria. It follows the stories of two characters from 1939 to 1954. Lakhdar-Hamina plays a madman whose message is ignored. The other story traces the life of Ahmed, a poor peasant, who is driven off his land by a drought where water is controlled by the colonists. In the city he is left with only one son during a typhus epidemic. He is conscripted after the Americans liberate Algeria from the Vichy government and is forced to assist the French government in suppressing a revolt in 1945. He finally joins the underground, and even though he dies, his son survives to continue the fight. While *Chronicle* dramatically personalizes the Algerian struggle for independence, some criticize its lavish production and lack of extensive political analysis. It was the first African film to win the Palme d'Or (the top prize) at the Cannes Film Festival.

While Lakhdar-Hamina's remaining films do not recapture the sweep of *Chronicle* they continue to explore Algeria's problems with Western cinematic techniques. In *Riâh al-Raml/ Sand Storm/ Vent de sable* (1982), the natural world is the force that provides the external conflict for people who must also deal with their personal problems in this hostile environment. He returns to historical narrative in *Al-qura al-akhira/ The Last Image/ La dernière image* (1986). Just before World War II, life in an Algerian village is disrupted by a new schoolteacher who brings her big city ways with her. As their subjects suggest, Lakhdar-Hamina's recent films still deal with Algerian conflicts, but he seems to be moving toward a more international cinema with European casts. His career demonstrates one approach to African filmmaking; he employs the more popular Western tradition to communicate Algerian themes. Lakhdar-Hamina is an important Algerian filmmaker who enjoys using the sweep, color, and drama of the cinema to tell his stories.

Filmography

Promesse de juillet/ July's Promise (1963)

Lumière pour tous/ Light for All (1963)

Tu cherches la science/ You Are Looking for Science (1963)

Guerre aux taudis/ War on Slums (1964)

La campagne de l'arbre/ The Tree Campaign (1964)

Prends soin/ Take Care (1964)

Mais un jour en novembre/ But One Day in November (1964)

Le temps d'une image/ The Time of an Image (1964)

Rih al-Awras/ The Wind from the Aurès/ Le vent des Aurès (1966), Best first film Cannes Film Festival

Hassan Terro (1968)

Décembre/ December (1972)

Waqai' sinin al-jamr/ Chronicle of the Years of Embers/ Chronique des années de braise (1975), Palme d'Or Cannes Film Festival

Riâh al-Raml/ Sand Storm/ Vent de sable (1982)

Al-çoura al-akhira/ The Last Image/ La dernière image (1986)

Bibliography

Armes, Roy. *Dictionary of North African Film Makers*. Paris: Editions ATM, 1996.
Malkmus, Lizbeth, and Roy Armes. *Arab and African Film Making*. London: Zed Books, 1991.

Lumumba: La mort du prophète/ Lumumba: Death of a Prophet (1992: Raoul Peck, France/Germany/Switzerland). This extraordinary documentary is really a meditation on its stated subject: the death of the African leader Patrice Lumumba, the first prime minister of what was then called Congo-Kinshasa, now known as Zaïre. Raoul Peck weaves together personal and public past and present to not only recall events in danger of being forgotten but also to analyze these events and how memory can be influenced by the media. The director reaches back to the beginning of colonialism in Zaïre and traces the effect of the Belgian presence up to the time of the making of the film, thirty years after the death of Lumumba. To the public record he adds interviews representing various opinions and his own personal reflections and home movies. Peck's parents were part of the educated Haitian professional class brought to Zaïre by those who replaced Lumumba. As the film states, people thought French-speaking blacks would be good choices to fill the vacant management positions, jobs held by white doctors, lawyers, and engineers who returned to Europe.

The film opens in Belgium with shots of dark, empty streets. A crash is heard and a voice-over narrator recites a poem about Lumumba's death, which begins, "In Katanga it is said that a giant fell in the night." The poem continues over other shots of the city. The viewer, who still has memories of Lumumba, knows he was killed in Katanga province. The rest of the audience should have some idea of the identity of the giant. The next shot—a silent, grainy image of Lumumba—is followed by words that complete the title of the film declaring a prophet tells of the future but the prophet is dead and so is the future. Over European faces the narrator wonders if his memory and his message should be revived.

If the opening sets up the opposition of Lumumba and colonialism, the next series of images establishes the Haiti of 1960 and Zaïre at the point of independence. In addition to his parents' move to Africa, his mother worked in the government as the secretary to the mayor of Leopoldville. Peck also recounts how his mother told him the story of the colonialization of the Congo. A photograph she gave him begins his examination of the role of the press because it seems to show Lumumba at a press conference. The various journalists Peck interviews and the newsclips he uses demonstrate how the press distorted Lumumba's character, which undercut his effectiveness before he began to govern. Peck's mother has explained Belgian rule was very simple. They treated the Negroes well but kept them stupid. The people rebelled at that stupidity and became nationalists. Even though Lumumba was elected by the people, the Belgian government distrusted him because he was an activist who in his first speech during the independence ceremonies insulted the king by daring to refer to the treatment blacks had received in the Congo. Lumumba's daughter explains how her father really believed the statements he made about the kind of freedom necessary in the Congo, and both the church and the press attacked him.

Peck reconstructs Lumumba from fragments of film using an empty screen where images have been lost. This is one example of a cinematic technique that reflects the themes of the film. He uses pieces to put together what remains of Lumumba's stories, using bits of film and scraps of memories recorded thirty years later. He moves through a natural history museum as he reflects on the process of reconstructing history. He stops on a setting of Africa, sculptures of Africans, and even an image of Tintin, the cartoon reporter whose Belgian creator, Hergé, depicted in the Congo. These are not just images of colonialism, but mediated images, constructed images that have become part of the European cultural memory and must have affected attitudes during the transition from colonialism to independence. These images are later contrasted with a series of names the press developed for Lumumba ranging from equating him with the devil to calling him the Elvis Presley of Africa. The greatest damage comes from his continued labeling as a communist. These reflections on the nature of memory and the creation of a history are intercut with a reconstruction of Lumumba's brief time in office (June-September 1960) and the causes of his failure.

Peck connects the past with the present because Lumumba's death still reverberates in Zaïre. When the director attempts to get permission to film in the country, the concern of the Zaire secret service in his project convinces him not to get on the plane. The Western powers undercut

Lumumba and felt more comfortable with those who murdered him because dictators often seem safer than true patriots. Lumumba's downward spiral toward his death is mirrored in the Belgian treatment of the Congo. Peck contrasts the early Congolese brought to Europe for the 1897 exposition with his family's vacation there. Before the war Congolese could not return home because they might tell others what life in Europe was really like. Those brought over for the exposition died of cold and were only buried because a vicar defied his parishioners and gave them coffins. Peck says his family took sweaters with them. Peck's first attempts at filmmaking, with his father's camera at a bullfight in Spain, provide another view of the press. When he is asked how he felt filming the killing of the bull, Peck responds that he was more concerned with keeping everything in focus. By implication, one wonders what the photographer was thinking when the film shows the last images of Lumumba, newsreel footage of his capture that cost Peck $3,000 a minute to reproduce. As he states, "Memories of a murder are expensive." After he describes Lumumba's final humiliation and death, Peck repeats the poem that he used in the opening. Even his body is destroyed. Patrice's story is not a nice story, the narrator concludes.

While the film may end with Lumumba's death, it suggests the story it tells is not over. The reconstruction of history, the reviving of memory, is a process. The very act of making this film creates new memories and a new history for its viewers. For those who have some knowledge of this past, the film may alter their concept of the events. For those with no knowledge of this past, the film may reveal much about occurrences in the past. For everyone, the film should illuminate the connections between past and present. While Peck deals with a very specific period in the life of a country, his meditations on how one can understand the interaction of Europe and Africa has implications for the recent history of the continent.

M

MAMBETY, DJIBRIL DIOP (Dakar, Senegal, 1945). Some of the most technically stunning films of African cinema come from Djibril Diop Mambety. As is true of many Senegalese, he is Wolof and comes from a Muslim background. Mambety came to film through theater, which he studied. He also worked in Dakar at the Théâtre Daniel Sorano as an actor and director. He began his film career with two short comic films before directing his first feature. While he has made very few films, only two features, he has gained an international reputation for the way he unites form and content to expand the possibilities for cinematic communication in Africa. Rather than the linear narrative and slow pacing, which is associated with many African films and which is seen as a means of transforming a lifestyle associated with the continent and the oral tradition into a different medium, Mambety constantly experiments with the medium. From his earliest films, Mambety challenges established norms of cinematic communication as he develops a voice that will represent his unique point of view and provide one way of representing postcolonial Africa.

Mambety's first film *Contrast-City/ A City of Contrasts* (1968) is considered to be one of the first African comic films. Along with *La noire de . . . /Black Girl** (1966) and other early films, it utilizes a nonsynchronous sound and French voice-over technique because of budgetary concerns, but it was shot in color. Mambety presents a satiric examination of Dakar's image as a cosmopolitan city. In this film he expresses his concern for the lack of any planning in the city's growth. With his next film, *Badou Boy* (1970), Mambety turned to the Wolof language for another critique of Dakar. In what seems to be a study for one aspect of his first feature, he follows the comic pursuit of a wicked young boy by a policeman through the city revealing some of its problems. Both of these films concentrate on Dakar and the problems facing a city that is emerging from a colonial past with little sense of direction for the future.

This city is the background for Mambety's first feature *Touki Bouki/ Le voyage de l'hyène/ The Journey of the Hyena** (1973). He follows the journey of two young people who are outsiders in a marginalized world. Dakar is a city in a country on a continent that exists on the fringes of Western consciousness. In the postcolonial period this continent only becomes of interest to the rest of the world in periods of crisis. But as Mory and Anta demonstrate, its young people are still oriented toward a colonial past; they dream of going to Paris. This couple tries a variety of schemes during the course of the film to get money for the trip. Their efforts take them to various locations and place them in contact with many different people. What distinguishes this film is not just its critique of the aims of African youth, but the way in which it portrays their quest for illusory goals. Mambety creates a quick moving narrative that incorporates dream and fantasy sequences and a complex symbolism to convey its messages. For example, images of cattle open and close the film and shots of slaughter are cut into the narrative. These images can be read as examples of the continued exploitation of African resources, the consumerism of the city, which does not produce what it uses, or as a connection to Mory's past as a shepherd. At the end of the film, Mory comes to the realization he will not find his dreams in France. Anta sails off, but he remains behind. While he is not exactly a hope for the future, Mory does embody the contradictions inherent in modern African life. The ox's skull he has attached to his motorcycle connects him to his former occupation. He rides around Dakar having lost his relationship with his past and longing for a future that is only a dream.

Parlons, grand-mère/ Let's Talk, Granny (1989) is a short that provides a kind of transition to Mambety's next feature. He documents the making of *Yaaba*, a film directed by Idrissa Ouedraogo, in Burkina Faso. *Yaaba*, which details life in a village, became an international success. *Hyènes/ Hyenas** (1992) also deals with life outside of a big city, but this film takes place in a backwater village which has seen better days, not the unspoiled precolonial site of *Yaaba*. *Hyenas* is an adaptation of the play by Frederich Dürrenmatt, *The Visit*. In this story a woman who was forced to leave the town returns to claim her vengeance against the man who was the source of her problems. She has become very wealthy and offers the inhabitants large amount of money if they will kill the man. In *Hyenas*, Linguère Ramatou was made pregnant by Draman Drameh. He avoided responsibility for the child and bribed two men to say they also had sexual contact with her. Linguère returns to Colobane with all of the treasures of the modern world, fashionable clothing, appliances, cars, and even a carnival with fireworks that blot out the stars. The temptation and transformation of the village is symbolic of conditions in Africa. A country like Senegal remains dependent on the West for consumer goods, which keeps it in debt and encourages corruption and desires for products that the economy cannot afford to support.

Mambety's most recent film is the longest segment in a compilation of three short films distributed under the title *Three Tales From Senegal.** Le Franc* (1994), his section, is the first in a projected trilogy called *Stories of Little People*. The devaluation of the West African franc and the hardships it causes provides the basis for the story of a man who has no money and is in danger of losing his room. His landlady has already confiscated his *congoma*, a musical instrument, for back rent. He finally joins many of the poor in his country by playing the lottery. Worried about the safety of his ticket, he glues it to his door under the poster of his hero, Yaadikoone Ndiaye, a Senegalese figure who operated like Robin Hood. When he wins he must transport the door to the lottery office only to be told important numbers are on the back of the ticket and it must be removed from the door. He takes the door to the seaside, removes the ticket, loses the ticket and finally ends the film with it located, plastered to his forehead. The film continues Mambety's stylistic and thematic concerns. He combines comic and serious elements with a form that employs fantasy and dreams in its presentation of its narrative.

Mambety is one of the most original directors working in African film. He moves freely from realistic observation of the lives of people to fantastic symbols that reverberate throughout the work. He often employs images of animals in his films to represent complex concepts. Hyenas appear as scavengers, outsiders, and folkloric emblems. They become part of the intricate narratives that characterize his work.

Filmography

Contrast-City/ A City of Contrasts (1968)

Badou Boy (1970), Silver Tanit Carthage 70 Film Festival

Touki Bouki/ Le voyage de l'hyène/ The Journey of the Hyena (1973), International Critic's Prize Moscow Film Festival 1973

Parlons, grand-mère/ Let's Talk, Granny (1989)

Hyènes/ Hyenas (1992)

Le Franc (1994), Gold Tanit Carthage Film Festival

Bibliography

"Diop-Mambety, Djibril." *Dictionnaire du cinéma africain*. Vol. 1. Paris: Editions Karthala, 1991. 284–86.
Malkmus, Lizbeth, and Roy Armes. *Arab and African Film Making*. London: Zed Books, 1991.

Shiri, Kenneth, comp. and ed. *Directory of African Films*. Westport, Conn.: Greenwood P, 1992.

Ukadike, Nwachukwu Frank. *Black African Cinema*. Berkeley: U of California P, 1994.

N

Neria (1992: Godwin Mawuru, Zimbabwe). The traditional form of the melodrama is the organizational basis for this film about family life in modern Zimbabwe. The director, Godwin Mawuru, incorporates both the thematic and structural elements of this genre to examine the changing roles of males and females in African society. As is customary in the melodrama, *Neria* concentrates on people who must deal with social problems; the characters and their interaction with the structures of society are foregrounded. The plot is closely related to these problems rather than growing out of character. This film even returns to the earliest meaning of the term melodrama, which combines music and drama, and the sound track is an important component of the narrative. Not only is one of the central characters a musician but also one of his songs frames the moment when Neria finally decides to act for herself, when she makes those choices that alter the course of the narrative. Mawuru employs a traditional genre as a means of making the didactic goals of his narrative available to all of the viewers. While the film presents memorable characters and a detailed view of aspects of life in Zimbabwe, it also aims to teach its viewers about their rights.

Neria opens with Connie—as images of her neighbors painting their house and interacting with family members overlay her face—as she naps. The picture of a sleeping woman is an apt metaphor for the entire film for as the story enfolds many of the women awaken and understand their situations and how they must act to exist in a changing world. Connie is contrasted with Ambuya, mother of Patrick and mother-in-law of Neria, who is dozing in a chair as she visits her son and his family. This opening establishes the basic relationships between these characters. The grandmother does not like her daughter-in-law who is too modern. She constantly criticizes her under her breath and to her face. Patrick and Neria have an excellent marriage in which they share everything including the financial responsibilities for their children and the household. Connie, a divorced neighbor, has already dealt with many of the problems that Neria will soon confront. She is wise and supportive of Neria's immediate frustrations with her mother-in-law. After these characters are presented, the scene shifts to a club where Jethro, Neria's brother, is performing with his group. He is played by the singer Oliver Mtukudzi, who wrote much of the music for the film and plays all of it. Patrick's brother, Phineas, waits impatiently for him to finish so Jethro can help him transport goods to Patrick's house for the trip back to the village. Phineas' actions immediately characterize him as a self-centered individual who has no concern for anyone else.

The contrasting attitudes of the two sides of the family are evident when Jericho praises his sister. That night Neria prays for the strength to deal with her mother-in-law, while Ambuya decides she will get up early and show her daughter-in-law how a wife should act. The next morning Ambuya sweeps the front yard while Neria sets off for her job. The conflict between these two women is not so much a result of their in-law relationship as it is an opposition between city and country lifestyles, modern attitudes, and tradition. Neria's world is defined by her job where she works with other women sewing and creating other handicrafts, which they sell. These women form a genuine supportive community that is contrasted with the false sense of tradition represented by Phineas in the village. The grandmother admits she does not understand city life, and she cannot see any advantages to it.

The differences between Patrick and the rest of his family are demonstrated during the trip to return Phineas and the grandmother to the village. Phineas constantly attacks Patrick because he wants to consult Neria before buying a bull for Phineas. Phineas cannot understand why she should be included in the decision even when Patrick points out that there are some months when she may even make more money. Phineas sees Neria as "our wife" because the family contributed to the bride price. He tells a story of a man who dies after making a will suggesting the wife may have killed her husband for the money. Mawuru intercuts two versions of another story told by Patrick and his mother to two different audiences. In this tale a woman helps her husband by working in the village while her husband goes to the city. The moral for both versions is good treatment of the wife.

The opposing views of social interactions are focused in the conflicts that arise when Patrick dies in an accident. Phineas arrives and asserts his rights to his brother's estate. He takes away the bank account. When Neria returns from the village funeral she finds he has even taken all of the furniture. As the oldest brother, he tries to take control of everything including Neria, but his mother objects because tradition dictates the inheritance ceremony take place after a year has passed. Neria finds it difficult to survive without the bankbook. The electricity is turned off, and she cannot pay the school fees. Phineas and his wife arrive, move in, and attempt to give the children material possessions to turn them against Neria. When they leave with her children Neria follows them to the village. She learns the children are not happy. Mavis is ill. When Phineas will not drive them to the hospital, Neria carries her daughter on her back to the bus. They arrive at the hospital just in time for the safe removal of Mavis' appendix.

While all of these events are troubling for Neria they also become important for her eventual victory. She decides to take Connie's advice and hire a lawyer. He informs her of her rights. As Neria takes charge of her life, Jethro sings a song about Neria. The film follows Neria's journey, which is intercut with shots of Jethro. This sequence marks the turning point in the story, and the music intensifies the experience. Even the grandmother rejects Phineas' actions. She tells him that he will have to go to court because of his greed; he also almost killed Mavis. The court does grant Neria the role of executor of the estate for the oldest child. Phineas must return everything, but he does not quit. He takes Neria back to court with his own lawyer who presents a very different picture of his sister-in-law. Luckily her own lawyer allows her to testify, and the judge believes her.

The film ends with shots that bring together the concerns of the film. A year has passed, and Neria participates in the inheritance ceremony in the village. The men line up as possible husbands, but she rejects them all. Even the grandmother agrees with her, stating that, "You have to bend tradition to changing times." The film closes with Neria dancing with the women of the village. They all share in her triumph.

Neria is a film that demonstrates how important points can be made in ways that both entertain and instruct the audience. Mawuru uses a traditional form to engage the audience in Neria's problems, but he allows the melodrama to have a happy ending to show positive solutions that are now possible. He reconciles the conflict between the modern and traditional worlds by using Phineas as an example of the worst possible version of the old ways. Even the grandmother comes to understand why some laws must be altered. Neria's positive character makes the best case for change. She is positioned between Connie, her divorced neighbor who has already learned how to use the law, and the grandmother who does not understand the need for change. By the end of the film all of the women share an appreciation of their rights. Those involved in the production of *Neria* want all of the viewers to come to the same understanding.

This film won Best Foreign film from Black Filmmakers Hall of Fame;

Best Film by a Black Filmmaker, from the Berlin International Festival of Black Film, and OAU Award for Best Director from the Carthage Film Festival.

La noire de . . . / Black Girl (1966: Ousmane Sembene,* Senegal). Many critics mark the emergence of full-length filmmaking in sub-Sahara Africa with the screening of this film in Dakar, Senegal, in 1966. *Black Girl* is based on a real story that Sembene converted into a novel before making the film. The work was originally 65 minutes long, the minimum for a feature, but it had to be cut to 60 minutes to conform to certain technical regulations in order to be shown in France such as the certification of members of the crew (Vieyra 31–32). As is true of many African films, *Black Girl* was made on a very small budget with a combination of amateur and professional actors. Even with all of these restrictions, the film is clearly structured as a full-length fictional film.

The film tells the story of Diouana, who is hired as a maid in Dakar and then is taken back to France by her employers. Sembene contrasts scenes in the Antibes with flashes back to Diouana's life in Senegal. The opening of the film traces her arrival and the details of her daily life. The viewer immediately sees the way the French employers and their guests treat the maid. Diouana believes she has been hired to take care of the children, but in France the children are not present, and she must cook and clean. The French see her as both servant and exotic object who will take care of the apartment and produce real African cooking on demand. When the film cuts back to her life in Dakar, Diouana is a very different person. She is hired because she is not as aggressive as the other women who are waiting for jobs. She is happy with the job and brings her employers an African mask as a gift.

The mask becomes a symbol both of her relationship with her employers and of their lack of understanding of her. In Africa the mask is, like Diouana, connected to the tradition that produced it. When the mask hangs on the wall in the apartment in France, it is alienated from its culture. It is just another decoration for the family just as Diouana is only a servant, a cog in the machinery of the household. Diouana gets the mask from her brother, a child like the children she is hired to care for. When the children are gone, she loses another important connection to her life in Senegal.

Most of the time Diouana has no voice; her thoughts are conveyed by voice-over narration. The French voices are dubbed. The audience hears the mistress speak her constant criticism, which indicates her lack of understanding; she retains a colonial mentality in a postcolonial situation. Diouana is a person who has doubly lost her voice, both as a woman and as a black in an alien society. As she withdraws from her life in France, Diouana becomes even more quiet. Her silence contrasts with her joy in the flashbacks, and her lack of voice is also related to her level of activity. She dances in Dakar but walks slowly in France as she moves deliberately toward her final rebellion, her suicide.

While Diouana is never presented as a politically conscious person, she is aware that the end of colonialism has not really changed French attitudes. Her voice-over commentary constantly repeats her resentment at being treated like a slave. Her sense of a lack of freedom leaves her with no apparent choices. She takes back the mask, carefully packs her suitcase, and commits suicide by cutting her wrists in the bath tub. Her employer is left to return her things and her pay to her mother in Dakar. Diouana's mother rejects what she sees as blood money, and her former employer quickly leaves followed by the brother wearing the mask. He and his friends pursue the man to a foot bridge, which marks the division between the African and European sections of Dakar. The film ends on the boy's unmasked face. While the image may suggest hope for the future, there is no impression of change in the lives of the individuals in the film.

Black Girl is an early film by Sembene, which begins to articulate some of the problems he deals with in greater complexity in later films. Images like the mask demonstrate a complexity that reverberates throughout the story. But the French couple present a simplified version of postcolonial society. A later film like *Xala** (1974) demonstrates the way that colonialism persists without the French presence. Diouana is the first of many rebellious women in Sembene's films. While her story is moving and can lead to an understanding of connections between economics and politics in Senegal, these issues are examined more deeply in those films where Sembene's female characters actively express their views in their own languages. The film won the Jean Vigo Prize for direction in 1966.

Bibliography

Dittmar, Linda. "The Articulating Self: Difference as Resistance in *Black Girl*, *Ramparts of Clay*, and *Salt of the Earth*." *Multiple Voices in Feminist Film Criticism*. Ed. Diane Carson, Linda Dittmar, and Janice R. Welsch. Minneapolis: U of Minnesota P, 1994. 391–405.

Malkmus, Lizbeth, and Roy Armes. *Arab and African Film Making*. London: Zed Books, 1991.

Vieyra, Paulin Soumanou. "Five Major Films by Sembene Ousmane." *Film & Politics in The Third World*. Ed. John D. H. Downing. New York: Praeger, 1986. 31–39.

O

OUEDRAOGO, IDRISSA (Banfora, Burkina Faso, 1954). Idrissa Ouedraogo is one of the few filmmakers from Burkina Faso to make more than one film. He became interested in the cinema at an early age. His farmer parents sent him to the capital, Ouagadougou, for his more advanced education. His first experience at film school was at the INAFEC (Institut africain d'education cinématographique). He worked in the management area of film production. He began his career as a director by making several short films. As with many other African filmmakers he turned to Paris for further education at IDHEC (Institut des hautes etudes cinématographiques) where he graduated in 1985. He began his feature career a year later. Ouedraogo's films exhibit a concern for the individual who is caught either by traditions that affect the quality of life or by attempts to make transitions from one world to another whether it be between children and adults or the city and the village.

His early films begin to explore themes he will deal with in greater detail in his features. *Pourquoi?/ Why?* (1981) is a very short film in which a man dreams of killing his wife, but he can't tell if it is dream or reality. *Poko* (1981), his second short film, deals with a tragedy in the life of some villagers. A pregnant woman who suffers from complications dies while being transported on a cart. The story points out the difficulties of villagers who do not have medical facilities or quick means of transportation available. They pay taxes but receive little from the government in return. In *Les écuelles/ The Platters* (1983), the life of the village is disrupted when the young people leave for the city. Only the old are left to continue the traditional crafts, a condition that is of universal concern. Ouedraogo continues to record traditions in danger of being lost with his next film about the funeral of a chief, *Les funerailles du Larle Naba/ Larle Naba's Funeral* (1983), which he co-directed with Pierre Rovamba. *Ouagadougou, Ouaga deux roues/ Ouagadougou, Ouaga Two Wheels* (1985) presents the film-maker's impressions of the circulation of vehicles in the city. *Issa le tisser-and/ Issa the Weaver* (1985) returns to his concerns for the survival of the artisan. Weavers need to adapt to modern styles in clothing in order to survive. In *Tenga* (1985), his last short, Ouedraogo's subject is the land itself and the lives of those who live on it as seen through the eyes of a person who has returned to the village after attempting life in the city. In these shorts the director begins to explore the various techniques and themes that will form the basis of his features. Each piece will later serve as the inspiration for important concepts in his view of the problems of Africa. While he is interested in the relationship between tradition and change, as these films indicate, he is not as concerned with the abuses of postcolonial society as he is with the individual's moral and ethical uni-verse.

Ouedraogo's early features deal entirely with aspects of life outside the city. He is interested in how people make the decisions that govern their lives. *Yam daabo/ Le choix/ The Choice* (1986) is not as well known as his later films. A family must decide whether to remain in a village on the edge of the desert dependent on international aid for survival or to move further south to an easier life where the family could become self-supporting. The director details the daily life of the family to demonstrate what is involved in such a decision. His second feature won prizes at fes-tivals and has been widely distributed. *Yaaba/ Grandmother* (1989) is a moving story of the relationship between youth and age in a village that has its source in a narrative from the oral tradition. Bila, a young boy, and Nopoko, a young girl, decide to befriend an elderly woman who is thought of as a sorceress by the rest of the village. Bila becomes especially close to the woman, Sana, whom the children call Yaaba, grandmother. The rest of the village blames her for anything that goes wrong, but she is more accepted when she is instrumental in saving Nopoko's life. The reason for her being an outsider is revealed after her death. She is an orphan and does not fit into a society in which family ties are of supreme importance. While this film is popular with audiences around the world because of its beauty and simplicity, some critics are concerned about its lack of a complex consideration of the serious issues that confront villag-ers.

Tilaï/ A Question of Honor* (1990) answered some of the fears ex-pressed by those who felt *Yaaba* lacked depth. This narrative deals with a moment of change on the Moré culture. The conflicts generated in a clash between parents and children and two brothers raise questions about the value of tradition, the position of women, and the difficulty of changing values that have been held by the community. Saga returns home to find his father has wed the woman promised to his son, Nogma. Saga and Nogma secretly see each other. When they are discovered, Saga's brother, Kougri, draws the lot that condemns him to kill Saga. Kougri spares his brother with the promise he will leave the village and never return. Nogma follows Saga to a relative's village where they are happy until he learns of his mother's illness. Saga returns arriving as his mother is about to be buried. This time Kougri accepts the law and kills him. Ouedraogo shows the damage created by an unwavering acceptance of tradition. While he does not suggest that everything from the past must be abandoned, he shows how certain conventions destroy the very community that they were created to protect.

After the success of *Yaaba* and *Tilaï* Ouedraogo was under a great deal of pressure to produce another comparable success. *A Karim na Sala/ Karim and Sala* (1991) was rushed to completion for the twelfth FES-PACO. It was not well received and has not been distributed widely. With his next film, Ouedraogo demonstrated further development of the themes that have interested him throughout his career. *Samba Traoré* (1993) combines the conflicts between tradition and change and the city versus the village into the life of a single character. The quality of life in the city is demonstrated in the rapid violent images that open the film. Samba Traoré participates in the robbery of a gas station. His partner is shot, and he runs back to his village. Once back home, he changes. He supports various activities in the village opening a business with friends and developing a relationship with a single mother. But he cannot get away from the guilt he feels. His actions raise questions about the nature of guilt and innocence and how ethical and moral decisions are made in a changing world.

Ouedraogo's work shows the kind of growth possible when a director can find the funds to make several films. He is concerned about the continuing problems confronting those who want to make films in Africa. He has been criticized for making films that will appeal to a wide audience both in Africa and in the West. But he realizes distribution that does not find a larger audience will not be financially viable in light of the tremendous cost of a film. He also feels films should be judged on their own merit and not just be viewed because they represent a certain region of the world. His career demonstrates what can be accomplished by a talented person who is willing to make the effort necessary to make films under extremely difficult conditions.

Filmography

Pourquoi?/ Why? (1981)

Poko (1981), Short Film Prize FESPACO 81

Les écuelles/ The Platters (1983)

Les funerailles du Larle Naba/ Larle Naba's Funeral (1983), co-director Pierre Rovamba

Ouagadougou, Ouaga deux roues/ Ouagadougou, Ouaga Two Wheels (1985)

Issa le tisserand/ Issa the Weaver (1985), Director's Prize Carthage 84, Grand Prize Short Film FESPACO 85

Tenga (1985)

Yam daabo/ Le choix/ The Choice (1986)

Yaaba/ Grandmother (1989), International Critic's Prize Cannes 89, INALCO and Jury Prizes FESPACO 89, Young Public Prize Tokyo 89

Tilaï/ A Question of Honor (1990), Special Jury Grand Prize and Critic's Prize Cannes 1990

A Karim na Sala/ Karim and Sala (1991)

Samba Traoré (1993)

Bibliography

Diawara, Manthia. *African Cinema: Politics & Culture.* Bloomington: Indiana UP, 1992.

"Ouedraogo, Idrissa." *Dictionnaire du cinéma africain.* Vol. 1. Paris: Editions Karthala, 1991. 55–58.

Ouedraogo, Idrissa. "Le cinéma et nous." *Africa and the Centenary of Film.* Ed. Gaston Kaboré. Dakar: Présence Africaine, 1995. 336–42.

Malkmus, Lizbeth, and Roy Armes. *Arab and African Film Making.* London: Zed Books, 1991.

Shiri, Kenneth, comp. and ed. *Directory of African Films.* Westport, Conn.: Greenwood P, 1992.

Ukadike, Nwachukwu Frank. *Black African Cinema.* Berkeley: U of California P, 1994.

Q

Quartier Mozart (1992: Jean-Pierre Bekolo, Cameroon). Recent African films work to achieve a style that is not just a reflection of Western cinema. *Quartier Mozart*, the name of a neighborhood in Yaoundé, combines modern techniques such as direct address to the camera—which are associated with modern American filmmakers like Spike Lee—with folklore from the oral tradition to produce a film that reflects the best of both worlds. The film demonstrates an awareness of the importance of the media in modern Africa, but it also acknowledges a certain sophistication on the part of its audience. While some decry the influence of the West, Jean-Pierre Bekolo, the director, accepts the universality of certain references and uses them to make his film accessible to its audience. Characters discuss the relative qualities of Princess Di, Denzel Washington, and Michael Jackson. Bekolo realizes such cultural icons are almost universal in their appeal. But he situates such references in a uniquely African culture.

The film, which takes place over a period of forty-eight hours, opens with a series of titles that explain its narrative focus and introduce the characters. The first says, "*Quartier Mozart* uses traditional Cameroonian folk beliefs to explore the sexual politics of an urban neighborhood." The various characters are presented with descriptive folk names. Queen of the Hood is the young heroine. She is concerned about having men take advantage of her. She goes to a local sorceress, Maman Thekla, who transforms her into My Guy. Maman Thekla takes on the form of a traditional comic character, Panka. The titles also introduce Mad Dog, the local policeman, who is in the process of acquiring a second wife and his daughter, Samedi (Saturday). While these titles provide a preview of some of the episodes in the film, they also establish a guide for the magic events that will follow. Rather than undercutting the usual suspense generated by a narrative, this information clarifies the transformations that might otherwise seem confusing.

The first part of the film reenacts the material covered by the introductory information and introduces additional characters such as Lady's Candy Man, Atango, a Sorbonne graduate who designs female clothing to attract women. He is part of the sexual politics of the quarter. Queen of the Hood, who is described as stuck up like a woman who has not known men, approaches Maman Thekla to make her a woman in the body of a man so she can remove herself from the sexual interactions that are a major focus of the community. That night Queen enters a car and emerges as My Guy. The transformation in a vehicle is an example of how the film unites modern technology with traditional magic. Maman Thekla's witchcraft is accepted. It is no different than the more conventional activities of the other characters. After the transformation, My Guy clothes himself with items taken off a clothesline and sews buttons on the jacket and patches on the pants. While he meets the people in the quarter, Maman Thekla transforms herself into Panka, a traditional comic character from the country, who arrives in the city on the train. Both of the transformed women will learn much and change those they come in contact with as they pass through the neighborhood.

The introduction of the two supernatural characters accelerates the comic and ironic interactions of the inhabitants of Quartier Mozart. Mad Dog hires Panka to guard his house. Mad Dog brings in his new wife. As he sits with his two wives and his daughter a glass breaks, and his new wife is afraid and wants the house blessed. The film takes a complex attitude toward this event and all of the other things that happen. While they may be taken seriously by those involved, the film takes a humorous view of them. The audience is closest to My Guy and Panka, but the viewer is not encouraged to identify with any specific point of view. My Guy becomes an object of interest for the women, while Panka has the ability to make men's genitals disappear. Even though nothing could happen, a story circulates about the sexual activity of My Guy and Samedi. My Guy discovers male freedom can be difficult to deal with. Both of these characters use their adopted masculinity to assist women who have suffered because of men. My Guy gets a character to acknowledge responsibility for a woman he made pregnant, and Panka aids the wife of a drunk. When My Guy has learned enough about men she and Maman Thekla return to their female personas from the beginning of the film.

While *Quartier Mozart* is a unique product whose style is not easily reproduced, the film both thematically and technically suggests important areas of cinematic exploration for African film. The film uses techniques that might be associated with modern films from many different countries, films that experiment with traditional narrative. Bekolo adopts what might be considered a universal modernism to the specific themes and customs of his own country. Many other African films seamlessly blend the supernatural and the realistic, a reflection of societies that have no need to make careful distinctions between the real and the magical. The film also takes on the teasing tone of the folklore it employs, a manner that blends extremely well with its modern style because both ignore a more traditional cinematic naturalism. The way the film combines its various styles make the usual interactions of the traditional and the modern in African society useless. *Quartier Mozart* demonstrates that the crossing of sexual boundaries draws into question the very idea of distinct categories. Its radical examination of the sexual politics that operate in the city shows the reactionary qualities that still exist among a group of people who consider themselves quite modern. While the film continues the concern for women's rights, which is central to many African films, it performs this activity in a context that challenges most boundaries at the same time that it employs traditional figures and magical transformation as the tools for its exploration.

Bibliography

Akudinobi, Jude. "Tradition/ Modernity and the Discourse of African Cinema." *IRIS* 18 (Spring 1995): 25–37.
Shohat, Ella, and Robert Stam. *Unthinking Eurocentrism: Multiculturalism and the Media.* London: Routledge, 1994.

R

RACHEDI, AHMED (Tebessa, Algeria, 1938). Ahmed Rachedi began his involvement with film as a member of the "groupe Farid," which was the filmmaking arm of the FLN (National Liberation Front). He received formal film training in Tunisia. Rachedi held many positions in Algerian production organizations such as director of the Centre de Diffusion Nationale (Center for National Distribution) from 1964–66, and the head of ONCIC (Office national du commerce et l'industrie cinématographique/ The National Office for Cinematic Commerce and Industry) from its inception in 1967 until 1971. He assisted in the production of several feature films and also worked on short films with the CAV (Centre Audio-Visuel d'Alger/ Algerian Audio-Visual Centre), a collective that he helped found in 1962.

Rachedi's first feature film demonstrates his involvement in documentary filmmaking. *Fajr al-Mu'adhdhabin/ Dawn of the Damned/ L'aube des damnés* (1965) is a compilation film that treats the history of liberation efforts on the African continent. He aims to reclaim African history from its colonialized myths. Mouloud Mammeri wrote the narration for this film, and his novel is the source of Rachedi's second film, *Al-afyun wal-'asa/ Opium and the Stick/ L'opium et le bâton* (1969). The novel's episodic structure interested him, and he was also attracted by its treatment of the Algerian revolution and its depiction of the people. The film takes place during the war of liberation when a doctor returns to the countryside and his home, which is divided. His brothers seem to fight on opposing sides. Rachedi uses this story to demonstrate the courage and persistence of the people in their fight against colonialism. In order to attract large audiences, he adopts a Hollywood production style where the story dominates the action and the film's messages are submerged in the action-adventure format.

In his next feature, *Le doigt dans l'engrenage/ A Finger in the Works* (1974), Rachedi steps back from the Hollywood style and creates a small film about an emigrant Algerian in Paris. He returns to his documentary roots and combines interviews and documentary footage with his fictional story of a person who arrives in Paris and immediately gets lost in the metro. Rachedi continues to explore the situation of Algerians in France in his next film *Ali fi bilad al-sarab/ Ali in Wonderland/ Ali au pays des mirages* (1979). Like many foreign workers, Ali can only observe a world where he must remain an outsider.

With *Tahunat al-sayyid Fabré/ Monsieur Fabré's Mill/ Le moulin de Monsieur Fabré* (1982), Rachedi returns to films set in Algeria. This film explores the problem of power and bureaucracy in a postcolonial society. A small village must have an example of how nationalization is progressing to show to an important visitor from the capital. Fabré, an immigrant who supported the Algerians and had joined the FLN, loses his heroic position in the community when he is honored by agreeing to have his small mill selected to be nationalized. The local officials find the whole ceremony meaningless especially in light of the very real problems the community faces. While Fabré—who does not realize that he is no longer part of the revolutionary direction of the community—enjoys the honor, the real local heroes gradually disappear because the visitor did not like their attitude.

Rachedi's most recent films continue to explore themes relating to the war of independence. *Es Silane/ Barbed Wire/ Barbelés* (1981) is an epic story of life in a village during the period preceding liberation through the war and its aftermath. *C'était la guerre/ It Was the War* (1992) explores the war for liberation from the dual perspectives of an Algerian soldier and a French teacher who fights for the French. These films continue to develop Rachedi's concern for the transition from colonialism to freedom and the effect of this transformation on the individual and the state. His career is a reflection of the development of Algerian cinema and its on-going analysis of the postcolonial situation in this country.

Filmography

Fajr al-Mu'adhdhabin/ Dawn of the Damned/ L'aube des damnés (1965)

La commune/ The Commune (1966)

Les élections/ The Elections (1967)

Al-afyun wal-'asa/ Opium and the Stick/ L'opium et le bâton (1969)

L'informatique en Algérie/ Computer Science in Algeria (1973)

Les transports/ Transportation (1973)

Le doigt dans l'engrenage/ A Finger in the Works (1974)

Ali fi bilad al-sarab/ Ali in Wonderland/ Ali au pays des mirages (1979)

Es Silane/ Barbed Wire/ Barbelés (1981)

Tahunat al-sayyid Fabré/ Monsieur Fabré's Mill/ Le moulin de Monsieur Fabré (1982)

C'était la guerre/ It Was the War (1992)

Bibliography

Armes, Roy. *Dictionary of North African Film Makers*. Paris: Editions ATM, 1996.
Hennebelle, Guy. *Les cinémas africains en 1972*. Paris: Société Africaine d'Edition, 1972.
Malkmus, Lizbeth, and Roy Armes. *Arab and African Film Making*. London: Zed Books, 1991.

Remparts de Argile/ Ramparts of Clay (1970: Jean-Louis Bertucelli). Like *La Battaglia de Algeria*,* this film is directed by a European who worked with Algerians to create a work that analyzes important political and cultural events in modern Algeria. The film's two sources are an indication of the range of ideas it covers. The ethnographic study, *Change at Shebika: A Report from a North African Village* by Jean Duvignaud (Austin: Texas University Press, 1977) gives the film the story of its central character and a setting that had to be moved from Tunisia to Algeria because of its criticism of postcolonial government. The quotation from Frantz Fanon's *Wretched of the Earth*, which condemns the bourgeois stage of political development in an underdeveloped country as a worthless position, provides the film's critique of postcolonial Algerian society. Bertucelli, because he was an outsider, had greater freedom in filming than an Algerian counterpart would have had. He was able to enlist the members of the village of Tehouda to participate in the film, and the central character is played by a professional actress, Leila Schenna.

Even though Bertucelli is French, the film's visual and narrative style are like those of many African films. *Ramparts* begins with the daily life of the village, focusing on the situation of one young unnamed woman. While there may be a hint of a fascination with the exoticism of the subject in Bertucelli's lingering presentation of her performance of her chores, he is providing the basis for her later actions. The evocation of the rhythms of everyday life is shared by many other films that deal with rural life on the African continent. Its focus on this particular woman allows Bertucelli to develop a critique of the patriarchal structure of the village at the same time that he explores the economic oppression common to all of its inhabitants.

As the audience learns, when an official arrives to take a kind of census, the young girl has no real place in the community. She is a nineteen-year-old orphan with no dowry and no hope of marriage who is to spend the rest of her life working for the family who adopted her. No one encourages her attempts to learn to read, and she exists on the margins of the village's social structure. But no one in the village has an easy life. The men either spend their time quarrying stone or cutting slabs of salt from the surrounding rocky hills. Bertucelli demonstrates the general hardship of life in this barren setting by detailing the variety of difficult jobs. But he also shows the isolation of the young woman who is confined by the society. Her repeated gestures of putting her black veil over her face every time she moves into the public world of the village becomes a poignant expression of her solitary life.

In addition to the visual style and narrative patterns he establishes in the opening segments of the film, Bertucelli uses sound to create a sense of place and to produce a thematic contrast between the intensity of the sounds created by work and the general lack of communication in the society. The men seldom speak, and there are points when their conversation is deliberately not translated in the subtitles to underline the inability of the audience to fully understand life in this village. The young woman's silence becomes another indication of her isolation. Her real voice is the squeaking of the pulley she uses to haul water up from the well.

Toward the end of the film her association with the pulley develops from a symbol of her oppression to a central moment of resistance. The men of the village go on strike against the bosses of the quarry because of a dispute over wages. This action illustrates Fanon's critique of the bourgeois elements of postcolonial society. Rather than supporting the men, who are being denied their correct pay, the government sends in troops to surround them. Independence has changed nothing for the villagers. The repressive colonial government, which supported the owners rather than the workers, has been replaced by a postcolonial government that takes the same position. The women watch as the soldiers eat and drink while their men can only sit in the sun. When the soldiers draw water from the well for their own, the squeaking pulley becomes a sound signaling the oppression of the entire village. During the night the young woman silently removes the rope and the bucket. When the soldiers try to get water in the morning they find an empty pulley. Her action results in the end of the strike.

As in *Emitai*,* the women take a role in the protest against injustice. But the young woman does not become a heroine as a result of her action. The village structure is as closed to change as is the larger world. At the end of the film the strike is over. In a final act of rebellion, the young woman runs out into the desert and her probable death. Bertucelli follows her in a helicopter until the viewer has to strain to see her disappearing body. He deliberately includes the interior of the helicopter in the image. Viewers must realize their distance from the action. He does not give the viewer the false illusion of identification with her and her situation. Bertucelli wants his audience to become aware of its role. He does not want his viewers to think that everything can be understood and that it is easy to identify with the villagers. The audience flies off in the helicopter unable to intervene.

In *Ramparts*, the filmmaker explores a world that is foreign to the Western audience. But he refuses to romanticize life in the village. He also does not cover-up the problems in a postcolonial society. Bertucelli wants his audience to understand the difficulty of examining the lives of people whose lives are different from those who have not experienced the effects of colonialism. He forces his viewers to acknowledge their position as outsiders at the same time that he demonstrates the difficulty of adjusting to a postcolonial situation.

Bibliography

Dittmar, Linda. "The Articulating Self: Difference as Resistance in *Black Girl*, *Ramparts of Clay*, and *Salt of the Earth*." *Multiple Voices in Feminist Film Criticism*. Ed. Diane Carson, Linda Dittmar, and Janice R. Welsch. Minneapolis: U of Minnesota P, 1994. 391–405.

S

Saaraba/ Utopia (1988: Amadou Seck, Senegal). Saaraba is the Senegalese name for a mythical place where everything will be perfect. Amadou
Seck uses this dream location to examine the problems in modern Senegal.
Like his fellow countryman and filmmaker Ousmane Sembene,* he is concerned about what has happened in postcolonial Africa. In *Saaraba* he
exposes the false dreams of all ages. The old are corrupt, the middle-aged
are trapped by tradition, and the young drop out of society. While they
try to live independent lives, all of the characters are still confined by the
legacy of colonialism. Either they imitate or buy into the corruption of
white society, or they spend their lives fighting against any connection with
it. Seck traces the search for a version of Saaraba in the lives of several
characters and examines the destructive potential in such dreams.

Tamsir is the central character who moves among all the rest. His return
after seventeen years in France opens the film. He encounters modern
Senegal the moment he leaves the airport as two men fight over carrying
his suitcases. His wealthy uncle meets him and takes him to his home.
Tamsir also renews his acquaintance with Sidy, his uncle's drop-out son
who refuses to take part in the corrupt society he sees around him and
instead takes drugs. Tamsir's uncle has a job for him in his firm, but the
young man must go back to his village first to see his family.

Tamsir's village is contrasted with the city. Tradition is central to village
life. Tamsir makes the last part of the journey on the back of a cart.
Tamsir's religious father teaches the children. But even in this location
modern influences intrude. Tamsir goes to the village to get away from
white influences. The MP comes and announces the changes he has arranged. There will soon be electricity, a water supply, and sewage disposal.

But the entire character of the village will change when the projected salt factory and tourist center are built. A herder protests these alterations in his lifestyle. What he wants is immediate help for his cows dying from the extended drought. Tamsir's sister, Daba, may live in the village, but she receives a letter from the father of her child, Thian, a situation her mother finds appalling. The two lovers wanted to marry, but their parents objected. Tamsir sides with his parents' support of tradition while Daba objects. Tamsir tells her that whites have confused us and influenced us. She tells him that he hasn't learned anything abroad; he is just like their mother.

In his relationship with Lissa, Daba's friend, Tamsir shows signs of taking a different attitude toward tradition. Lissa attracts the attention of both the MP and Tamsir. She likes Tamsir, but her parents promise her to the MP. This conflict presents one of the film's basic confrontations between modern life and tradition. She wants to please her parents and also be an obedient daughter, but she does not agree with their decision. Tamsir wants to uphold tradition against the erosion of it by white influence, but he too is trapped. He tries to promote a sexual encounter between them, but she supports her parents and insists on remaining a virgin. When she is forced to accept the MP, she and Tamsir do make love, an action that results in her pregnancy and disgrace.

In the central section of the film, the characters all pursue misguided quests for false dreams. The most extreme example of blind adherence to tradition occurs in the life of the herder. His cows are still dying, and he consults a witch doctor. He is about to follow the orders and sacrifice his only child, his daughter, until he is stopped by a member of the village. Tamsir's return to the city places him in the opposite situation. He feels an obligation to his uncle and joins his firm, but he really is not able to contribute. Some of the characters, like the herder, act out of a false belief; others, like the MP, work to gratify personal greed or lust; many of the young, like Sidy, abandon the possibility of a dream.

There are some characters who have a more balanced view of life. Tamsir's dying father cautions him to find this balance. Tamsir wants to avoid the mistakes of the whites. His father points out how tradition can also be stifling and how technology is already an integral part of their age. He councils Tamsir to live in his own time rather than look backward to a past that is not his. No matter how much one might inherit from a father one can never be that father.

Tamsir is still unable to take his father's advice. Instead he is gradually drawn into Sidy's world of drugs. In an ironic scene, the young people complain about their lack of control over their lives while smoking dope in front of posters of Bob Marley, whose music plays under this scene. They have adopted the form of Marley's actions but have not understood his active protest against white domination. In the village, Lissa tries to escape from her forced marriage; even though she is pregnant, the MP refuses to give her up. Tradition does save her from an immediate wedding because, according to Islamic law, a pregnant woman cannot marry. The MP will wait until after the child is born.

As the film moves toward its close all of the dreams begin to disintegrate. Tamsir is arrested by the police in a drug sweep. His uncle gets him out of jail by bribing the police. Sidy, his own son, has left a letter detailing his father's corruption, his shady deals, and his misuse of foreign aid meant for the poor. Sidy leaves for Paris. The uncle's connection to the MP's deal is also revealed. Most of the characters come together at a village party to celebrate the coming electricity and sewage control provided by the MP, as well as the ambulance he has gotten free but claims to have bought as a gift. A young man, Demba, has been repairing a motorcycle left to him by a white missionary for a trip to Saaraba that he believes is an actual place. He tinkers with the MP's car because he believes Lissa and Tamsir should marry. Tamsir accompanies him on his mad drive to Saaraba, which results in a crash. As Demba dies, he tells Tamsir he has found his Saaraba, but Tamsir should fight for humanity and take care of Lissa. Tamsir promises that if Lissa has a boy they will name it Demba. The MP also crashes and is tended by Thian who has come home from his medical studies. The accident convinces the MP to give up Lissa. The film ends as Demba dies.

In *Saaraba*, Seck chronicles the confusion, corruption, and despair of Senegal. While some of the characters have bought into the legacy of colonialism and promoted their greed over any concern for the rest of the country, others have abandoned any responsibility for their own lives. A few try to make some sense of the conflicting demands of the modern and traditional worlds they encounter. Seck does not suggest any easy answers for the questions he raises. He does advocate a return to a worldview based on reality. Saaraba does not exist except in death. The characters will have to spend their lives working out their balance between the old and the new rather than pursuing that which does not exist.

Sambizanga (1972: Sarah Maldoror, Angola). This film is a record of a world in transition made at yet another period of change in the history of Angola. Sarah Maldoror (born Ducados in Guadeloupe), while not African, is married to the Angolan leader, Mario de Andrade. She acquired cinematic experience as an assistant on *La Battaglia de Algiera*.* She made *Sambizanga* while Angola was still involved in its fight for independence from the Portuguese. The film, which is adapted from a novel by the Angolan author Luandino Vieira, *La vraie vie de Domingos Xavier*, takes its name from one of the poor suburbs of Luanda. As a result of the fighting in Angola, the film was shot in Brazzaville in the People's Republic of the Congo with the participation of the MPLA (Popular Movement for the

Liberation of Angola). The film begins with the daily activities of a couple, Domingos and Maria, whose lives are dramatically transformed when the husband is arrested. From this point the film traces three connected narratives: the wife's search for her husband, the militant group's search for Domingos, and his torture and death in prison because he refuses to reveal the name of the European construction worker who is his contact in the underground movement. In *Sambizanga*, the fictional story is closely interwoven with the didactic themes of the importance of revolutionary activity. Individual characters are carefully developed, but they are also part of a larger movement of national liberation.

The opening images contrast enduring images of water with the work of a construction crew. The first words are an exchange between Domingos and his European contact establishing a meeting later that night. Maldoror wants the viewer to understand that the conflict in Angola may be between colonialism and the forces of liberation, but those forces are not limited to one race. Domingos tells his African helper that whites can be friends. The director then establishes Domingos' home life, introducing his wife, Maria, their child, and his close relationship to them. But the mood is destroyed the next morning as Africans round up other Africans for their colonial bosses. Domingos' imprisonment is the beginning of the education of both Maria and the viewer.

Maria has no idea of her husband's political activity. She even goes to the wrong prison because she is certain he would not be held with the political prisoners. At the same time that she undertakes her search for Domingos, his capture is noted by members of the underground who watch the prison and try to identify those who have been interred. As the film follows the searchers, the audience learns about the revolutionary movement through its members. Both Maria and the audience learn political divisions are not the same as racial divisions. Africans and Europeans torture Domingos. Africans and Europeans share jobs in the revolutionary movement. As a tailor explains to those who come to listen while he works, the real divisions are between rich and poor, and these divisions are universal. The growth in Maria's understanding and the search for information about Domingos help alleviate the horror of his torture. If his graphic suffering is still startling for those who have not seen the effects of this activity on the individual, its intercutting with the searchers provides a more hopeful focus for the film.

Maldoror alternates the torture with scenes of Maria and of the revolutionaries because she has set this film in a historical past. She wants the events from the past to inspire the present. When Domingos finally dies without revealing any information, he is honored by his comrades both inside and outside the prison. The prisoners wipe off his battered face as they speak of their friendship and how they will never forget him. Maria cries when she learns the news, but the women around her tell her she must stop crying and take care of her child. While death is honored, the future cannot be ignored. Plans continue for a party that is part of the plans for the immediate future. Domingos is mourned at the dance. He has died a true nationalist, and he will live forever in the hearts of the Angolan people. The film ends with plans for the first major effort of the revolution, the storming of the Luanda prison on February 4, 1961.

Just as she alternates torture and hope in her story, visually Maldoror alternates shots of Maria that isolate her from the background with shots of the militants that emphasize communal action. She is often shot with a telephoto lens, which flattens the background behind her and has the added effect of making her trip seem even more lengthy. Motion is extended through the use of this lens, and it seems people travel much longer to reach a goal. But she too gradually finds a community of women in Luanda who help her and educate her. Society becomes increasingly important in *Sambizanga* until, by the end of the film, the full extent of the organization is suggested at the party. While revolutionaries may often operate alone or in small numbers, a large organization is necessary for the kind of change that will expel a colonial power. The end of the film lets the viewer believe such a change is possible with its increased emphasis on group action: the reaction of his fellow prisoners toward Domingos' bloody corpse and the actions of the militants at the social function, which is a cover for their political activities.

Maldoror does not disguise her political goals in *Sambizanga*, but she places her message within a strong narrative that reflects the realities of African life. The film, like many others, also relives a lost moment in African history. For a continent whose history has only been told from the point of view of the invader, the recapturing of the past is an ongoing project. Maldoror also does what directors like Ousmane Sembene* have also done, reclaim the role of women in this history. The film is a call to action, but even after the revolution it remains a moving testament to the difficult and painful project of the elimination of colonial rule. The film was awarded the Tanit d'Or and Catholic Office prize at the 1972 Carthage Film Festival.

Bibliography

Diawara, Manthia. *African Cinema: Politics and Culture*. Bloomington: Indiana UP, 1992.

Hennebelle, Guy. "Sambizanga" and "Entretien avec Sarah Maldoror." *Ecran* (May 1973): 69–71.

Malkmus, Lizbeth, and Roy Armes. *Arab and African Film Making*. London: Zed Books, 1991.

Ukadike, Nwachukwu Frank. *Black African Cinema*. Berkeley: U of California P, 1994.

Sango Malo/ The Village Teacher (1991: Bassek ba Kobhio, Cameroon).
Two different approaches to education are the focus of this film. Opposing
views of teaching serve as a focus for an examination of the lingering
effects of colonialism and the need for change, which is tempered by an
understanding of the force of tradition. Many African films provide examples of how the residue of colonialism distorts the educational system.
In *Keïta,** the teacher concentrates on European history and languages,
and the students learn nothing about their own past. Bassek ba Kobhio,
the director, believes lasting change can only come about with a change
in the education of the young. But the director also recognizes that not
all ideas can be altered quickly. Arrogance is not just a quality associated
with colonial attitudes. In examining both sides of the educational system,
Sango Malo should teach the Western viewer not to assume that the imposition of liberal values across the culture is always positive. Anyone who
comes into a community must be willing to compromise and learn even if
such a person comes to effect change.

The film begins with the introduction of the new teacher who is assigned
to a village school. Malo's arrival in the village generates a great deal of
interest among the people. The simplicity of his quarters establishes the
lifestyle he will be expected to maintain. The villagers are also interested
in him as a single man who is a potential husband. Malo's first day generates controversy. The headmaster criticizes him for not maintaining iron
discipline. When he is told he must present himself to the village chief, he
stays with his students. Malo combines work with education and connects
his lessons to their lives. By not showing the proper respect to the authority of the chief and the headmaster, he angers both of them. The
headmaster does not understand why the students should work. The new
teacher knows it is important to make connections between education and
life and wants them to learn work-related tasks that relate more directly
to their needs. The headmaster is only concerned that they pass their
exams.

The conflict between the headmaster and the new teacher becomes a
test of two views of the direction modern Africa should take. The teacher
wants the students to learn how to think for themselves, and he wants
their education to be connected to their lives. The headmaster wants them
to master a body of knowledge that will prepare them for life in the city
or in the Eurocentric world outside of the continent. A visiting airline
steward who shares his views of the United States—the site of pop music
and hamburgers—and Paris—the gourmet land of wine and cheese—with
villagers who have never experienced what he calls good wine as compared
with palm wine illustrates the differences in the two approaches. The new
teacher wins over the students because he connects with their lives, especially when he teaches them about their exploitation by the local shopkeeper. He helps them set up their own cooperative to circumvent his

excesses. The headmaster see this as an example of the teacher's communist tendencies and refuses to abandon his own methods of dictation and rote learning about France.

While the new teacher's methods are attractive to his students, the headmaster and others in the village continue to resist. The shopkeeper, whose business is ruined by the cooperative, goes to the city, brings back prostitutes, and turns his store into a nightclub. Malo is recalled to the head office to explain his position. He refuses to become involved with politics; he wants to serve the people not the government. He must deal with the conflict between dreams and reality. He decides to stay in the village no matter what controversy he creates. Another new teacher arrives in the village. She is a student teacher from the area. She begins by repeating the headmaster's style with a dictation lesson, but she then takes the students out into the natural world. Malo falls in love with her and wants to marry her, but he refuses to pay, as custom dictates, for a feast and dowry. He does not care what others think as he opposes these traditions.

The refusal to observe marriage customs is the first example of the conflict Malo generates by his total allegiance to modern methods. He wants the village to create a collective plantation in their sacred forest. He can only see the potential for cooperative growth, but he does not understand the ritual significance of such a space in their lives. While Malo is innovative in his desire to take his classes outside into the real world, he can only see the natural world as another classroom. He also is too self-impressed to understand that he must recognize what the villagers want, not just what he thinks they want. Many people do change their attitudes. His wife teaches the women to count. The headmaster begins to see the value in Malo's approach and decides the world is too complicated and plans his retirement. The village dropout, a drunk who became an alcoholic when his entire family was killed, joins the cooperative. But the attempt to work in the sacred forest goes beyond what the village wants, and Malo who has become too arrogant is arrested and sent to prison. The villagers have learned much from him and are able to continue the cooperative without his leadership. Even though he will be in prison, his life will continue through his wife who is pregnant.

Sango Malo presents a complex view of how a country like Cameroon can move forward without abandoning its past. The film critiques the pretensions of those who think being modern means becoming like the former colonial power. This side believes important knowledge, which will ensure the economic future of the people, is tied to Western technology and European history and values. An alternate view introduces the innovative idea that education should be directly related to the needs of the people who are to be educated. Those who hold this position believe it is critical for citizens to learn how to think and act on their own. While the film is clearly on the side of this more radical view of education, it also recognizes the importance of retaining ties to the past. Learning, which makes no connection with tradition, can lead to an education that loses contact with important lessons from the past. The sacred forest is part of a relationship with the earth that goes beyond its economic exploitation. The film condemns arrogance on every side. True progress comes from working with the people and giving them control over their own lives.

Bibliography

Akudinobi, Jude. "Tradition/ Modernity and the Discourse of African Cinema." *IRIS* 18 (Spring 1995): 25–37.

SEMBENE, OUSMANE (Ziguinchor, Senegal, 1923). Ousmane Sembene is the best known and most influential of sub-Saharan African filmmakers. As a result of his parent's divorce, he spent his childhood with various members of his family. His father was not upset when Sembene quit the French school he was attending because the boy hit back when a teacher slapped him. Sembene practiced a number of different trades such as automobile mechanics and carpentry. He also worked with his father as a fisherman. He was drafted at the beginning of World War II and served in the French army in both Europe and Africa. He worked in France after the war in an automobile factory and became involved in a trade union. Much of his early life became the source for his fiction and films. His first book, *Le docker noire/ The Black Docker*, was published in 1956 and was based on his experiences as a dock worker in France. Subsequent novels continue to explore both personal and historic events, but the focus is always on the effects of colonialism. With *Les bouts de bois de Dieu/ God's Bits of Wood* (1960), Sembene turns to another theme that will also become central to his cinematic work: the role of women in the struggle for freedom.

When Senegal achieved independence in 1960, Sembene continued to present the conflicts that he sees as creating problems for both the individual and the state. At the same time he continued to write, Sembene decided to work in film to reach those large numbers of Africans who could not read. He went to Moscow and studied at the Gorky Film Studio. His first film, *L'empire Songhaï/ The Songhaï Empire* (1963), a documentary funded by the Republic of Mali, has never been released. His next film, *Borom Sarret/ Le charrier* (1963), is considered by many to be the first professionally produced African film. This short deals with a day in the life of a cart driver in Dakar. In a French voice-over narration, the central character describes his day and the confiscation of his cart when he enters a part of the city that used to be reserved for the colonists but now is inhabited by a new African elite. This work demonstrates the way Sembene transfers his literary concerns to film, but this early film also indicates the difficulty of presenting authentic African experiences for the masses while still being economically tied to a French language narration.

In his next film, Sembene turns to the position of women in the community. *Niaye* (1964) is narrated in French by the village griot who tells the story of a girl made pregnant by her father. The story is set in the colonial period. The villagers try to hide the scandal from the French. Sembene's first feature film, *La Noire de . . . / Black Girl** (1966), combines his interest in women's roles with his concerns abut postcolonial Africa. In this work he exposes the attitudes of the French employers of a Senegalese woman and how their treatment of her and her growing sense of isolation lead to her suicide. The central character's inability to make her employers understand her feelings is mirrored by the sound track that features a voice-over presentation of her thoughts.

Sembene continues to examine the postcolonial situation in his country with the novel *Le mandat, précédé de Véhi-Ciosane/ The Money Order, with White Genesis* (1966). This is also the first novel that he translated into a cinematic work, *Mandabi/ Le mandat/ The Money Order* (1968). This film also marks the first use of the native language, Wolof, in Sembene's work, and his first full film in color. Even though he still had problems with finances, he shot the film in two versions, French and Wolof. His story of the illiterate villager, Ibrahima Dieng, whose nephew in Paris sends him a money order, exposes the gaps between classes that exist in postcolonial Senegal. Even the imam tries to get money from this poor man who can find no one who will cash his gift. Sembene demonstrates the effect of greed on all elements of Senegalese life, especially those whose jobs should involve them in the lives of the people they choose to exploit rather than serve.

While his next film deals with everyday life in Dakar, the seventies marks the emergence of Sembene as major feature film director. *Tauw* (1970), Sembene's last short film, deals with the problem of unemployment in the life of a young dockworker who also tries to provide for his pregnant girlfriend. The following year Sembene directed *Emitai/ Dieu du tonnerre/ God of Thunder** (1971). In this production he finally gets the opportunity to explore many of the themes that have been so important to him in a major film. *Emitai* is the true story of a village that is forced to give both men and rice to the French during World War II. The women of the village rebel, and the French respond with a massacre. Sembene reclaims a piece of lost history at the same time that he restores women to positions of importance in African society. In *Xala/ L'impuissance temporaire/ The Curse** (1974), he turns to contemporary comedy to continue his critique of postcolonial Senegal. A businessman displays his wealth by taking a third wife. He is cursed with impotence by a beggar he has mistreated. The film focuses on the continued presence of colonial structures that have been adopted by the Senegalese bourgeoisie and are the real curse of modern life in this country. *Ceddo**(1976) reaches back into the past to demonstrate the foreign roots of Senegal's religious institutions. The ceddo are a class of society that resists conversion to Islam. They attempt to enforce their resistance by kidnapping the daughter of the king who has already converted. Sembene assumes a very controversial position when he demonstrates that Islam is not native to Africa and is, instead, another example of colonialism. The film was banned in Senegal.

Camp de Thiaroye/ Camp Thiaroye* (1988, co-directed with Thierno Faty Sow), also deals with an event from Senegal's colonial past. Like *Emitai*, whose massacre is also an element in this film, *Camp de Thiaroye* traces the results of accelerating confrontations between the Senegalese and the French. African soldiers who have just returned from service and, in some cases, incarceration in German POW camps protest their treatment by the French as they wait to be processed out of a demobilization camp outside of Dakar. The men are betrayed by the French who put down their protest by bringing in tanks to level the camp and kill the mutineers. *Guelwaar** (1992), Sembene's most recent film, combines the historical reality of his films about events during World War II with the comic attack on present-day life of *Xala*. As with his other films dealing with contemporary African life, he shows that independence has not solved all of the problems created by the colonial experience. Pierre Henri Thioune, a Christian activist who protests over dependence on foreign aid is killed and the body is mistakenly buried in a Muslim cemetery. The complex negotiations necessary to retrieve the body illustrate many of the problems in Senegalese society. Sembene also uses this incident to reiterate his points about how both religions are part of colonialism.

Thematically, Sembene's films deal with the director's concerns about Senegalese society, the legacy of colonialism, the role of women, the importance of the group, and the hope for the future. In addition to his development of these social and political problems, Sembene also explores ways of making films that reflect African life in their narrative organization. Rather than emulating Hollywood suspense techniques, he attempts to reproduce the linear structure of the tales of the griot, who maintains the oral tradition by telling stories that focus on time and place and introduce the past through flashbacks. Sembene's films also reflect the pace of African life. The village films move at a slower speed than those situated in the faster moving city. While he turned to film to teach his audience about their history and reveal the problems in their current society, Sembene, the artist, developed a style that genuinely reproduces his world.

Filmography

L'empire Songhaï/ The Songhaï Empire (1963)

Borom Sarret/ Le charrier (1963)

Niaye (1964)

La Noire de . . . / Black Girl (1966), Jean Vigo Prize for Direction

Mandabi/ Le mandat/ The Money Order (1968)

Polygamie (1969)

Problème de l'emploi (1969)

Tauw (1970)

Emitai/ Dieu du tonnerre/ God of Thunder (1971), Silver Medal Moscow Film Festival

The Munich Olympics (1971), part of a collective film

Xala/ L'impuissance temporaire/ The Curse (1974)

Ceddo (1976)

Camp de Thiaroye/ Camp Thiaroye (1988, co-directed with Thierno Faty Sow)

Guelwaar (1992)

Bibliography

Diawara, Manthia. *African Cinema: Politics and Culture.* Bloomington: Indiana UP, 1992.

Gadjigo, Samba, Ralph Faulkingham, Thomas Cassirer, and Reinhard Sander, eds. *Ousmane Sembene: Dialogues with Critics and Writers.* Amherst: U of Massachusetts P, 1993.

Ghali, Noureddine. "An Interview with Sembene Ousmane." *Film & Politics in The Third World.* Ed. John D. H. Downing. New York: Praeger, 1986, 41–54.

Malkmus, Lizbeth, and Roy Armes. *Arab and African Film Making.* London: Zed Books, 1991.

Shiri, Keith, comp. and ed. *Directory of African Films.* Westport, Conn.: Greenwood P, 1992.

Ukadike, Nwachukwu Frank. *Black African Cinema.* Berkeley: U of California P, 1994.

The Silences of the Palace/ Les silences du palais/ Çoumt al-Quçour (1994: Moufida Tlatli, Tunisia). A woman director, Moufida Tlatli examines a subject that has been largely overlooked by the filmmaking community, the lives of women who work in a closed world. She moves smoothly back and forth between the past and the present, ten years later, as she details the story of Alia who grew up in the palace of the beys, Tunisia's royal family of rulers, during the period of the end of French control in the fifties. While *The Silences of the Palace* is her first feature film, Tlatli—who was educated in France—has spent many years as a film editor in Tunisia. As Amy Taubin indicates, Tlatli made this film as a way of exploring her mother's life and death. She nursed her mother during the illness of her last five years. Once Tlatli's mother became ill she never spoke again. When women of *The Silences* speak they rarely express their true thoughts. Their bantering exchanges and frequent arguments mask their true feelings. Their hidden world is the center of the film. The conflicts that lead to Tunisia's independence occur at the edges of the palace kitchen where they congregate. As the film demonstrates, women's lives are not changed by independence. *The Silences* moves back and forth between the past and the present to show how Alia's current dilemmas are based on the events that took place in the palace. The closed society of beys reverberates into the modern world. For Alia there is no postcolonial world.

The film opens with a close-up of Alia's face as she sings. The camera pans around the room where men and women sit at separate tables. Her head hurts. She leaves the stage, puts on her coat and goes to a waiting car. The moment she enters the car the reality of her life is evident. The man who waits is impatient because she is late. When they discuss the usual harassment she experiences in her job he reassures her. No one will really harm her because she is with him. But being with him does not mean being married to him, and her tenuous situation is leading to yet another abortion. She cannot have a child because they are not married. Her lover is the one who pushes her toward the abortion. While the complex connections between mothers and children form the central theme of the film, Alia's long-term but barren love affair with Lotfi is actually the most positive male-female relationship in the work. Lotfi insists on the abortion because a child must have a name and a family. The lack of a last name, a real sense of father and family have haunted Alia all of her life. The connection between her present dilemma and her past is made when Lotfi tells her Houssine came by to tell her Sidi Ali has died. She is overwhelmed by the memories of the palace and the horrifying night when she left ten years earlier. The rest of the film retraces the steps leading to her flight and the effect of her early life on the present.

The next day Alia returns to the palace to pay a condolence call. While the people are important elements of her reclaiming of her past, the actual spaces she revisits—the rooms of the palace, the kitchen and bedrooms of the servants' quarters, the gardens—embody the class and gender relationships that controlled her youth. She greets Jneina, the childless widow of Sidi Ali, and Sarra, the daughter of Sidi Ali's brother who was born the same night as Alia. She moves downstairs to the servants' quarters to see Khalta Hadda, mother of Houssine, and Alia's mother's oldest friend in the palace. As they talk about the day Alia was born and how happy Sidi Ali was, the film shifts to the first of many flashbacks to life in the palace. Both Ali and his brother pace the floor. First the film shows Sarra's mother giving birth and then moves from the grandeur of the palace to Khedija's labor with Alia. In the first scene, the husband enters and holds his new daughter. In the second, Ali walks outside the room. His concern for Alia is joined to his inability to acknowledge her. The greatest silence in the film is connected to Khedija's cries as she gives birth to Alia. Alia can never get anyone to actually say the words that will reveal her father's identity. No one will say she is Sidi Ali's child.

Aside from one brief scene of her as a young child receiving a gold necklace she wears throughout the film, the rest of *The Silences* moves between a period of time in her early adolescence and the present of the film. She and Sarra share a friendship, but the gulf between them is marked by a musical instrument. Sarra takes lessons on her lute. Alia loves music but can only secretly borrow her friend's instrument. For a servant to have a lute places her in danger. As she takes it away one day she is threatened with a sexual look by Sarra's brother. The lute is connected to Alia's voice. She sings beautifully, but her voice also places her in danger. It brings her to the attention of the men of the palace. When she goes upstairs to sing for them, she moves into the world where female servants must be available whenever the men desire them, the world where servants have no lives and do not own their own bodies. Khedija has already been trapped by the beys. Her relationship with Sidi Ali seems to give her some privileges, such as Alia's freedom to associate with Sarra, but Khedija is not protected from a violent sexual attack by Sidi Ali's brother, which takes place in her room in front of her not quite sleeping daughter.

The complex connections between masters and servants are exacerbated by the closed world of the palace. The outside only intrudes through news on the radio, Houssine's experiences on the streets of Tunis, and Lotfi (Houssine's friend and tutor to Sarra and her brothers) who must take refuge in the palace to avoid arrest. During Lotfi's stay he forms a relationship with Alia that culminates in their leaving together on the night of her mother's death. Even though Lotfi is a representative of the new world that will liberate Tunisia, he still speaks for the patriarchy. While he is more concerned for Alia than Sidi Ali was for her mother, Khedija, he too will not give their child a name. Khedija dies during her attempt to abort yet another child of the masters of the palace. But her death scream does not break the silence. Alia encounters it when she returns and Khalta Hadda refuses to confirm her suspicions about the identity of her father. She states the one rule of the palace: silence. But in a voice-over commentary at the end of the film Alia finally breaks the silence. She speaks of her connection to her mother, the suffering they have shared. Alia sees her life as a series of abortions, of still-born songs, of a lack of self-expression. She decides to have the child she is carrying. She sees her choice as a means of reaffirming her connection to her mother. But she will choose to live openly with a child, and her child will know about the past. Alia hopes her child will be a girl, and she plans to call her Khedija. Alia gives a voice to the silences of the palace by giving a name from the past to her child. This film was given a special jury mention and the Camera d'Or at the Cannes Film Festival.

Bibliography

Armes, Roy. *Dictionary of North African Film Makers*. Paris: Editions ATM, 1996.
Bouzid, Nouri. "Our Inspiration." *African Experiences of Cinema*. Ed. Imruh Bakari and Mbye Cham. London: British Film Institute, 1996. 48–59.
Taubin, Amy. "Speak, Memory." *Village Voice*, 16 April 1996: 78.

T

Ta Dona/ Fire! (1991: Adama Drabo, Mali). While many recent African films deal with the problems of modern life, *Ta Dona* uses a blend of magic and realism to examine the possible solutions to an ecological crisis. Rather than setting up the usual opposition of country and city, government and people, tradition and modern life, this film demonstrates the need for various people to cooperate. The central character comes out of the modern world. Sidy works for the Ministry of Rivers and Forests as an agronomist. He is aware that his knowledge can help the villagers he lives with, but he is also willing to learn from them and embrace traditional healing methods. Adama Drabo, the director, also accepts both worlds in his presentation of the narrative. He moves back and forth between the realism of daily life, the struggle of the country and the corruption of the city, and the supernatural events that can occur in any setting. Drabo's film argues for a world where everyone can have value and where both past and present can work together for the future.

The film sets up its various points of view early in its presentation. The contrast between Sidy on a bicycle, which is friendly to the environment, and bosses in large cars establishes its ecological position. Sidy is also looking for an important Bambara herbal cure, the seventh *canari*, and part of the film traces his quest for this almost lost part of his cultural heritage. *Ta Dona* also shows wives of officials exploiting craftsmen, officials planning reforestation without any regard for the needs of the people or the land. As one of the character states, "A goat among the hyenas has to howl or it will get eaten." Sidy and others realize that conditions must change. They have to take risks and become active in the transformation of their society.

While high officials divide illegal money and plan new villas, Sidy works with the villagers to restore the land that is suffering from drought. He also learns by participating in the rituals of the community. But the villagers have found that tradition is not always effective. The offering of a sheep to the marabouts, religious teachers, for rain did not work the previous year, and the harvest was almost lost. Many doubt the bull-calf offered now will be any more effective. The government hierarchy does not understand the workings of the land. Taxes make the villagers' situation even worse as does the ban on brush fires. These traditional fires burn off the useless vegetation, encourage new growth, and discourage wild animals. But the government imprisons those who set them and fines their villages. The ordinary people see the officials as an extension of the colonizers who ruled with the whip. One villager in desperation tries to set a fire, but it is found and extinguished. Ironically, an official who arrives in a car throws a cigar into the brush and really starts the cleansing fire. Sidy is ordered to find the person responsible. Luckily someone has photographs of how the fire was started.

In addition to the problems in the village, Sidy is involved in his quest for the seventh *canari*, which is needed for its medicinal properties to heal his future mother-in-law's mysterious illness. Armed with symbols such as bracelets that magically appear and fit together, he sets out for the land of the Dogon. He finally finds a very old woman, a midwife who never had children. She supplies the secret medicine created from a plant, passing on her knowledge before she dies. Sidy's experience demonstrates the close connection between the natural and the supernatural when the ties to tradition are maintained.

Meanwhile, the political corruption continues. Even an anticorruption movement is taken over by the very officials it is to investigate. Token changes will be made to avoid any significant alteration in their lifestyles. Friends sacrifice allies to save themselves. Sidy's medicine is effective. He cures his girlfriend's mother, but their future is uncertain. Her father is one of those accused of corruption. Sidy can make a difference in individual lives, but the film leaves the viewer with the idea that the true transformation of the society can only come about through radical activity. The thieves who run the country must be thrown out instead of the prosecution of a few to save the others. In fact, soon after the film's opening in Mali, there was an uprising that deposed the dictator, Moussa Traoré. One of the most corrupt officials in the film is named Samou Traoré as a reference to this man.

Ta Dona deals with serious issues about life in Mali. But in his depiction of the world of the village Drabo presents moments of humor. He also shows the ongoing cycle of life and death, which is connected to the land and its rituals in this community. The community in the village also represents a world where people attempt to remain in harmony with the land.

Drabo does not suggest that all tradition is good, and he also demonstrates the need for the kind of scientific knowledge Sidy brings with him to correct the problems created by abuse of the land. But he shows how those who have taken over from the colonizers have adopted their attitudes toward consumer goods. Their vision of progress leads to lifestyles that cannot be sustained in countries with poverty and limited resources. Drabo questions the blind acceptance of Western values and posits instead a path that combines the best of the traditional and modern worlds. The film also unites the real and the magical in its use of cinema as a medium that can present both worlds in the same image, a union that mirrors the connection between past and present in modern Africa.

Three Tales From Senegal (*Le Franc*, 1994, Djibril Diop Mambety*; *Picc Mi/ Little Bird*, 1992, Mansour Sora Wade; *Fary l'Anesse/ Fary the Donkey*, 1989, Mansour Sora Wade; Senegal). This compilation unites three recent short films from Senegal united by their presentation of the interaction of the real and the magical in everyday life. They are also joined in their adaptation of the oral tradition to cinema. Even though they share many elements, each film is also a unique statement about modern African life. The first film also provides insight into the films of one of Senegal's most experimental directors. The two remaining films introduce a less well-known director's work.

Le Franc is the longest and most complex of the three tales. Djibril Diop Mambety is best known for his two feature films, *Touki Bouki** (1973) and *Hyènes** (1992). This film is part of a trilogy of shorts called *Histoires des petits gens/ Stories of Little People*. In this story he combines the general effect of the French government's devaluation of the West African franc on the people with a magical and comical tale of one man's struggle to survive. This story can also be seen as a parable of world economy where the poor are forced to play a similar lottery to the one the central character enters. His win is magical; in the real world the odds are definitely not in favor of the poor and their countries.

Marigo, the hero, is behind in his rent and at the mercy of his landlady who has taken his one joy, a *congoma*, a guitar-like homemade instrument, until he pays his back rent. When a lottery winner drops some money as he purchases a ticket, Marigo grabs it. The dwarf who sells tickets sees Marigo's good fortune and convinces him to buy a lottery ticket. The dwarf is identified with Kus, the god of fortune. He warns Marigo to guard the ticket well, and Margio returns to his house and pastes it to the inside of his door, placing a poster of his hero, Yaadikoone Ndiaye, a legendary Senegalese Robin Hood figure, over it. Marigo's activities seem to exist on a realistic level even though his movements and gestures are often exaggerated for comic effect. Once his ticket actually wins, magic and realism blend in the film. He removes the door to take it to the lottery office. His journey provides a realistic vision of the disparity between the poor sections of the city and the large office buildings in the distance. Marigo's trip is intercut with images of his alter ego who wears a costume and appears in various locations playing the *congoma*. His comic journey ends at the lottery office where he is told the ticket must be removed from the door because of the control number on the back. Marigo is dejected until he thinks of taking the door to the sea. As he staggers toward the water, the *congoma* player appears as a mystical figure on a boat. Once the door falls into the sea and Marigo struggles to find the ticket, the figure on the boat passes by in more realistic colors. The film ends with two different visions of Marigo, one splashing in the water happy to have found his ticket, the other making heroic poses on the beach.

The director's style perfectly conveys the content of this film. Except for the images of the *congoma* player in the boat, he uses realistic techniques to present both the real and the magical. But his realistic style is filled with camera movements, abrupt cuts, point of view shots, and images that must take place in the character's mind. Rather than the seamless technique which foregrounds the story and hides the artifice so favored by Hollywood, Mambety uses the tools of cinema such as sound, editing, shot selection, and color, which separate the film world from the real world. In his films, the magic of his view of life is matched by his use of the magic of the camera. He uses the art of cinema to recapture of the art of the storyteller.

Mansour Sora Wade's two films also combine fantasy and reality, but his world is concerned with the traditional magic of transformation and the blurring of identities as characters are changed into animals. He presents his films with a combination of synchronous and voice-over narration to convey the world of the storyteller. The films also use traditional fables as their base.

Picc Mi/Little Bird uses the story of the crocodile who tries to tempt the baby bird from the nest in the absence of its mother to examine the life of poor children. The tale is both told and sung at key moments as the film follows Modou, a young boy who has been given to a marabout by his mother. The Muslim teacher or holy man sends his charges out to beg each day. Modou meets Ablaye when he falls for the boy's cripple act and helps him across the street. Ablaye scavenges for his father who has lost his farm because of the drought. The boys explore the city together. At one point they watch a bird seller. A customer comes, and the seller discards one dead bird. The customer uses the live one as an offering in a ritual against bad luck. The boys note the captive birds are afraid. The crocodile song underscores the lives of the boys. As Modou returns to the marabout who asks for the money the boy has begged, the tale recounts how the bird is hungry and tired and so is the crocodile who wants to eat him. The next morning Modou runs along the edge of the sea. He stops for a moment and is transformed into a bird that flies away.

Fary l'Anesse/Fary the Donkey also ends with a human changing into a animal. But in *Picc Mi* the transformation can be seen as wish fulfillment. In *Fary* the opposite is true. Fary is a donkey because Ibra has an unreasonable desire. This film is set in an undefined past. Ibra, the hero, is introduced as a man who wants a perfect woman for his wife. The smallest blemish makes the candidate unacceptable. A voice-over narration sets the tone as "once upon at time." The camera pans across an expanse of water, settling on a figure, Fary, who walks toward it, the perfect beautiful woman. As in any magical tale, the hero marries the beautiful woman and all goes well for a while. One day the town womanizer follows Fary as she delivers Ibra's lunch in the field. He watches as she transforms herself into a donkey. Word of his discovery races through the village. Finally Ibra sees the truth for himself. He forces her transformation that night. At first Fary grows donkey ears, and then a donkey leaves Ibra's home. The film ends with a moral about men who fall in love with beauty forgetting a woman's other qualities. The narrator questions whether things have changed since Ibra's time.

While Wade uses fables to comment on modern life, his films are not as complex as those of Mambety. Wade makes simple correlations between the specific and the general, the bird and the boy for example. His magic is limited to character transformation. Wade's style is effective in presenting his story. He represents the oral tradition through traditional fables, songs, and voice-over narrations. While the ending of *Picc Mi* may be seen as either fantasy or imagination, the viewer is not lead to believe Modou has really escaped any more than the audience thinks Fary becomes a donkey in a real world. Mambety's use of magic is more complex. The boundaries between worlds in his films are constantly blurring. The viewer seeks for clues as to what is real and what is part of the film's fantasy. Each viewer may have a different perception of how the film operates and exactly what it means. Mambety actively involves the viewer in the creative process. The audience tries to anticipate but is continually surprised in his films. The viewer often must wait for several clues before a piece of the narrative is clear. Mambety extends the magic of the griot to the telling of the story and the attitude of the viewer. *Le Franc* won the Gold Tanit award at the 1994 Carthage Film Festival.

Tilaï/ A Question of Honor (1990: Idrissa Ouedraogo, Burkina Faso). *Tilaï* examines the tragic consequences of rigid adherence to certain aspects of the Moré tradition. Unlike many films that directly attack what are seen as outmoded customs, Idrissa Ouedraogo, the director, presents a poetic narrative of a society on the verge of change. The film shows the viewer individuals who reject any change and those who cannot obey the restrictions their society places on them. Ouedraogo deals with society on the level of the individual and the small village. While the director is clearly on the side of change, he leaves the job of generalizing how change might operate on a scale larger than that of his film to others. The beautiful photography demonstrates a real love of the lifestyle of the village. The problem does not lie with simple customs but rather with those who hold onto the past with a fanatical fervor.

The first image of the film introduces the central character Saga, but, in a foreshadowing of the ending, he rides away from the camera and finally disappears from view. The next shot has him coming toward the camera. He descends and looks down on the village below him. He ceremonially blows a horn three times to announce his presence and claim his place back in the village. People come out to see who is approaching. Immediately there are suggestions that his arrival may create problems. His brother Kougri tells Nogma not to worry because Saga will understand. Kougri goes to meet his brother and is forced to explain that their father has married Nogma. Nogma's father had promised her to Saga before he left, but changed his mind. Saga turns his back on the village after this news. Nogma looks out, obviously still in love with Saga.

The scene shifts to night; many of the most moving events in the film take place in the dark when complex relationships can develop in secret. Saga visits his mother and explains that he must leave because of his father. When he leaves her hut he hears Nogma singing softly to herself. When she says his name he walks away. The world of the village looks different in daylight. Kougri and his mother discuss the problem with Saga. At this point Kougri is torn between his love of his brother and his father. The father is rigid throughout the narrative and refuses to make any conciliatory gesture toward his son. Meanwhile Saga begins repairing an abandoned hut outside the village. Whenever he is in a village setting he is engaged in the construction of a house, an action that demonstrates his desire for a real home. In this village it is made of straw. Later in his aunt's village, he begins a brick house for Nogma and their future child. Nogma and her sister, Kuiga, discover Saga as they go to get water. In another night scene Kuiga waits while her sister makes love with Saga. They admit their love for each other. But such an affair is soon discovered by members of the small community.

Adultery cannot be tolerated. Nogma is tied up so she cannot warn Saga. In another nighttime scene, the men of the village draw straws. Kougri gets the short straw and must kill his brother. The men move through the village by the light of torches. When Kougri goes into the hut he pretends to kill Saga and makes him promise to leave and never come back to the village. Kougri burns the house that hides the evidence of his failure to kill his brother. Nogma's father is so shamed by her actions that he hangs himself. The others see his action as a question of honor; only

Kougri is disturbed by it. Kougri's refusal to kill his brother Saga is his first act that goes against tradition. The extremes to which custom forces those who believe disturb viewers as well as some of the members of his family who are relieved with his solution to his dilemma.

In daylight, the film traces Saga's long and difficult journey to his aunt's village. The original village sends out riders to locate him, but they come back without finding him. Saga's aunt is thrilled with his arrival. Once Nogma learns that her lover is alive she sets out to find him. Even though she has a brief affair with a man on the way, Saga welcomes her. Their life together in the new village is the only idyllic segment of the film. The entire village is enchanted by their love, and the aunt is even more pleased when she learns of Nogma's pregnancy. But their happiness cannot survive the pressures of their family obligations. Nogma sadly accepts the absence of her mother and sister aided by the aunt's love. Saga cannot stop himself from returning home when he learns of his mother's serious illness. When the others learn where he has gone they follow.

Once again Saga approaches the village. He looks down and sees his mother's funeral procession. He announces his presence with his horn, but this time his brother does not come to greet him. While Kuiga tells her mother things are going to get really difficult, Saga runs down to embrace his mother's body. Kougri states he was not to come back, even though he was the one who sent word to his brother of her illness. Saga explains he had no choice because of his love for his mother. His father tells him not to touch her. As Saga puts his arms around her, the father banishes Kougri who gets a gun, shoots his brother in the back, and walks off. The film cuts to a close-up of the father and a shot of Kuiga and her mother. In a long shot Nogma and the aunt walk toward the village. Kougri passes them without acknowledging their presence. Realizing something is wrong, the two women run toward the village.

The tragic end of the story is a profound illustration of the effect of strict adherence to the rules of a social order. The film does not condemn the simple life of the village, just its resistance to change. The agents of change are the young people who cannot understand why unreasonable laws should be obeyed. Kuiga spends most of her time observing others and trying to figure out the logic of adult behavior. The older siblings fight with their own desires and the decisions of their parents. Among the older adults, the men are the worst. Saga's father indulges his own desires with no concern for anyone else. Nogma's father blames his wife for everything their children do but finally succumbs to others by committing suicide to save his honor. While no character is able to survive outside of a community, the film suggests the need for individuals to take charge of their own lives and make their own decisions. Ouedraogo also points out the difference between the father's repressive village and the aunt's more free and loving one. Men may make the decisions and be the agents of change, but one element of that change is the role of women. As the world of the village adjusts to the desires of its youth, women will begin to have a greater role in the control of their lives. *Tilaï* won the Special Jury Prize at the 1990 Cannes Film Festival and the Grand Prize at FESPACO.

Bibliography

Diawara, Manthia. *African Cinema: Politics and Culture.* Bloomington: Indiana, UP 1992.

Ukadike, Nwachukwu Frank. *Black African Cinema.* Berkeley: U of California P, 1994.

Touki Bouki/ Le voyage de l'hyène/ ***The Journey of the Hyena*** (1973: Djibril Diop Mambety,* Senegal). *Touki Bouki* is a remarkable film that challenges both Western and African cinematic traditions. Mambety uses a simple story of the relationship between two young people as the framework for a complex study of cultural values in postcolonial situations. While some critics see in the film an extension of the film techniques pioneered by French filmmakers in the sixties, other argue that its particular perspective is uniquely African. *Touki Bouki*'s natural incorporation of magic and ritual into the narrative certainly places it with other films from the continent. Even the jump cuts and radical spatial shifts can be seen as adaptations of the oral tradition. As Lizbeth Malkmus and Roy Armes point out, the organization of space is expanded from mere realism to the inclusion of memories of the countryside and a vision of France. Community is introduced through the treatment of the secondary characters who are featured as the central characters pass through their lives (191). These authors also suggest that the disjunction of the narrative is contained by a thematically organized three-act structure that moves from love and death in the first, to various schemes to leave Senegal in the second, and the resolution of the first two with a possible arrest and final separation in the third (206).

The first image of the film is a key to what is to come. Cattle are lead to market by a small boy and then slaughtered. The film then cuts to a point of view shot of Mory, one of the central characters, riding his motorcycle through Dakar. The horns of the ox's skull, which Mory has attached to the front of his bike, connect this shot to the preceding one. The motorcycle ride reveals the contractions in a modern African city as Mory goes from slums to office buildings or rides by a mosque with an ancient Dogon symbol on the back of his cycle as prayers let out. He goes to pick up his friend Anta, whose ambiguous sexuality is only revealed as female in a scene where he makes love to her. In this sequence, suggestions of their sexual contact are intercut with shots of the slaughter of animals and waves, a series of images which convey what has happened without being explicit.

After establishing the relationship between the couple and the world around them, the narrative moves on to their attempts to fulfill their dream of leaving Africa and going to France, symbolized by French songs on the sound track. The couple attempts a variety of schemes to get money. They run off with the proceeds of a wrestling match only to find that they have a contestant's amulets. They then go to the home of Charlie, a homosexual, where they take his clothes and a wallet. As they leave they experience the fantasy of a parade through Dakar celebrating their triumphant return from Paris. Unfortunately, in reality Anta and Mory are pursued by the police for the theft of Charlie's things. They actually purchase tickets for a ship, the *Ancerville*, which will leave later that day. Mambety presents French people on the boat who make negative statements about Africans and their culture. These comments suggest that running away may not really be a solution. The Paris of their dreams has little to do with reality as is shown by the introduction of shots of animals being slaughtered. Anta decides to follow her dreams, and she gets on board. At the last moment Mory returns to the city. He is left with the broken skull from his motorcycle; the former shepherd has lost his bike and is left with a symbol of his former profession. The boat leaves with Anta. The film ends with the images that opened it: the herd of cattle.

The events that happen to the major characters are intercut with other smaller stories. A person waits for a letter from France, and the film tracks the mailman as he follows his daily routine. Other characters continue with their everyday jobs or the rituals that frame their lives. In addition, the film connects the couple to such characters as a wild white man who gets Mory's bike or the child who leads the herd. These characters contribute to the complexity of the film. Mory and Anta exist on the edges of a society that contains its own richness—a richness they ignore in their hurry to escape.

The film's complex visual organization forces the viewer into an interactive role. While the basic story is easily followed, the often-startling images, which are inserted into the narrative, require interpretation. The images as well as the events that surround them are important in an understanding of their role in the film. The slaughter of the animals can be seen as the destruction of Africa's resources to feed those who do not contribute to its development or as a symbol of a consumer society where the city despoils the countryside. The endless killing is contrasted with the ritual sacrifice of a goat, an action that maintains a connection to the traditions of the country. While Mory and Anta exist as outlaws outside of conventional society, their alienation is representative of their generation—a generation that has lost its ties to history and has found nothing to replace them. Anta thinks she can substitute the colonized dreams of Paris for her lost culture. Mory at the last moment returns to Dakar. This city represents similar sites across the continent. The film does not make overt didactic statements about postcolonial society. The connections arrive through the conjunctions of the images and the lifestyles of its youth. Like the hyenas that live on the fringes of the animal kingdom and exist as clever scavengers, Mory and Anta live off of the carcass of a dying society that must be revived if Africa is to have a positive future. *Touki Bouki* won the International Critic's Prize at the 1973 Moscow Film Festival.

Bibliography

Malkmus, Lizbeth, and Roy Armes. *Arab and African Film Making*. London: Zed Books, 1991.

Ukadike, Nwachukwu Frank. *Black African Cinema*. Berkeley: U of California P, 1994.

U

Udju Azul di Yonta/ The Blue Eyes of Yonta (1991: Flora Gomes, Guinea-Bissau) In Guinea-Bissau the fight for independence was a difficult and hard won battle as with other Portuguese colonies. In *The Blue Eyes of Yonta* Flora Gomes examines the result of the revolution in the lives of those who fought, as well as in the lives of their children who are the hope for the future. The film is also a story of generations: parents who fought for a better life but find it hard to accept the kind of lives their children want. The reality of everyday life in Bissau is contrasted with the dreams of both generations. Gomes uses what seems like a realistic style to tell this story, but at certain moments an image appears that takes the film beyond the real into the magical. These moments culminate in a final sequence that ends the film in the realm of fantasy.

The film opens with such a transition from the real to the magical. The camera moves along a road gradually entering the city of Bissau. *The Blue Eyes of Yonta* is full of such movement along roads. The characters' lives are all in motion; they restlessly reach destinations only to set out again. The camera follows a car that is driven by Vicente, one of the central characters. The scene shifts to what seems to be a race among a group of children. They take off down the road pushing tires decorated with various years written on their sides. The race comes to a stop when they almost run into a lumber truck at a crossroads. The angry driver is finally calmed by Vicente who recognizes Amilcar, the son of one of his former comrades, among the children. Amilcar introduces Vicente as one of the heroes of the revolution and explains to him that the tires are decorated with the year of independence, 1974, and the years after independence. Significantly, Amilcar's tire points to the future with the year 2000. This scene introduces two of the central characters at the same time that it establishes the complex connections between past and present.

The film intercuts Vicente taking Amilcar home with shots of Yonta, Amilcar's sister, and her friend, Mana. As they walk Yonta bumps into a young man, Zé. She does not really notice him, but he is attracted to her and later sends a love letter that he copies from a book about a Swedish girl. A phrase from this letter about the author's beloved's blue eyes becomes the source of the title of the film. The Westernization of modern life leads to Africans using European models for love letters and impossibly praising their loves' blue eyes. But Zé does not have much chance of success with Yonta who is dazzled by Vicente. Vicente has no idea of her interest because he either spends his time dealing with the problems of his business or thinking about the past. Vicente is the real focus of the film. He has just returned from a trip to Europe to confront a series of conflicts which raise questions about the impact of the revolution. While all of the major characters pursue some kind of dream, his is the most elusive.

The nature of these dreams and their pursuit forms the body of the film. Amilcar wants to be a football (soccer) player. His dream may not be realistic, but he knows he must spend time practicing in order to achieve it. His father wants to beat Vicente at draughts and has also been practicing. His mother, Belonte, the most grounded of the characters, wants her friend and neighbor, Mrs. Santas—whose husband has disappeared—to be able to retain her home. When her friend is evicted they consult a fortune teller, and Belonte forces the most positive reading possible of the cards. The eviction itself provides another magical moment in the film. All of Mrs. Santas' things are put out on the street in piles. Suddenly the camera returns to the scene, and the woman is dusting her furniture, which is set up as though there are invisible walls in the middle of the street. When she goes to the fortune teller, Amilcar breaks open the lock on her door and the children return all of her possessions to her house. As with many of the dreams in this film, such as the game of draughts, the viewer never learns exactly what happens to Mrs. Santas.

Vicente works to put his business back together. Vicente is actually keeping alive the ideals of the revolution, giving an opportunity to poor fish sellers and fishermen. He manages to restore the electricity to his plant and find a new buyer who will take as much fish as he can get. But Vicente views his life as a failure because the revolution still has not reached everyone. Nando, the missing husband of Mrs. Santas and a revolutionary comrade, visits him. Nando is a wanderer who disappears from Vicente's house. He is the extreme example of someone who cannot deal with the reality of postrevolutionary life. After Nando leaves Vicente is overcome by despair and identifies with the vultures he sees flying over the city as he sees himself eating the dead carcass of the revolution. He does not realize what Belonte learned from the fortune teller: "Vultures only take from us what is already dead." His country has moved on from the revolution and will still change. He does not see the impact of his actions and feels a failure.

Yonta's search for her dream is frivolous. She encounters Zé, the source of the letter, receives clues to his identity, but never notices him. While she shares much with Zé, her infatuation with Vicente and her search for the author of the love note blind her to the reality of the young man in front of her. But she is a product of both her father and her mother, the revolutionary dream and the real. Her faults come from her youth. Gomes shows her positive relationships with her friend and her family. When she argues with Vicente she is aware of the reasons for the revolution, and she wants her right to choose her own way. Her role in the future is suggested by her presence in the final magical moments of the film.

The film ends with Mana's wedding. An earlier celebration in the African tradition is followed by a legal ceremony in Western dress. The elaborate reception features strange motorized carts bearing food and drink that propel themselves around a pool. The guests indulge. The scene abruptly shifts from the night of the wedding to the next morning. Most of the guests sleep by the side of the pool. Two children float on Amilcar's inner tube in the pool as fishermen move their nets in slow motion. Two of the carts have stopped, but a third moves along coming to a quick stop at the edge of the pool and dumping the three tiers that held the wedding cake into the water. Laughing children appear and, joined by Yonta, dance around the pool and out of the frame. The film closes as the camera holds on a couple barely moving on the dance floor.

The film ends as it began—with the children. They are alive and dancing in a world where the natural has been transformed into the artificial, the ocean into a swimming pool. The scene also recalls the moment when the children return Mrs. Santas' belongings to the house. In all three magical moments the children provide a link between the present and the future. They cannot reclaim a revolutionary past, but they can commemorate it in their race. They can change the present by reclaiming a house. They see the humor in the mechanical cart, but they create their own magic when they dance out of the film and into the future leaving behind the present. Gomes does not show how the characters' dreams come out. He knows better than to predict the future. But the revolution, which began with dreams, did lead to independence. He ends the film with the hope that other dreams will also change the world.

V

La vie est belle/ Life is Rosy (1987: Ngangura Mweze and Bernard Lamy, Zaïre/ Belgium). Unlike many African films *La vie est belle* is not concerned with examining the shifting relationship between the traditional and modern worlds in an era of postcolonialism. This film chooses instead to celebrate the Zairian culture and examine the survival of folklore and its connection to the music of Kinshasa, the capital. The film is dedicated to the inhabitants of this city. *La vie* is like a modern fairy tale about an average man who overcomes tremendous odds and finds love and success at the end of his quest. The central character, Kourou, is played by a famous musician, Papa Wemba. For those who recognize him there is added pleasure in seeing a celebrity play a poor man from the country who struggles to succeed. The tone of the film creates an atmosphere where a happy ending is not really in doubt. The narrative generates its interest in watching how the characters will work out their problems and how justice will prevail. The film is also important because of its acceptance of the continued presence of ritual in everyday life. Despite colonialist efforts to discount the impact of the supernatural, the people of this capital still believe in the role of the diviner in their lives. The film demonstrates how this belief is justified.

La vie opens in the country where a ragged Kourou sings for the villages. His homemade instrument smashes when he leaves for the city, but, like everything else in the film, no event is ever really tragic. As Kourou arrives in the city, he sees a group of young women in school uniforms. Although he does not know her, Kabibi, his future wife, is a member of this group. He later encounters Emoro, the dwarf, in the market, and enters Nvaunda's club where the musicians mock his countrified appearance. The initial scenes in Kinshasa are reversed at the end of the film. The events that form the story are framed by these night scenes, which feature the city and its inhabitants. They also introduce key characters and themes. Kabibi represents Kourou's quest for a true love. Emoro connects many of the characters as he travels the streets selling chicken for Mama Dingari, Kabibi's mother. He voices the title of the film at several key moments. The words "la vie est belle" also become part of Kourou's song. The owner of the nightclub, Nvaunda, becomes Kourou's boss and Kabibi's suitor. Nvaunda must learn about love before he can be reconciled with his first wife. Nvaunda's visit to a witch doctor, Nganga, to find a cure for his impotence presents this personality, who also serves as a connection to the various characters.

Both Emoro and Nganga establish a magical atmosphere for the film. Emoro voices its theme, which erases the possibility of a tragic conclusion, and Nganga's actions ensure the romantic unions that leave all the characters happy. While the spells and potions Nganga provides are treated as real in the film, the supernatural is also a source of humor. The witch doctor gives Nvaunda a cure for his impotency. He is to marry a virgin but avoid contact with her for thirty days, and he is to dance by hopping first on one foot and then the other singing "push, push, piston." While the viewer never sees actual evidence of the cure, Nganga's spells do control the actions of other characters. His injunction about not touching the new wife creates a situation that prevents Nvaunda from consummating his marriage to Kabibi. Nganga also draws her true love, Kourou, toward her.

Nganga's spells often occur in humorous contexts as the witch doctor must work within the various comic episodes of Kourou's life in Kinshasa. While Kourou is attempting to gain his love, his employer actually marries Kabibi and battles with his first wife because of this second wife. The film explores the world of the wife and her woman's group and the life of Kabibi's mother who runs several businesses. While Kourou is constantly in trouble with his employers, the film never deals with the reality of poverty or the threat of the loss of a job. At various points he performs his song, and the persona of Papa Wemba, which always lurks behind the character, ensures Kourou's eventual success. Because Papa Wemba is a star the audience never doubts Kourou will become one.

The end of the film is the culmination of the magic and the humor. When Kabibi rejects him, Kourou attempts to hang himself, but the branch breaks. Kabibi appears to be dead because of a potion she has taken. The lead singer in the nightclub also falls down, and Kourou must be found to take his place. While the children of the neighborhood dance to save Kabibi, Kourou is found and brought to the club. When he puts on a new, fancy shirt he is transformed into the star he actually is in real life. Kabibi awakens and is drawn to the club. Once there she is also transformed. She is also played by a famous singer, Bibi Krubwa, and she performs with Papa Wemba in the final scene. All of the other conflicts are resolved; characters are reconciled. Emoro is correct: la vie est belle.

This film chooses to examine the positive aspects of modern African life. Rather than displaying a concern for the effects of colonialism, *La vie* celebrates the survival of traditions in the modern world. The characters clearly trace their ancestry to folklore and oral storytelling. While the consequences of their actions could be serious, the tone of the film focuses on the comic. The viewer never worries about the eventual outcome of the complicated events. The film concentrates on demonstrating how things will work out even though the characters seem to be in serious trouble. The music brings in elements of modern life to combine with the folk tradition. A ragged Kourou rises from his life in the country to success in the city as he follows his destiny and plays his role as a buffoon at the same time he pursues his dreams of professional singing. While *La vie* may not explore the serious challenges of a postcolonial world, it does give the viewer hope that some dreams may survive in a modern world.

VIEYRA, PAULIN SOUMANOU (Porto Novo, Benin, 1925–87). Paulin Soumanou Vieyra was one of the elder statesmen of the African cinema. He received much of his education in France where he studied biology at the Université de Paris. His first involvement with film was as an extra in Claude Autant-Lara's *Le diable au corps/ Devil in the Flesh* (1946). He was the first African graduate of IDHEC (Institut des hautes etudes cinématographique) in 1954. Vieyra's first short film was a student production. His next film, which he co-directed with Mamadou Sarr, is considered the first short made by black Africans. He took many different jobs with both film and television and became central to the development of filmmaking in Africa when he returned to Senegal. He headed the film division of the Ministry of Information and was involved in preserving many of the events surrounding the end of colonialism in several African countries. He continued making documentary films. Vieyra also became the leading historian of African cinema and authored numerous articles and four books: *Le cinéma et L'Afrique/ Cinema and Africa* (1969), *Ousmane Sembene cinéaste* (1972), *Le cinéma africain: Des origines à 1973* (1975), and *Le cinéma au Sénégal* (1983). He spent his life dedicated to the development of African cinema either through making films or recording its history.

Afrique sur Seine/ Africa on the Seine (1955), the short film Vieyra co-directed with Sarr, was made in France because they could not get permission to film it in Africa. The film dealt with the problems Africans faced when they lived in France as students or artists alienated from their own culture in a racist French society. During this period, he joined others to form Le Groupe Africain du Cinéma to consider how to establish an

African film industry after independence. As the leader of the group, he was interested in establishing a film center to organize production for French-speaking countries. After he returned to Africa he made several films dealing with the independence of many West African countries and continued to document Africans in other countries. In addition he made a film about the very special type of wrestling in Senegal called "Lamb" in Wolof, (*Lamb/ Senegalese Wrestling* [1963]).

After making other documentaries dealing with aspects of African public life, Vieyra turned to the first of several short fiction films. *N'Diangane* (1965) is taken from a story by Birago Diop. When his father is killed by a lion a son calls himself N'Diangane, little husband, to maintain the sense of a man in the house for his mother and sister. When he is teased by other children, he drowns himself and is then accompanied in death by his mother and sister who cannot deal with their grief. This film was followed by a ballet about marriage. In *Sindiély* (1965) a father wants to marry off his daughter to a man of his choice, but she loves another. The film ends happily when the father is convinced to let his daughter marry her love. Vieyra uses traditional African dance to present his story as a means of ensuring a permanent record of an art in danger of being lost. *Mol: Un homme un idéal une vie/ Les pêcheurs/ Fishermen* (1966) was begun in 1957 and was not finished until 1966 because of a lack of funding. This short traces the efforts of a fisherman to motorize his boat. This act emphasizes the need for industrialization and examines its conflict with traditional values, which sometimes must be sacrificed for progress.

Vieyra continued to make documentary and short films, including some dealing with literary and cinematic figures. *Birago Diop, conteur/ Birago Diop, Storyteller* (1981) features the author, Birago Diop, who speaks of his past. *L'envers du décor/ Behind the Scenes* (1981) records the filming of *Ceddo** by Ousmane Sembene.* While his films never achieved the critical approval or expertise of other directors who were able to move more easily into the longer format, he did make *En résidence surveillée/ Under House Arrest* (1981), which deals with serious concerns. In this work Vieyra documents the power struggles in an African country, a topic that had been taboo for filmmakers. But Vieyra's main contribution remains as a pioneer who helped open the way for others and who recorded, both in film and in his books, the history of an important era.

Filmography

C'était il y a quatre ans/ Four Years Ago (1954)

Afrique sur Seine/ Africa on the Seine (1955), co-director Mamadou Sarr

L'Afrique à Moscou/ Africa in Moscow (1957)

Le Niger aujourd'hui/ Niger Today (1958)

Les presidents Senghor et Modibo Keita/ Presidents Senghor and Modibo Keita (1959)

Avec les africains à Vienne/ Africans in Vienna (1959)

Présence africaine à Rome/ The African Presence in Rome (1959)

Independence du Cameroun, Togo, Congo et Madagascar/ The Independence of Cameroon, Togo, Congo and Madagascar (1960)

Une nation est née/ A Nation Is Born (1961)

Lamb/ Senegalese Wrestling (1963)

N'Diangane (1965)

Sindiély (1965)

Mol: Un homme un idéal une vie/ Les pêcheurs/ Fishermen (1966)

Le Sénégal au festival mondial des arts nègres/ Senegal in the World Festival of Black Arts (1966)

La bicyclette/ le gâteau/ au marché/ rendez-vous/ The bicycle/ the cake/ at the market/ meeting (1967)

Ecrits de Dakar/ Letters from Dakar (1974)

Diarama/ Welcome (1974)

L'art plastique/ Plastic Arts (1974)

L'habitat urbain au Sénégal/ Urban Housing in Senegal (1976)

L'habitat rural au Sénégal/ Rural Housing in Senegal (1976)

Birago Diop, conteur/ Birago Diop, Storyteller (1981)

L'envers du décor/ Behind the Scenes (1981)

En résidence surveillée/ Under House Arrest (1981)

Iba N'Diaye, peintre/ Iba N'Diaye, Painter (1983)

Bibliography

Diawara, Manthia. *African Cinema: Politics & Culture*. Bloomington: Indiana UP, 1992.

Hennebelle, Guy. *Les cinémas africains en 1972*. Paris: Société Africaine d'Edition, 1972.

Malkmus, Lizbeth, and Roy Armes. *Arab and African Film Making*. London: Zed Books, 1991.

Shiri, Kenneth, comp. and ed. *Directory of African Films*. Westport, Conn.: Greenwood P, 1992.

Ukadike, Nwachukwu Frank. *Black African Cinema*. Berkeley: U of California P, 1994.

"Vieyra, Paulin Soumanou." *Dictionnaire du cinéma africain*. Vol. 1. Paris: Editions Karthala, 1991. 315–19.

Visages des femmes/ Faces of Women (1985: Désiré Ecaré, Ivory Coast).

It is interesting to compare *Faces of Women* with the documentary *Femmes aux yeux ouverts*.* Both films are directly concerned with the role of women in modern Africa, and they both cover similar problems. While the documentary deals directly with a wider range of issues, Désiré Ecaré, the director of the fiction film uses innovative techniques to pursue two important topics: women's control of their economics and their sexuality. As with many African films, financing was a problem, and it took the director twelve years to complete this project. Ecaré employs elements from ritual and tradition to unite the two stories, which he shot ten years apart. He incorporates dance, music, and song at the beginning and end of the film, between the two stories, and within the stories. In addition to providing connections between the two narratives, these elements underscore the thematic examination of women's rights and relate modern issues to traditions. Ecaré shows how positive elements from the past can be retained at the same time that repressive customs should be abandoned. The first story takes place in a small village while the second takes place in the capital, Abidjan. The dances and songs are located in a larger village, a point somewhere between the extremes of the two narratives.

The music and dance build gradually at the beginning of the film. Ecaré assembles the women with a series of cuts of groups of females and several shots that concentrate on their faces. A close-up of the foot of a drummer and a pan up to the drum marks the beginning of the music that leads to an extended dance sequence featuring men and women dancing as couples. The sequence ends with men alone, dancing as warriors, which is gradually transformed into men going to work in the fields, a transition to the first story. The city is not entirely absent even among the workers in the fields. In the second story a relative comes from the country to ask for money. In the first narrative the city dweller is Kouassi, Brou's brother who is visiting. While Kouassi resists doing any work and most of the time speaks in French to people who answer in their own language, he is not above flirting with the women, especially N'Guéssan, his brother's wife, and her friend Affoue. N'Guéssan reciprocates his attention even though she worries about being seen by others. In this narrative, women's desires are often in conflict with the social order that is concerned with maintaining the status quo.

The relationship between sister and brother-in-law is mirrored in an article N'Guéssan reads in the newspaper about mutual infidelities in the European community. A man and his daughter-in-law form a relationship, and his wife gets back by having an affair with her son-in-law. As N'Guéssan says, "These white folks keep surprising us." But she does not operate out of a sense of revenge. She merely wants to pursue her own desires. Her husband Brou is the one who reacts with jealousy. Broy sends his brother Kouassi off to visit their grandmother, but N'Guéssan goes to visit her mother in a village only a short distance from the grandmother's. The relationship between the villages is described by a return to the dancers. This time a group of women sing the story of the connection between the villages. When she returns Brou makes accusations against N'Guéssan, and she denies anything has happened. N'Guéssan loses all respect for

Brou when he threatens her. She is his wife, his possession, his thing. Brou follows her around the village claiming he is her master, and he owns her body. N'Guésan tells him she no longer loves him. The film returns to the group of women who sing about men's inability to trust women. A man who can't trust deserves to be deceived because he sees the worst in everything. The women claim they will demonstrate what happens to a man who spies.

While the song suggests an encounter between N'Guéssan and Kouassi, Affoue comes down to the river to get water. She sees Kouassi, takes off her clothes, and bathes in the river. The scene that follows has been both praised and criticized for its explicit eroticism. Nwachukwu Frank Ukadike points out, "The traditional African moral code does not permit such public exposure . . ." (221). One defense for the detailed presentation of the sexual encounter is the foregrounding of Affoue's desire. She is the one who initiates it, and the camera focuses on her enjoyment. At one point she encourages Kouassi to continue. The narrative's concern for women's rights to choose a mate expand to a right to enjoy sex. Such an assertion certainly strongly supports those who oppose female genital mutilation in a film like *Femmes aux yeux ouverts*. This story ends with Brou still angry with N'Guéssan after he tricks her into thinking she is meeting Kouassi. Brou drags her off threatening to beat her.

Violence against women directly connects this story to the second where a mother, Bernadette, talks to her daughter about a man beating his wife. She says women need to learn how to fight back because men are stronger. She suggests her daughter go to military school after she graduates to learn how to fight. The film shifts back to the group of women who are transformed into marchers. Shots of women marching are intercut with a woman learning self-defense. The woman is N'Guéssan who is learning how to defend herself against Brou. She almost succeeds until he gets her on the ground and has his hands around her throat.

The film returns to Bernadette's story. She is a successful business woman. She buys fish, smokes it, and exports it to other countries. She works very hard and wants to open a small restaurant because she will be able to control an aspect of the retail sales and hopes to work less hard. She goes to the bank to ask for a loan. The banker reviews her finances. While she feels that she is not making much money she is really in charge of a large enterprise. She employs two hundred workers. She is amazed to see the actual figures of what she makes each month because she is left with no money. The banker refuses the loan because her house is not sufficient collateral, and she cannot provide anything else to secure the loan. The awareness of how much money is spent each month changes her view of her family. Rather than continuing to give money to one relative she buys a van and sets him up in business. When he comes back after three months because the van has broken down, she refuses to help him further. She also rejects the request of another relative to send money back to family in the country. Her husband has gotten fat off her money, and her children live well. She wants something for herself. She finally decides, "With people like this there is no hope for economic progress." She makes money to provide food, but anything that is left also gets consumed. A male voice-over councils joining the others and dancing with them. The film closes with images of the dance. A sentence appears on the screen: "In the end the festival becomes the refuge."

While the film shows women who have confronted repressive situations, women have not really triumphed. In the end they must accommodate to a society that resists change. The film does not hold much hope for the future. Bernadette's daughters think they can use their sexuality to get ahead. They visit the banker who is attracted to them but is still not very encouraging about the loan. Ecaré demonstrates that traditional ways need to change just as the dancers have incorporated modern moves. He also knows that men are not going to give up their power easily. Bernadette's husband takes her money at the same time he asserts his position in the family. Women may take control of their sexuality or their economics, but they are still not really free from the societal constraints that keep their husbands in power. *Faces of Women* won the International Film Critic's Award and the UNESCO International Film and Television Council Award.

Bibliography

Ukadike, Nwachukwu Frank. *Black African Cinema*. Berkeley: U of California P, 1994.

W

Wend Kuuni/ God's Gift (1982: Jean-Marie Gaston Kaboré*, Burkina Faso). This film is one of the early films to attempt to develop a uniquely African cinematic language. The story returns to an earlier precolonial period in the Mossi empire. Gaston Kaboré, the director, presents a deceptively simple story in a style that interacts with elements of the oral tradition and the documentary to suggest the necessary connections between tradition and modern life. *Wend Kuuni*'s depiction of the past is also part of an ongoing project by many African filmmakers to recapture their history and to represent their own vision of a life that has been distorted by a Western colonial view of a preindustrial society. As Manthia Diawara points out in an essay on this film, the narrative is actually composed of three different stories, parts of which are taken to create a new story that challenges the role of the traditional social structures and of the griot whose tales support those structures: the missing husband, the wanted son, and the emancipated daughter (202–3). The film seems to present a linear narrative, but as *Wend Kuuni* eventually reveals, it is actually an extended flashback. The ending reveals crucial elements of the story that force a reconsideration of the entire narrative.

The film opens by introducing a woman and her son. Her husband, a hunter, has been missing for thirteen months, and she is informed by her village that it is time to take a new husband. The next shot is of a young boy who is unconscious. A peddler finds him and takes him to the nearest village where he is left with a family consisting of a husband, wife, and daughter. The family agrees to take the boy until his parents can be located. The boy cannot explain what has happened because he is unable to speak. The boy's thoughts and other events are explained throughout the film by a voice-over narrator. The boy's inability to talk is even more difficult in an oral culture where he can only express himself with hand signals. The family attempts to find the boy's parents, but when they are not successful the village decides he can stay with his foster parents who call him Wend Kuuni, God's gift.

The boy becomes part of the life of the family and forms a close connection with his new sister, Pongneré. The central section of the film details their daily life. While Wend Kuuni's jobs take him into the countryside to herd the goats, Pongneré's role as a girl confines her to the household. Their routine is punctuated by trips to the market and village. In a scene in the village a young woman wants to be rid of a husband she thinks is impotent and too old, another aspect of male/female relationships examined in the film. The fields are the locations for the real changes in the story. The home guards tradition; Pongneré is trained in her future role by her mother. Pongneré challenges her predetermined place when she follows Wend Kuuni into the field, a space that is off limits for women. Wend Kuuni makes a flute that becomes another means of communication. But he is still limited by his lack of voice.

As the film moves toward its close, various events come together. Pongneré dreams Wend Kuuni can speak. He, too, senses a change. In the woods he discovers a man who has hanged himself, the old impotent husband who had been shamed by his wife. The shock of this encounter restores Wend Kuuni's voice. He tells Pongneré of his past, which is visually represented through flashbacks. He and his mother were poor, and he was often ill. Her refusal to remarry causes the village to decide she is a witch. They burn her house and force her into the countryside. Her dying moments are intercut with images of her hunter husband. Wend Kuuni falls asleep, and when he awakens his mother is dead. He runs away, which is how he is found by the peddler. The flashback fills in critical events in the narrative.

Wend Kuuni gains his own voice, and by telling events out of order he challenges the linear narrative of the oral tradition. While the compression and expansion of time usual in storytelling is part of the film, the events occur in a sequential order in which time always moves forward. The flashback moves the events into a cause-effect relationship, which is usual in the Western cinematic tradition. These kinds of connections encourage time shifts because the narrative is not dependent on linearity for coherence; one occurrence is the cause of the next. Kaboré uses this shift from one technique to another as a means of exploring the interaction of the oral tradition and Western narrative. As Diawara suggests, Kaboré juxtaposes pieces of stories from the oral tradition to construct his film and comment on the restrictive nature of this tradition (205). The flashbacks also allow him to incorporate a different perspective on narrative. A cause-effect interaction at the end of the film suggests the possibility for change in society. The narrator does not control the tale; the griot preserves history by repeating the same story from generation to generation. Wend Kuuni's story does need to be retained and retold. But the boy has no role in the shaping of his story until he regains his own voice. The end of the film provides the balance necessary to retain tradition and also change the restrictive elements that should be altered. *Wend Kuuni* won the silver Tanit at the 1982 Carthage Film Festival, the Francophone Prize at Cesar 1985, and prizes at the Locarno and Monpellier Film Festivals.

Bibliography

Chirol, Marie-Magdeleine. "The Missing Narrative in *Wend Kuuni*." *Research in African Literatures* 26 (Fall 1995): 49–56.

Diawara, Manthia. "Oral Literature and African Film: Narratology in *Wend Kuuni*." *Questions of Third Cinema*. Eds. Jim Pines and Paul Willemen. London: British Film Institute, 1991. 195–211.

"Kaboré, Gaston." *Dictionnaire du cinéma africain*. Vol. 1. Paris: Editions Karthala, 1991. 48–51.

Malkmus, Lizbeth, and Roy Armes. *Arab and African Film Making*. London: Zed Books, 1991.

Ukadike, Nwachukwu Frank. *Black African Cinema*. Berkeley: U of California P, 1994.

A World of Strangers/ Dilemma (1962: Henning Carlsen, South Africa). Nadine Gordimer's novel, *A World of Strangers* is the source of this film. It was shot secretly in South Africa and is remarkable for the amount of documentary footage it includes. The director, Henning Carlsen, spends a great deal of time recording the daily life of South Africans, especially the blacks within the context of a story about an outsider's encounters with apartheid. The film is shot in black and white because of the technical necessities of filming clandestinely without elaborate lighting or a large crew. The documentary footage is not just used for atmosphere; it gives the story an authenticity and sets the tone and pacing that also adds to its realism. In addition to the visuals, the film makes extensive use of live music. As the central character, Toby Hood, moves through the different social milieus he inhabits, the music changes to correspond to the setting as well as providing the usual support of the dramatic action.

The footage that opens the film chronicles the daily life of the people of Johannesburg. They leave areas bound by high fences as they go toward the European section of town. The shots emphasize people going to work or to school. As the crowd increases in number, the sounds of the drums that accompany these scenes becomes more intense. The camera also pans over headlines that become part of the film's use of newspapers and books to transmit its antiapartheid message. In the city the film continues to pay attention to the blacks as they set up stalls along the road. The camera finally concentrates on one man, staying with him as he walks along the street. There is a cut to a window as the shot reveals another man working on a musical composition and a woman bringing in a tray. The camera moves into the room; the man who has been walking enters. This gradual introduction of two of the central characters becomes a pattern for the rest of the film. Stephen Sitole is visiting his friend, Sam and his wife.

Although it isn't evident until later, Stephen is one of the characters who provides an anchor or connection for others in the film. Stephen, who has recently returned to South Africa from Great Britain, links the other blacks to the whites. The camera follows him and then shifts to the person he is going to see, Anna Louw. She is an Afrikaner lawyer who works at the Legal Help Centre. Stephen comes to her with a complex problem about a borrowed car, which reveals her concern for him. She is worried that something senseless will happen to him that will not be worth the loss of his life, an unfortunately prophetic concern. They share a common involvement in South African politics. While Stephen is there, Anna calls a publisher to speak to Mr. Hood about another situation. Toby Hood, the newcomer from Great Britain who is now running a family publishing business, is the real center of the film even though his role is revealed gradually. Another set of characters is also interested in Toby. The Alexanders, a wealthy family, have connections to his relatives and invite him to their home. Anna goes to Toby's office to explain a situation concerning one of his workers, and they go out for drinks and to a party. Stephen is at the party, and he and Toby become friends.

In the middle section of the film, Toby moves among the various groups he has met. He has affairs with both Anna and Cecil Alexander. While Anna does not know about his other affair, she cautions him about trying to keep a foot in different camps. His rich friends know nothing about his interest in Anna or Stephen. The problems of relationships between blacks and whites is illustrated by Stephen's visit to Toby's office. The secretary tries to prevent Stephen from entering Toby's room. She resigns after she is forced to obey Toby's request to get some lunch for him and Stephen. Interspersed with the main story are shots of Anna helping a woman whose husband has been arrested followed immediately by wealthy whites at play. Images of the interior of a church accompanied by a voice-over reading of the twenty-third psalm are followed by whites playing golf and blacks dealing with the police. Both on the level of the individual characters and on the broader societal level, the film blends reality and fiction to create its images of South Africa.

A World of Strangers ends with its various plots coming together around Toby. As Toby makes love to Cecil, Stephen slips a note under his door. Anna has been arrested. Cecil leaves, and Stephen and Sam arrive at Toby's apartment. Carlsen creates emotional depth in the scene by allowing the characters to sit in silence with just brief attempts at conversation as they are all overwhelmed by events. The mood is broken by the entry of the landlady who informs Toby that he cannot have blacks in his apartment. As they leave, Toby lends Stephen his raincoat. Stephen refuses Sam's offer of a ride and sets off on his own. Toby looks down on them from his window. As Stephen goes toward the train station he is knifed to death by robbers and left on the ground. Toby is called to the police station. They want to return his raincoat, which they assume has been stolen. He throws the coat over his shoulder. As he walks through the streets, both Cecil and Anna speak in voice-overs. The film ends with Anna's words about the difficulty of keeping a foot in different camps.

The credits for *A World of Strangers* close with a statement explaining that the film was shot entirely in South Africa without permission from the authorities. Carlsen is clear about the focus of the story and its antiapartheid message. He carefully attempts to convey his points without either understating or overstating them. He accomplishes this tone by allowing many of the images to speak for themselves. The spaces in the narrative, which he fills with real shots of real people, both lend a sense of authenticity to the fiction and chronicle a world that needed exposure. The very ordinary and unexceptional nature of the images demonstrates the banality of the evil of apartheid. The quiet ending of the narrative reinforces this point. As the voices of Cecil and Anna indicate, Toby has experienced a world where prejudice is the norm and only a few fight it. He has also been a part of the privileged world that flourishes side by side with oppression. He cannot maintain a foothold in both worlds unless he wants to remain an outsider everywhere. The film combines documentary and fictional footage so that the audience can understand something of the social structure created by apartheid.

X

Xala/ L'impuissance temporaire/ The Curse (1974: Ousmane Sembene,*
Senegal). With this film Sembene turns his attention away from the historical events of *Emitai* (1971)* to a satiric exploration of the ongoing
effects of colonialism in Senegal. Sembene contrasts the postIndependence
members of the Chamber of Commerce with the beggars whose lives have
not changed with the removal of colonial rule. The film opens with a satiric
version of the ceremony of independence. The symbols of colonialism are
rejected including the white rulers. But the whites soon return operating
behind the scenes at the chamber meeting providing the new African
members, who are dressed in European clothes, with briefcases full of
money. Sembene demonstrates the sorry reality of the difficulty of re-
moving colonial influences. For the poor people nothing is different.

Sembene personalizes his story by concentrating on one of the members
of the Chamber of Commerce, El Hadji, a Muslim whose name means
pilgrim and can reflect a pilgrimage to Mecca. The director uses this name
as an ironic commentary on this character's lack of holiness, his hypocrisy.
He has the beggars outside of his business removed, an uncharitable act
that results in the *xala*, the curse, which makes him impotent. El Hadji
decides to celebrate his rising fortunes with a marriage to a third wife, the
beginning of a series of excessive acts that lead to his destruction. Sembene
suggests the curse is also effective because El Hadji rejects the traditional
ceremony suggested by his future mother-in-law to ensure potency on the
wedding night.

The wedding is a demonstration of the division that exists between the
classes in Senegal. The wealthy guests arrive in fancy cars. El Hadji must
mediate quarrels between his first and second wives. The wedding dem-

onstrates the ways that the ruling class straddles the two worlds of Africa
and Europe without really existing in either. Polygamy is part of the African tradition, but the wealth El Hadji demonstrates through this action
is only possible because of the money he has taken from the Europeans.
The guests drink Johnny Walker and smoke cigars. The bride and groom
remain in Western dress at the same time many guests offer El Hadji pills
to guarantee potency, a universal concern that is even more important in
a polygamous society.

Even El Hadji's attempts to rid himself of his curse combine elements
of both worlds. He wears a Western suit as he rides out into the countryside to consult a marabout. He pays a second marabout with a check that
bounces and this marabout restores the *xala* even though he no longer
wears Westerrn clothing. The *xala* itself becomes a complex symbol. The
curse extends beyond his sexual life to the business world. El Hadji loses
his position on the chamber. But his impotency also suggests the inability
of modern Africa to act even after independence. El Hadji's business con-
sists of importing items from Europe, but he cheats his own countrymen.
He uses money from the business to get his third wife. When he is removed from his position on the chamber he asks to speak in Wolof, his
native language. The others laugh at him and insist on speaking French.
The symbol of his loss of power is the removal of his briefcase as he is
ejected from the chamber.

All of El Hadji's Western possessions are taken away. The man who
comes to repossess his Mercedes can't drive it, and the car is pushed down
the street. Finally El Hadji realizes he can only remove the *xala* by a return
to tradition. He discovers that a beggar is the source of the *xala*. The
beggars invade the house of El Hadji's first wife where he has taken refuge. He has lost everything and stands in front of them in his underwear.
The beggars spit on him completing the ritual that will restore his virility,
the one thing he can get back.

In *Xala*, Sembene attacks the pretenses of postcolonial societies. His
criticism is so sharp that parts of the film were censored when it was shown
in Senegal. He combines elements of the African oral story-telling tradition, which are in evidence in most of his films, with the more traditional
Hollywood techniques of using a variety of shorter shots to convey the
conflicting elements in the film. Sembene indicates the ways in which the
rise of an African bourgeoisie merely continues the situations created during the colonial period. Throughout most of the film, El Hadji's African
values are subordinated to his desires to accumulate wealth and the status
it confers according to Western standards. African traditions, like his wedding, become moments for displays of Western consumer goods. Only
when he loses power and the class status it confers does he really return
to African traditions. Sembene offers hope for the future in El Hadji's
daughter, one of the children of his first marriage. She is able to combine

the best of both worlds. She speaks both Wolof and French. She admires traditional values at the same time that she condemns polygamy. She is successful because she can combine the best elements of her father and mother. Sembene does not suggest most young Africans are like this woman, but he does indicate that she is the only hope for the future.

Bibliography

Gadjigo, Samba, Ralph Faulkingham, Thomas Cassirer, and Reinhard Sander, eds. *Ousmane Sembene: Dialogues with Critics and Writers*. Amherst: U of Massachusetts P, 1993.

Ghali, Noureddine. "An Interview with Sembene Ousmane." *Film & Politics in The Third World*. Ed. John D. H. Downing. New York: Praeger, 1986. 41–54.

Malkmus, Lizbeth, and Roy Armes. *Arab and African Film Making*. London: Zed Books, 1991.

Ukadike, Nwachukwu Frank. *Black African Cinema*. Berkeley: U of California P, 1994.

Vieyra, Paulin Soumanou. "Five Major Films by Sembene Ousmane." *Film & Politics in The Third World*. Ed. John D. H. Downing. New York: Praeger, 1986. 31–39.

Y

Yeelen/ Brightness (1987: Souleymane Oumar Cissé,* Mali). *Yeelen* is one of the most celebrated of African films. The director, Souleymane Oumar Cissé, re-creates a past and depicts a sacred ritual to bring to life an epic of the Bambara oral tradition. Even though this film does an excellent job of recalling the past, it also has implications for the present and future of Mali. The son who sacrifices himself to destroy his father's tyrannical power reflects the filmmaker's hope for an end to the dictatorship that controlled Mali at the time of the making of the film. The father is part of a repressive secret society, the *Komo*. He refuses to teach his son the secrets because he is afraid his son will be greater than he is and destroy him. Cissé's hope for the future was fulfilled when the dictator was overthrown. This film was also one of the first modern African films to explore the mythic past of the continent. Economic considerations and the shooting situation forced the director to create supernatural events very simply making a virtue out of necessity and establishing a magical realism that now appears in many African films.

   Yeelen opens with symbols that establish the ritual character of the narrative. These symbols represent a statement about creation: "Heat makes the fire and the two worlds (earth and sky) exist through light." A series of titles present further information of the *Komo* as a body of divine knowledge taught by signs. The vulture, bird of space and knowledge, is the symbol of the Kôré, the seventh stage of the Bambara initiation society, its emblem is the wooden horse that symbolizes the human spirit, the scepter is the Kôré wing. The Kolonkolanni is a magic pylon that finds what has been lost and punishes thieves, traitors, and perjurers. The final explanation tells the viewer that "the Kôré wing and the magic pylon have been used in Mali for centuries.'' The film cuts from the black of the introductory statements to a shot of a sunrise, a true beginning, a symbol of creation, and then inserts a shot of a flaming chicken. A child brings a goat to the sacred grove and leaves. Soma sacrifices so he can locate Nianankoro. The next shots are of the beginning of the flaming sacrifice of the chicken that appeared earlier. The film begins in ritual and transformed time.

Soma wraps up the magic pylon. The first image of its movement is the reflection in the water, which Nianankoro sees to track his father. His mother warns him about his father. He wants to confront his father, but she knows he is not ready yet. She gives him a fetish to wear around his neck and one to take to his Uncle Djigui, his father's blind twin brother who lives beyond the Peul. The film cuts between Soma's brother Baafing and his two rather comic helpers who are controlled by the power of the pylon they carry as they track Nianankoro. The son and his mother separate. She performs a twilight bathing ritual to assist him and to counteract his father's magic. Nianankoro's lonely journey produces visions of his fortunate future as he traverses the dry, cracked land. His father is accompanied by the two men carrying the pylon, and his trip is full of noise and excitement.

Nianankoro's capture and accusation of stealing cattle marks his entry to the land of the Peul. He freezes a warrior as an example of his powers. He helps the Peul defeat their enemies through his magic, which creates an attack of bees, and he also cures the king's wife, Attu, of her sterility. Unfortunately, he succeeds too well at the last task, and they make love. He confesses to the king who banishes both of them. Attu is pregnant with Niankoro's son who will carry on after him. Baafing follows Nianankoro to the land of the Peul. The king tells Baafing that the young man has gone on. Baafing continues his pursuit and disappears.

At this point Cissé brings together various relatives and the film's most impressive rituals. First Cissé returns to Soma and presents a *Komo* ceremony, a secret ritual, a part of the society most Malians had only heard about in song. The rituals of the Komo are contrasted with the arrival of Nianankoro and Attu at his Uncle Djigui's home in the land of the Dogon. Before Nianankoro actually encounters Djigui, he and Attu receive permission to cleanse themselves in the holy spring, a magical site in this arid land. The final stage of Nianankoro's maturation takes place during his encounter with his father's twin brother. Djigui explains that their family used to be central to the Bambara, but recently there has been a curse on the family. He also tells the couple that Attu is pregnant, and the son she is carrying will be a bright star for his people. He also foretells disasters that will befall the Bambara. Djigui was blinded because he wanted to share the secrets of the *Komo*. Soma blinded him with the light from the wing of the Kôré. Djigui gives Nianankoro the wing. The young man places the fetish his mother gave him in it, which completes its magic. He is now ready to face his father.

Nianankoro sets out alone. When he meets his father, who is now accompanied by the two men and the pylon, the men run off. The pylon plants itself in the ground opposite the wing. The stones in the two sacred objects generate such a great light that the two protagonists disappear. In the final scene the young son of Attu and Nianankoro discovers two eggs in the sand. He carries one to his mother who gives him the cloak his father left him and the wing of the Kôré. He carries these objects away in the sand toward the future. His father's spirit lives on. The flash of light that occurred when his father sacrificed himself for the future has been reborn in the glowing light that surrounds his son.

In this film Cissé restores a sense of a heroic and mythic past to the present. He shows his contemporaries a vision of precolonial Africa where conflicts between good and evil are enacted within an indigenous tradition. He accomplishes this task by using a new medium, film, to re-create a sense of the oral tradition and its narrative style. The story is presented in a series of episodes. The cuts between Soma's life and that of Nianankoro are not established as parallel actions as they would be in Western cinema. The events do not always take place at the same time, and they are not connected by cause-effect relationships the way they would be in the Western narrative style. The passage of time is also not signaled as it would be in a Hollywood film. Nianankoro's meeting with his uncle takes place over the course of an evening. But other events take place at specific times because those are the appropriate times for the ritual rather than because the event fits into a specific story time. The action is connected to the rituals of the *Komo*, the magic Nianankoro performs, and the ceremonies the characters enact rather than the real time it would take for the characters to travel the great distance from the land of the Bambara to that of the Dogon. The film opens and closes at sunrise with an undefined time in between. Cissé creates a unique style to convey the myths of creation and the triumph of freedom for both the past and the future. *Yeelen* won the Cannes Film Festival Jury Prize in 1987.

Bibliography

Diawara, Manthia. *African Cinema: Politics & Culture*. Bloomington: Indiana UP, 1992.

Ukadike, Nwachukwu Frank. *Black African Cinema*. Berkeley: U of California P, 1994.

Z

Zan Boko/ Homeland (1988: Jean-Marie Gaston Kaboré*, Burkina Faso). The title, *Zan Boko*, is the term in Moré for "the place where the placenta is buried." The film deals with the problems that occur when sprawling urbanization overtakes a village. While *Zan Boko* is set in modern Africa, it deals with the relationship between tradition and change in similar ways to those explored by Gaston Kaboré in his first film *Wend Kuuni* (1982).* In the earlier film a return to the distant past allows the director to make distinctions between the positive and negative elements of traditional culture. Kaboré's second film is less critical of customary practices and more involved with a critical evaluation of change. As many countries have discovered, the blind belief in the equation of progress with an improved lifestyle is not always true. Not only can traditional observances be important in maintaining a continuity with the past but also such observances may be critical in dealing with the truly important aspects of life. More modern is not always better, and much can be lost in the name of progress.

The film opens by establishing the importance of tradition in the daily life of the individual. A water ritual to help with labor during childbirth is part of the ongoing connection with the land and the past. Villagers visit each other bearing special foods. There is a rhythm to the lives of the people as they are in tune with the natural world and the flow of the seasons. There is also no distinction made between magic, ritual, and existence. All flow together. But gradually changes occur. A stranger comes to measure the land. He numbers the houses. A young boy tries to erase the number from his house. Tinga, the husband in the central family in the film, is concerned that the numbers chase away sleep. The city becomes visible from the village as it slowly moves toward them.

Finally the city swallows up the village. A couple in a new imposing house use their relationship with government officials to buy up the land to add a swimming pool to their property. Tinga's children do go to school. But the new rich neighbors complain about flies and the smell of the soumbala, a traditional dish, Tinga's wife prepares. For this family the land becomes dead, killed by its incorporation into the city. The easy social relations of the village are replaced by the antagonism between neighbors who do not understand each other, who may not even speak the same language. Even the children seem to live in different worlds. Tinga's child makes a toy bicycle that the neighboring child wants. In the village such a transaction would take the form of a gift from one friend to another. Now the wealthy child insults Tinga's son by trying to buy the toy. While Tinga was comfortable in dealing with problems in the village, he is unable to solve the ongoing loss of land in the modern world. As he tries to hold onto his land an architect appears to survey for the swimming pool. The water ritual of the opening will be transformed into an imitation of the real world, a pool for the rich.

The second half of the film changes its focus from Tinga to a television journalist, Yabre, who attempts to use the tools of the altered society to effect change, or, as in Tinga's case, restore elements of the past. Kaboré foregrounds the role of the television journalist as a means of discussing the importance of the media in presenting and recording an accurate version of events. But Yabre works for the government; he is not free to speak as he would like. It is a touch of irony that the very system Kaboré critiques is the one that has financed his film. Yabre arranges a television show to give a voice to Tinga's concerns. Various officials present their positions. Tinga is obviously out of place in this alien environment. The moment his problem is introduced the program is taken off the air, replaced by "The Golden Dream," which will take their viewers to the Riviera. The viewers are cut off from present reality and are to view the glories of a colonial past. Tinga does not understand French, but, at the end of the film, he encourages Yabre to hold fast to his convictions and his sense of self.

Zan Boko ends with a sense of loss. The rich and the corrupt are taking over the land. But the collision of past and present raises important questions about modern values. The film does not take the easy approach of condemning all progress. If television is replacing the oral tradition it can also record and preserve it. Yabre understands how to use modern technology to reveal modern excesses. He also takes the advice of a griot when he searches for Tinga. But, for many, traditional values have been lost. Officials are no longer representatives of the entire community. They only support the rich and influential among their constituents. Money becomes the only medium of exchange; even among the young, items are only valuable if they are purchased. When a neighbor becomes upset with the smells from another kitchen he calls for the health inspector to do away with an element of a traditional cuisine. The swimming pool is the ultimate symbol of the Westernization of modern life. The rich family cannot see how their desire for yet another status symbol will destroy Tinga's life. Artificial consumer goods replace a sacred relationship with the land, which has gone on for generations. By implication, the pool gives lie to the idea of progress. Those who see these symbols as essential do not understand how such items consume the very resources their country needs for genuine progress. The connection between Tinga and Yabre demonstrates the possibilities for the future, but the corruption that prevents their accomplishing their goals demonstrates how the connections between past, present, and future are delicate and difficult to maintain.

Bibliography

Akudinobi, Jude. "Tradition/ Modernity and the Discourse of African Cinema." *IRIS* 18 (Spring 1995): 25–37.

"Kaboré, Gaston." *Dictionnaire du cinéma africain.* Vol. 1. Paris: Editions Karthala, 1991. 48–51.

Ukadike, Nwachukwu Frank. *Black African Cinema.* Berkeley: U of California P, 1994.

DISTRIBUTORS

The following companies distribute African films. I have not identified specific films with companies because the rights of distribution can change. The first section cites companies who may have both film and video versions of a film and who may have titles for both sales and rental. In all cases a renter or purchaser should be aware of the copyright regulations for the showing of films. The companies in the second group rent videos for private use.

SALES AND RENTAL OF FILM AND VIDEO

California Newsreel
  149 Ninth Street/ 420
  San Francisco, California 94103
  415–621–6196
  This company has one of the most extensive lists of sub-Saharan African films, both features and documentaries.

First Run/Icarus Films
  153 Waverly Place, 6th Floor
  Sixth Floor
  New York, NY 10014
  212–727–1711
  800–876–1710
  Fax: 212–989–7649
  E-Mail: FRIF@echonyc.com
  This company distributes many African documentaries. Most are short films and many are not directed by Africans.

Filmakers Library
  124 East 40th Street

New York, NY 10016
212–808–4980
Fax: 212–808–4983
This company distributes many African documentaries. Most are short films, and many are not directed by Africans.

KJM3 Entertainment Group
274 Madison Avenue, Suite 601
New York, NY 10016
212–689–0950
Fax: 212–689–6861
This small company distributes a few African films.

Mypheduh Films
403 K Street N.W.
Washington, DC 20001
202–289–6677
Fax: 202–289–4477
This company distributes several African and African American films and is the major source of the work of Haïlé Gerima.

New Yorker Films
16 West 61st Street
New York, NY 10023
212–247–6110
Fax: 212–307–7855
This large company distributes many of the better-known sub-Saharan directors.

Third World Newsreel
335 West 38th Street, 5th Floor
New York, NY 10018
212–947–9277
Fax: 212–549–6417
This company distributes some African and African diaspora films among its extensive collection of documentaries.

Women Make Movies, Inc.
462 Broadway, Suite 500 D
New York, NY 10013
212–925–0606
Fax: 212–925–2052
E-Mail: DISTDEPT@ WMM.COM
This company distributes documentaries and feature films directed by women.

VIDEO TAPE RENTAL COMPANIES

Both of these companies have extensive lists of international videos or films for rent and purchase including several African films. They both charge a membership fee for rental privileges.

Facets Video
1517 West Fullerton Avenue

Chicago, IL 60614
800–331–6197, purchase
800–532–2387, rental
Fax: 773–929–5437
E-Mail: sales@facets.org

Home Film Festival
P.O. Box 2032
Scranton, PA 18501
800–258–3456, rental and purchase

BIBLIOGRAPHY

Akudinobi, Jude. "Tradition/ Modernity and the Discourse of African Cinema."
    IRIS 18 (Spring 1995): 25–37.
Appiah, Kwame Anthony. *In My Father's House: Africa in the Philosophy of Cul-*
    ture. Oxford: Oxford UP, 1992.
Armes, Roy. "Culture and National Identity." *Cinemas of the Black Diaspora:*
    Diversity, Dependence, and Oppositionality. Ed. Michael Martin. Detroit:
    Wayne State UP, 1995. 25–39.
———. *Dictionary of North African Film Makers*. Paris: Editions ATM, 1996.
———. *Third World Film Making and the West*. Berkeley: U of California P, 1987.
Bachy, Victor. *Le cinéma au Mali*. Brussels: OCIC, 1983.
———. *Le cinéma en Côte d'Ivorie*. Brussels: OCIC, 1983.
Bakari, Imruh, and Mbye Cham, eds. *African Experiences of Cinema*. London:
    British Film Institute, 1996.
Balogun, Françoise. *Le cinéma au Nigeria*. Brussels: OCIC, 1984.
Boulanger, Pierre. *Le cinéma colonial de "l'atlantide" à "lawrence d'arabie."* Paris:
    Editions Seghers, 1975.
Bourgault, Louise M. *Mass Media in Sub-Saharan Africa*. Bloomington: Indiana
    UP, 1995.
Bouzid, Nouri. "Our Inspiration." *African Experiences of Cinema*. Ed. Imruh Bak-
    ari and Mbye Cham. London: British Film Institute, 1996. 48–59.
Brown, Georgia. "*Sankofa*." *Village Voice* 12 April 1994: 56.
Cameron, Kenneth M. *Africa on Film: Beyond Black and White*. New York: Con-
    tinuum, 1994.
Centre d'Etude sur la Communication en Afrique. *Camera Nigra: Le discours du*
    film africain. Brussels: OCIC, n.d.
Cham, Mbye. "Official History, Popular Memory: Reconfiguration of the African
    Past in the Films of Ousmane Sembene." *Ousmane Sembene: Dialogues*
    with Critics and Writers. Ed. Samba Gadjigo, Ralph Faulkingham, Thomas

Cassirer, and Reinhard Sander. Amherst: U of Massachusetts P, 1993. 22–28.

Chazan, Naomi, Robert Mortimer, John Ravenhill, and Donald Rothchild. *Politics and Society in Contemporary Africa*. Boulder: Lynne Rienner, 1988.

Chirol, Marie-Magdeleine. "The Missing Narrative in *Wend Kuuni*." *Research in African Literatures* 26 (Fall 1995): 49–56.

"Cissé, Souleymane." *Dictionnaire du cinéma africain*. Vol. 1. Paris: Editions Karthala, 1991. 191–94.

Dauphin, Gary. "Continental Divides." *Village Voice* 16 April 1996: 82.

Diawara, Manthia. *African Cinema: Politics & Culture*. Bloomington: Indiana UP, 1992.

———. "Oral Literature and African Film: Narratology in *Wend Kuuni*." *Questions of Third Cinema*. Ed. Jim Pines and Paul Willemen. London: British Film Institute, 1991. 195–211.

"Diop-Mambety, Djibril." *Dictionnaire du cinéma african*. Vol. 1. Paris: Editions Karthala, 1991. 284–86.

Dittmar, Linda. "The Articulating Self: Difference as Resistance in *Black Girl*, *Ramparts of Clay*, and *Salt of the Earth*." *Multiple Voices in Feminist Film Criticism*. Ed. Diane Carson, Linda Dittmar, and Janice R. Welsch. Minneapolis: U of Minnesota P, 1994. 391–405.

"Faye, Safi." *Dictionnaire du cinéma africain*. Vol. 1. Paris: Editions Karthala, 1991. 287–90.

Ferro, Marc, ed. *Revoltes, revolutions, cinéma*. Paris: Centre Georges Pompidou, 1989.

Gadjigo, Samba, Ralph Faulkingham, Thomas Cassirer, and Reinhard Sander, eds. *Ousmane Sembene: Dialogues with Critics and Writers*. Amherst: U of Massachusetts P, 1993.

Georgakas, Dan, and Lenny Rubenstein. *The Cineaste Interviews on the Art and Politics of the Cinema*. Chicago: Lake View, 1983.

Ghali, Noureddine. "An Interview with Sembene Ousmane." *Film & Politics in The Third World*. Ed. John D. H. Downing. New York: Praeger, 1986. 41–54.

Hennebelle, Guy. *Les cinémas africains en 1972*. Paris: Société Africaine d'Edition, 1972.

———. *Quinze ans de cinéma mondial: 1960–1975*. Paris: Éditions du cerf, 1975.

———. "Sambizanga" and "Entretien avec Sarah Maldoror." *Ecran* (May 1973): 69–71.

"Hondo, Med." *Dictionnaire du cinéma africain*. Vol. 1. Paris: Editions Karthala, 1991. 215–17.

Hondo, Med. "The Cinema of Exile." *Film & Politics in The Third World*. Ed. John D. H. Downing. New York: Praeger, 1986. 69–76.

"Kaboré, Gaston." *Dictionnaire du cinéma africain*. Vol. 1. Paris: Editions Karthala, 1991. 48–51.

Kaboré, Gaston. "L'image de soi, un besoin vital." *Africa and the Centenary of Film*. Ed. Gaston Kaboré. Dakar: Présence Africaine, 1995. 21–23.

———. "Mon rapport au cinéma." *Africa and the Centenary of Film*. Ed. Gaston Kaboré. Dakar: Présence Africaine, 1995. 373–74.

Leprophon, Pierre. *L'exotisme et le cinéma*. Paris: Les éditions J. Susse, 1945.

Loizos, Peter. *Innovation in Ethnographic Film: From Innocence to Self-Consciousness, 1955–1985*. Chicago: U of Chicago P, 1993.

Malkmus, Lizbeth, and Roy Armes. *Arab and African Film Making*. London: Zed Books, 1991.

Martin, Michael, ed. *Cinemas of the Black Diaspora: Diversity, Dependence, and Oppositionality*. Detroit: Wayne State UP, 1995.

Mpoyi-Buatu, Th. "Sembene Ousmane's *Ceddo* & Med Hondo's *West Indies*." *Film & Politics in The Third World*. Ed. John D. H. Downing. New York: Praeger, 1986. 55–67.

"Ouedraogo, Idrissa." *Dictionnaire du cinéma africain*. Vol. 1. Paris: Editions Karthala, 1991. 55–58.

Ouedraogo, Idrissa. "Le cinéma et nous." *Africa and the Centenary of Film*. Ed. Gaston Kaboré. Dakar: Présence Africaine, 1995. 336–42.

Petty, Sheila, ed. *A Call to Action: The Films of Ousmane Sembene*. New York: Praeger, 1996.

Pfaff, Françoise. *The Cinema of Ousmane Sembene, A Pioneer of African Film*. Westport, Conn.: Greenwood P, 1984.

———. *Twenty-five Black African Filmmakers: A Critical Study*. Westport, Conn.: Greenwood P, 1988.

Pines, Jim, and Paul Willeman, eds. *Questions of Third Cinema*. London: British Film Institute, 1989.

Porton, Richard. "*Hyenas*: Between Anti-Colonialism and the Critique of Modernity." *IRIS* 18 (Spring 1995): 95–103.

Rayfield, J. R. "*Hyenas*: The Message and the Messenger." *Research in African Literatures* 26 (Fall 1995): 78–82.

Reid, Mark A. "Dialogic Modes of Representing Africa(s): Womanist Film." *Cinemas of the Black Diaspora: Diversity, Dependence, and Oppositionality*. Ed. Michael Martin. Detroit: Wayne State UP, 1995. 56–69.

Sadoul, Georges. *Dictionary of Films*. Trans., ed., and update Peter Morris. Berkeley: U of California P, 1972.

Sherzer, Dina, ed. *Cinema, Colonialism, Postcolonialism: Perspectives from the French and Francophone Worlds*. Austin: U of Texas P, 1996.

Shiri, Kenneth, comp. and ed. *Directory of African Films*. Westport, Conn.: Greenwood P, 1992.

Shohat, Ella, and Robert Stam. *Unthinking Eurocentrism: Multiculturalism and the Media*. London: Routledge, 1994.

Taubin, Amy. "Speak, Memory." *Village Voice* 16 April 1996: 78.

Tomaselli, Keyan, coordinator. *CinémaAction 39: Le cinéma sud-africain est-il tombé sur la tête?* Paris: Cert/Afrique Littéraire, 1986.

———. *The Cinema of Apartheid: Race and Class in South African Film*. New York: Smyrna P, 1988.

———, Alan Williams, Lynette Steenveld, and Ruth Tomaselli. *Myth, Race and Power: South Africans Imaged on Film and TV*. Bellville, South Africa: Anthropos, 1986.

Ukadike, Nwachukwu Frank. *Black African Cinema*. Berkeley: U of California P, 1994.

Ukadike, N. Frank. "The Other Voices of Documentary: *Allah Tantou* and *Afrique, je te plumerai*." *IRIS* 18 (Spring 1995): 81–94.

Video Hound's Golden Movie Retriever.

"Vieyra, Paulin Soumanou." *Dictionnaire du cinéma africain*. Vol. 1. Paris: Editions Karthala, 1991. 315–19.

Vieyra, Paulin Soumanou. "Five Major Films by Sembene Ousmane." *Film & Politics in The Third World*. Ed. John D. H. Downing. New York: Praeger, 1986. 31–39.

Index

Page references to main entries appear in **boldface type.**

About the Author
SHARON A. RUSSELL is Professor of Communications and Women's Studies at Indiana State University. She has published *Stephen King: A Critical Companion* (Greenwood 1996) and contributed to *Great Women Mystery Writers*: *A Biocritical Dictionary* (Greenwood 1994). She has published many articles on popular fiction and film.

ISBN 0-313-29621-9

90000>

EAN

9 780313 296215

HARDCOVER BAR CODE